D0775119

BACKCOUNTRY
SKI & SNOWBOARD
ROUTES

UTAH

BACKCOUNTRY SKI & SNOWBOARD ROUTES

UTAH

JARED HARGRAVE

FOREWORD BY CRAIG GORDON

MOUNTAINEERS
BOOKS

Mountaineers Books is the publishing division of The Mountaineers, an organization founded in 1906 and dedicated to the exploration, preservation, and enjoyment of outdoor and wilderness areas.

MOUNTAINEERS BOOKS 1001 SW Klickitat Way, Suite 201, Seattle, WA 98134
800.553.4453, www.mountaineersbooks.org

Copyright © 2015 by Jared Hargrave
Foreword © 2015 by Craig Gordon
All rights reserved.

No part of this book may be reproduced or utilized in any form, or by any electronic, mechanical, or other means, without the prior written permission of the publisher.

Printed in the United States of America
Distributed in the United Kingdom by Cordee, www.cordee.co.uk
First edition, 2015

Copy Editor: Joeth Zucco
Design and Layout: Peggy Egerdahl
Cartographer: Pease Press Cartography
    The background maps for this book were produced using the online map viewer
    CalTopo. For more information, visit caltopo.com.

Cover photograph: *Dylan Freed drops in to the Wasatch at sunrise.* (Jay Beyer, www.jaybeyer.com)
Frontispiece: *Booting up the summit ridge of Mount Tukuhnikivatz with Mount Peale behind*
Back cover photograph: *Mike DeBernardo drops into Granny Chute in Wolverine Cirque,
    Big Cottonwood Canyon.*
All photographs by the author unless otherwise noted

Library of Congress Cataloging-in-Publication Data
Hargrave, Jared.
    Backcountry ski & snowboard routes : Utah / Jared Hargrave.—First edition.
        pages cm
    Includes index.
    ISBN 978-1-59485-831-4 (Paperback) — ISBN 978-1-59485-832-1 (ebook)
    1. Skiing—Utah—Guidebooks. 2. Snowboarding—Utah—Guidebooks. 3. Natural
resources—Utah—Guidebooks. 4. Utah—Guidebooks. I. Title. II. Title: Backcountry ski
and snowboard routes.
    GV854.5.U8H37 2015
    796.9—dc23
                                    2015021049

Mountaineers Books titles may be purchased for corporate, educational, or other promotional sales, and our authors are available for a wide range of events. For information on special discounts or booking an author, contact our customer service at 800-553-4453 or mbooks@mountaineersbooks.org.

♻ Printed on recycled paper

ISBN (paperback): 978-1-59485-831-4
ISBN (ebook): 978-1-59485-832-1

CONTENTS

———··—— Featured ascent/descent		**℗** Trailhead parking
-------- Alternate descent		▪ Landmark
·········· Alternate ascent		▲ Peak
---------- Other trail		⊢⊣ Gate
——— Highway		**⋀** Campground
——— Local road		**⊼** Picnic
===== Dirt road		)(Bridge
		)(Pass
⑳ Interstate		_chairlift_ Chairlift
⑧⑨ US highway		⌒ Stream
⑫⓪ State highway		▬ Lake
⑦③ County road		Gentle terrain
①②③ Forest Service road		Steep terrain
▬ ▪ ▬ ▪ National forest boundary		40-foot intermediate contours
▬ ▪ ▬ ▪ Wilderness boundary		200-foot index contours

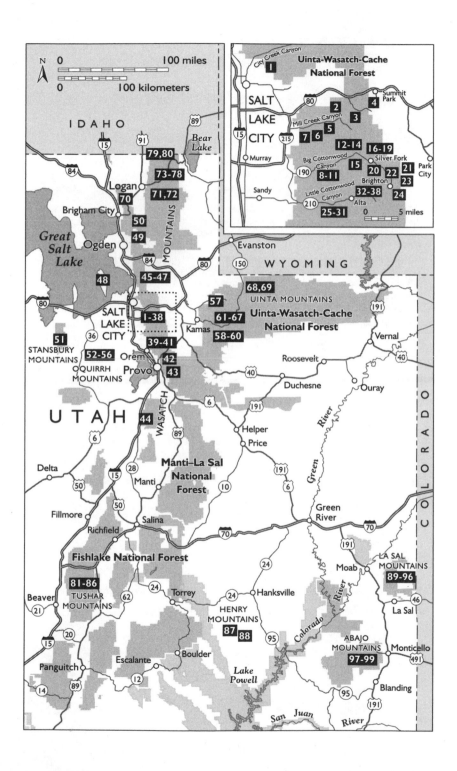

TOURS AT A GLANCE

No.	Tour	Skill Level	Roundtrip Distance (in miles)	Trail Time (in hours)	Best Season
NORTHERN SALT LAKE CANYONS					
1.	Salt Lake City Foothills	Intermediate	3	2	Winter
2.	Mount Aire	Intermediate	5	4	Winter
3.	Millvue Peak	Intermediate	5	3	Winter
4.	Summit Park Peak	Beginner/ Intermediate	3	2	Winter
5.	Porter Fork	Advanced	8	5	Winter
6.	Neffs Canyon	Advanced	8	5	Winter
7.	Thomas Fork	Advanced	7	5	Winter
BIG COTTONWOOD CANYON					
8.	Bonkers	Advanced/Expert	8	6	Winter
9.	Mill B South Fork	Advanced	9–10	8	Winter
10.	Mineral Fork	Advanced	8	5	Winter
11.	Kessler Peak	Advanced/Expert	3	4	Winter
12.	Circle All Peak	Intermediate	4	2	Winter
13.	Gobblers Knob	Intermediate/ Advanced	8	6	Winter
14.	Mount Raymond	Advanced	8	5	Winter/ Spring
15.	Gods Lawnmower	Advanced	4	3	Winter
16.	Short Swing	Beginner/ Intermediate	3	2	Winter
17.	Reynolds Peak and Toms Hill	Intermediate	6	4	Winter
18.	Little Water Peak	Intermediate	6	4	Winter
19.	Lake Desolation Area	Intermediate	8	5	Winter
20.	Greens Basin	Intermediate	5	3	Winter
21.	Beartrap Fork	Intermediate	4	3	Winter
22.	Silver Fork Meadow Chutes	Intermediate	4	3	Winter
23.	Willow Fork and USA Bowl	Beginner/ Intermediate	4	3	Winter
24.	Brighton Hill and Point 10420	Beginner/ Intermediate	3	2	Winter
LITTLE COTTONWOOD CANYON					
25.	The Pfeifferhorn	Expert	10	9	Winter/ Spring
26.	Red Pine Trees	Intermediate	6	4	Winter
27.	Pink Pine Ridge	Intermediate	4	3	Winter

No.	Tour	Skill Level	Roundtrip Distance (in miles)	Trail Time (in hours)	Best Season
28.	Lake Peak (No Name Peak)	Advanced	7	5	Winter/ Spring
29.	Red and White Baldy	Advanced/Expert	8	6	Winter/ Spring
30.	Red Top Mountain	Advanced	8	5	Winter/ Spring
31.	Scotties Bowl	Advanced	3	3	Winter
32.	Mount Superior	Advanced/Expert	5	4	Winter/ Spring
33.	Cardiff Pass	Beginner/ Intermediate	3	2	Winter
34.	Flagstaff Mountain and Upper Days Fork	Intermediate/ Advanced	3	2	Winter
35.	Davenport Hill and Upper Silver Fork	Intermediate	3	3	Winter
36.	Grizzly Gulch and Patsey Marley	Beginner/ Intermediate	4	3	Winter
37.	Wolverine Cirque	Advanced	4	3	Spring
38.	Catherine Pass Area	Intermediate/ Advanced	5	3	Fall/ Winter
SOUTHERN WASATCH					
39.	Lone Peak	Advanced/Expert	9	7	Spring
40.	Box Elder Peak	Advanced/Expert	9	7	Winter/ Spring
41.	The Three Temptations	Advanced	8	6	Winter
42.	Mount Timpanogos South Summit	Expert	7	6	Spring
43.	Big Springs Hollow	Advanced	11	9	Spring
44.	Mount Nebo	Expert	8	8	Spring
NORTHERN WASATCH					
45.	Gold Ridge	Beginner/ Intermediate	5	3	Spring
46.	Bountiful Peak	Intermediate/ Advanced	5	3	Spring
47.	Mud and Rice Bowls	Intermediate	5	3	Spring
48.	Frary Peak	Intermediate	7	6	Winter
49.	North Ogden Divide to Chilly Peak	Intermediate/ Advanced	8	6	Winter
50.	Ben Lomond Peak and Cutler Ridge	Intermediate/ Advanced	9	7	Winter

No.	Tour	Skill Level	Roundtrip Distance (in miles)	Trail Time (in hours)	Best Season
WEST DESERT MOUNTAINS					
51.	Deseret Peak	Advanced	6–13	8–12	Spring
52.	Flat Top Mountain	Advanced	8	7	Spring
53.	Lewiston Peak	Advanced	7–9	7–8	Spring
54.	Serviceberry Canyon	Intermediate/ Advanced	6	4	Winter
55.	Picnic Canyon	Intermediate	6	5	Winter
56.	Lowe Peak	Advanced	6–9	5–7	Spring
UINTA MOUNTAINS					
57.	Smith and Morehouse	Advanced	6	4	Winter
58.	Wolf Creek Pass	Beginner	2	2	Fall
59.	Wolf Creek Peak	Beginner	1.5–3	1–2	Fall
60.	Phelps Brook Slide Path	Intermediate	1.5	1	Fall
61.	Castle Peak Yurt	Intermediate	10, 5	5, 4	Spring
62.	Mount Watson	Intermediate	5	4	Spring
63.	Bald Mountain	Intermediate/ Advanced	3	2	Spring
64.	Murdock Mountain	Beginner/ Intermediate	1.5	1	Spring
65.	Reids Peak	Advanced	3.5	3	Spring
66.	Mount Marsell	Advanced	5	4	Spring
67.	Hayden Peak	Advanced/Expert	3	2	Spring
68.	Ridge Yurt	Beginner	10, 4	4, 2	Winter
69.	Boundary Creek Yurt	Intermediate/ Advanced	13, 2.5	6, 1.5	Winter
BEAR RIVER AND WELLSVILLE MOUNTAINS					
70.	Wellsville Mountains	Advanced	7	5	Winter
71.	Millville Peak	Intermediate/ Advanced	6–9	4–7	Winter/ Spring
72.	Logan Peak	Intermediate/ Advanced	9	6	Winter
73.	Wood Camp Hollow	Advanced	7	5	Winter/ Spring
74.	Tony Grove	Beginner/ Intermediate	2	1	Fall
75.	Upper Cottonwood Canyon	Intermediate/ Advanced	9	10	Fall/ Winter
76.	Cornice Ridge	Intermediate/ Advanced	4	3	Fall
77.	Bunchgrass Creek	Beginner/ Intermediate	8, 1	5, 1	Winter

No.	Tour	Skill Level	Roundtrip Distance (in miles)	Trail Time (in hours)	Best Season
78.	Hells Kitchen Canyon and Steam Mill Yurt	Beginner/ Intermediate	7, 4	4, 3	Winter
79.	Garden City Bowls	Beginner/ Intermediate	5	3	Winter
80.	Swan Peak	Intermediate	6–9	6	Winter
TUSHAR MOUNTAINS					
81.	Shelly Baldy Peak	Advanced	9, 4.5	4, 5	Winter
82.	Delano Peak	Intermediate/ Advanced	9, 4	4, 3	Winter
83.	The Great White Whale	Intermediate/ Advanced	9, 4, 3.5	4, 3, 4,	Winter
84.	Mount Holly	Beginner/ Intermediate	3–7	2–6	Winter
85.	Lake Peak	Intermediate	2.5–5	2–4	Winter
86.	City Creek Peak	Intermediate	3–5.5, 2	1–2, 2	Winter
HENRY MOUNTAINS					
87.	Mount Ellen North Summit Ridge	Advanced	7	6	Spring
88.	Mount Ellen South Summit Ridge	Advanced	9	7	Spring
LA SAL MOUNTAINS					
89.	Corkscrew Glades	Intermediate	5	4	Winter
90.	Noriegas Peak	Intermediate	3	3	Winter
91.	Laurel Highway	Intermediate	6.5	4	Winter/ Spring
92.	Mount Tukuhnikivatz	Advanced/Expert	8	6	Spring
93.	Mount Mellenthin	Advanced/Expert	8	6	Spring
94.	Haystack Mountain	Intermediate/ Advanced	7	6	Spring
95.	South Mountain Glades	Advanced	12	8	Winter/ Spring
96.	South Mountain	Advanced	14	10	Winter/ Spring
ABAJO MOUNTAINS					
97.	Old Blue Mountain Ski Resort	Intermediate	5	4	Winter
98.	Abajo Peak	Intermediate/ Advanced	9	7	Winter
99.	Horsehead Peak	Advanced	7	5	Winter

FOREWORD

MY LIFE TOOK AN UNEXPECTED TURN toward snow and avalanches in the late seventies when I first visited Utah with a local ski club from back East. I stumbled on a killer deal that included airfare, hotel, and lift tickets—$365 landed me behind the Zion curtain. I had read stories in *Powder* magazine about Little Cottonwood Canyon and all its amazing snow. Honestly, I could hardly sleep in the weeks leading up to the trip.

Our group stayed downtown in the City of Salt, and for the first few days it pounded snow in the mountains. Big, fat, dry flakes like I had never seen before. I had no idea it had been a relatively dry winter until our visit; I thought it was always over-the-head powder. We skied a few days in Park City before migrating to Little Cottonwood Canyon. Problem was, I couldn't see any of the terrain—true skiing by Braille. But then it happened. On the fourth day we navigated the Econoline rental van up to Alta, and there was energy in the air. Overnight, the storm deposited the last of its ultralight fluff, and like Moses parting the sea, the skies started to clear as the storm migrated to the east. As we got off at the top of the old Collins chairlift, I looked up at Mount Baldy and saw a few Alta patrollers traversing the face of Ballroom. As they broke trail, they threw bombs and skied powder. I was in awe. My best friend Don was itching to ski, but I couldn't move. I was mesmerized, watching the patrol do their thing. "Take a run," I said. "I'll meet you here."

Time evaporated, and in an instant Don was back and telling me about an amazing run he'd discovered. To this day I remember the moment. I gazed back at him with a stony look in my eyes and said, "Man, I'm comin' back to do that. Throwing bombs and skiing powder. I'm all over it." It was all he could do to keep from bustin' a gut laughing. A kid from Jersey is going to move to Utah and become a bomb-throwing ski patroller . . . right. But in his best westernized Jersey accent, and a back-at-ya grin, Don looked at me and said, "Sure you will, Craig, sure you will."

I returned to Utah under the guise of college in the mid-eighties, but school and I never really worked out. As a matter of fact, a nighttime dishwashing job sealed my fate, and I got to ski every day. It was an amazing time; everything was so new to me. Sure, I grew up skiing the big mountains of northern New Jersey, but here in Utah skiing was a way of life and everyone spoke a different language. Face shots, 4 percent density, interlodge. I was still speaking Jersey. Calzone, mobster, "Tramps like us, baby, we were born to run."

There was only one guidebook when I arrived, and the Utah Avalanche Center was still in its infancy. The backcountry was ruled by a handful of three-pinners wearing

Opposite: *Ascending Box Elder Peak near the Shotgun Chutes, Southern Wasatch* (Adam Symonds)

Red Top and Red Baldy crouch at the head of White Pine as a skier goes down Lake Chute in Little Cottonwood Canyon.

wool knickers, Peruvian hats, and big backpacks. However, within the confines of the resorts an even rowdier bunch of hippie punks on free-heel gear was emerging. These cats were shredding steep terrain and pushing the boundaries of what their fragile equipment could accomplish. Soon they brought their Sid Vicious, street-infused style to the backcountry—it was less of a clash of cultures and more of a fusion. Sorta like Lou Reed, Bob Marley, and Jimi Hendrix collaborating on an album with Joe Strummer as the producer. In any case, telemark skis and flimsy leather boots were the counterculture snow vehicle of choice. This crew was totally different—out there, in fact—and that's where I wanted to be.

I was smart enough to know that it would be a suffer-fest without a mentor. When it comes to mentoring, a few sports stand out: climbing, surfing, and, of course, backcountry skiing. I hooked up with a small posse that I thought had a lot of experience. Sure, we had all the avy gear, but we never practiced. As a matter of fact, a closer look at my partners made me re-evaluate my direction in life, and that's when I began a fulfilling career working with snow and avalanches. First, as a ski patrolman and part of the snow safety team at Brighton Ski Resort, next as avalanche forecaster for a heli-skiing operation, and finally, for the past fifteen years, with the Utah Avalanche Center.

A lot has changed in the past three decades, but in many ways so much remains the same. Let's face it, gear technology has advanced a hundredfold since I landed on planet Utah, and the backcountry is getting loved to death. However, that basic, instinctual starting point of "I wanna get in the backcountry" remains. And while there's a ton of information available through the interwebz and other forms of social media, it's often hard to decipher who's giving you the true lowdown and who's just spraying.

I've been following Jared Hargrave's work for a number of years and had the pleasure to get to know him better at an avalanche workshop I was leading in 2014. I was impressed by Jared's attention to detail while covering the workshop for KSL Outdoors and by this fact: most media peeps show up to do a story about snow and avalanches in street threads and loafers. Not that there's anything wrong with that. In fact, that's how I roll to most of the outdoor affairs I attend, though I prefer shorts and flip-flops. But what's even more amazing—I might even put it into the stunning category, truth be told—is that this guy can ski. Not only is he a solid skier, but he does it while schlepping around a shit-ton of camera gear. So with Jared you get the entire package—a journalist who can navigate the backcountry with finesse and can come home at the end of the day to deliver an accurate account. That being said, *Backcountry Ski and Snowboard Routes: Utah* is the real deal, from an author who's deeply devoted to his craft. Jared's easy-going writing style, peppered with detail-oriented descriptions, allows you to clearly navigate terrain, attain your goals, and, better yet, get the goods. It's like Jared is next to you on your journey. Plus, it's got ya covered from the moment you get in the car to when you land at the trailhead. Coffee shop to peak . . . you're good to go. Quite frankly, I'm not too surprised Jared compiled a straightforward, easy-to-understand, yet very comprehensive guidebook.

I wish a guidebook of this caliber, written by someone I could connect with, had been around as I started to break trail and explore this amazing backyard we have. On his first attempt at a full-blown guidebook, Jared scores a huge success by writing a fact-based, detailed account of his travels. Tours are rated on ability level, travel time, and distance traveled. In addition to the classics, Jared outlines the soon-to-be classics of the western Uinta and Logan areas. Whether you've been teleported to Utah from a cornfield in Iowa for the duration or are just passing through on your intergalactic travels, Jared lays down a road map that's easy to follow while citing credible resources you can use along the way.

So I salute your moment when you think to yourself, "I wanna ride Utah's backcountry terrain safely." Fortunately for you, Jared Hargrave has taken a lot of the guesswork out of the equation and his guidebook is one to add to your arsenal. It's a great honor to be part of this project, and I wish you, the reader, a life filled with deep powder days, tight turns, and safe travels.

—Craig Gordon

Craig Gordon has been involved in Utah's ski, snow, and avalanche community since 1986. For the past fifteen years, Craig has worked for the Utah Avalanche Center as a forecaster in the western Uinta and Manti-Skyline mountains. In addition, Craig developed the wildly popular "Know Before You Go" avalanche education program in 2004. In the past ten years, "Know Before You Go" has become the national standard for basic avalanche awareness, and in Utah nearly two hundred thousand people have participated in the program.

PREFACE

BACKCOUNTRY SKIING AND SNOWBOARDING, for many, is a revelation. I will never forget my first time leaving the restrictions and boundaries of a ski resort and venturing into untracked, wild terrain. I was a freshman at Basalt High School, located in Colorado's Roaring Fork Valley just downstream from Aspen. To prepare for a hut trip with the school's outdoor club, I rented backcountry ski gear available at the time—leather boots and scaled skis. My science teacher, Andre Willie, took me to Buttermilk Ski Area near Aspen. After riding lifts to the top, we promptly ducked the boundary rope and skied away from the crowds into a powder-filled emptiness like I'd never seen or experienced before. It was terrifying, exhilarating, and even came with a thrill of disobedience, like I was getting away with something. It was my moment of revelation.

After that first encounter, I was hooked. I went on to cut my teeth on hut-to-hut trips through the Elk Mountains. I was constantly in search of fresh powder and untrammeled lands. And I experienced the hard labor and immense satisfaction of ski mountaineering for the first time on 12,966-foot Mount Sopris, which then became a spring-skiing ritual every season until graduation.

Post-college, I moved to Utah, and my whole perspective on backcountry skiing turned upside down. Here's the secret about Utah, and the Wasatch Mountains in particular: it's the best backcountry skiing in the world. "The Greatest Snow on Earth" is Ski Utah's motto. From my perspective, the saying is true. Moist storms that track across the desert west of Salt Lake City slam into a wall of mountains east of the Great Salt Lake and dump huge amounts of snow. Alta Ski Area in Little Cottonwood Canyon reports an average of 514 inches every season. But it's not just the quantity, it's the quality that matters. Most storms come in right-side up, meaning they begin wet, with thick snow falling first, followed by colder air that dries the snow, leaving fluffy, dreamlike powder on top. That's the recipe for perfect powder skiing, and Utah has it in spades.

But the aspect of backcountry skiing and snowboarding in Utah that really makes it shine is easy access. Salt Lake City, a metropolitan area of more than a million people, hums alongside the Wasatch Mountains. Seven world-class ski resorts are just a half-hour drive from downtown skyscrapers. The canyons that split the range are bisected with plowed, paved highways. Just off the roads, dozens of trailheads with winter parking provide access to trails that meander into the high alpine. Day tours are quick and easy, sometimes taking only a few hours car to car. The Wasatch is the birthplace of "Dawn Patrol," where weekday skiers get a pre-dawn start for a few backcountry turns before they have to be in their cubicles at 9:00 AM. There literally is nowhere else quite like the Wasatch. It's no wonder so many skiers flock here for a single winter season and then never leave.

After I moved to Utah, all this bounty was at my doorstep. I dove right in. I continued my old ways of skiing out of bounds but found, to my delight, that times had changed, and Utah resorts allowed backcountry access through boundary gates. With ski-touring gear improving at light speed, my friends and I were able to venture far away from the resorts, exploring every nook and cranny in the Cottonwood Canyons, and eventually around the state. It wasn't long before I was logging more days in the backcountry than at ski areas.

After nearly a decade of skiing in Utah, I started a website, www.UtahOutside .com, where I could document all my backcountry ski tours with route descriptions and photos. Rather than a full-on guide, I intended it to be more like an online ski journal. That journal became this book.

After Mountaineers Books commissioned me to write this guide, my wanderlust became an obsession. With ski buddies piled into a truck camper we dubbed the "Yurt on Wheels," we scoured the state from border to border. We reacquainted ourselves with otherworldly descents above red rock deserts in the Henry, La Sal, and Abajo mountains of southern Utah. We booked almost every yurt available in the Tushar,

Booting up on the slabs above Bonkers, Big Cottonwood Canyon, with the Salt Lake Valley far below

Uinta, and Bear River ranges. And we revisited old classics in the Wasatch for reliable powder turns. Backcountry skiing was no longer just a hobby, it was a lifestyle.

Essentially, this volume is a collection of all the routes I've personally skied in Utah. It is far from exhaustive. Including every possible ski tour in the state would result in a book the size of Homer's *Iliad*, which would not be suitable for tossing in a pack. With this guide limited to ninety-nine routes, there are assuredly some obvious classics that I failed to mention. On the other hand, there are bound to be secret stashes that haven't appeared in a guidebook before. I apologize in advance if your favorite backcountry haunt appears in these pages.

My intention for this book was to create a guide easy enough for skiers and snowboarders to use who have never been in the backcountry before, or for travelers of all abilities who have not yet visited Utah. With that mindset, I decided to zoom in on specific routes, down to single skin tracks in some cases, rather than providing a bird's-eye view of possible ascents and descents in a given area. As such, this book shows what I consider the best, most efficient, and safest routes for individual tours, though alternative routes are absolutely out there and are no less valid. That's the beauty of backcountry skiing—it's ultimately your choice to ski where and how you want.

Also of note is that I generally chose to exclude lift-accessed backcountry from ski resorts, instead focusing on tours that require human power. There are exceptions, such as tours around Alta, Snowbird, Solitude, and Canyons, but I only included these routes because they have the added option of skinning from roadside trailheads to reach the same popular destinations. I also excluded routes in areas that are so remote that snowmobiles are required to reach them.

Hopefully this book will inspire some wanderlust in you as well. These routes are a good foundation for further exploration in Utah's urban and rural mountain ranges. As you ski or snowboard these routes, stop to scan the horizon or scope out lines in adjacent drainages. Build up the courage to see what's on the other side of the next ridge. Explore. Because exploration is ultimately what backcountry skiing is about. Well, that and shredding waist-deep powder.

ACKNOWLEDGMENTS

MY FRIENDS, FAMILY, AND COLLEAGUES were vital to the research and writing of this book. Without them, I would have failed several times over. Many thanks to everyone who participated in some way, large or small, in the creation of this guide.

First, I want to thank Kate Rogers and Kirsten Colton at Mountaineers Books for choosing and trusting me to write this book. Their unflappable encouragement convinced me to take on the project, which I was hesitant to accept at first. Without them, as well as the hardworking copy editor, proofreaders, cartographers, promotions crew, production crew, and the rest of the publishing staff, this book would not exist.

Backcountry skiing is a dangerous activity—and not something one does alone. Numerous touring partners came along for the adventure, which entailed countless hours of researching, driving, skinning, skiing, and standing around in the cold while I set up for photos. My comrades include Mason Diedrich, Zach Scribner, Mike DeBernardo, Lexi Dowdall, Jon Strickland, Eric Ghanem, Dave Thieme, Vince Pierce, Steven "Sherpa" Clark, Jeff Monroe, Chris Brown, Tim Cauby, Jon Monstrola, John Gilchrist, Jason True, Dan Finn, and my fellow members of the Niños Jugando, which include Justin Lozier, Sean Zimmerman-Wall, Brian McKenna, and Chad Burt.

Above all, I thank Adam Symonds for coming along on almost every single tour described in this book. He was truly dedicated to the project, had endless energy, and rarely said no when I called to see if he wanted to go skiing for the book. Plus, his "Yurt on Wheels" camper was absolutely vital to our statewide research.

The work that went into researching and writing this book took a lot of time away from my family, so I especially thank my wife, Callista, for her patience, love, and encouragement. Plus, she kept me on task whenever I didn't feel like sitting in front of the computer to do my "homework."

A huge shout-out goes to the Utah Avalanche Center for their tireless work in keeping us safe in the backcountry. And mucho thanks to UAC forecaster Craig Gordon for his contribution. I am honored to have Craig's unique perspective and humor included in the book.

I had never skied in Utah until I moved here fifteen years ago, so old guidebooks literally showed me the way as I ventured into the backcountry. Fellow authors David Hanscom, Alexis Kelner, Tyson Bradley, and Andrew McLean wrote books that I devoured during my early Utah years, so I thank them as well.

Finally, I'd like to thank the entire Utah backcountry skiing and snowboarding community. Your unwavering passion for our mountains and love for "getting after it" are constant inspirations to me. Basically, I wrote this book for you all. Hopefully it inspires you as much as you have inspired me.

INTRODUCTION

UTAH IS HOME to a diverse variety of mountain ranges. In the far north, the Bear Rivers near the Idaho border have lower-elevation summits, but they are cold mountains that harbor dry, deep snow. As you travel south, the Wasatch Mountains rise dramatically from the valley floor, without any foothills, for thousands of vertical feet. All manner of skiing is found along the Wasatch Front: from glade-filled forests to risky steeps in avalanche zones. The Uintas are the highest peaks in Utah, with rounded massifs that are constantly nuked by high winds. The West Desert ranges see less snow, and also fewer people, making for unforgettable skiing in no-man's land. The mountains of southern Utah have been described as "Islands in the Sky," as these snowcapped peaks appear to float above the desert floor when viewed from afar. Snowfall is unpredictable in the south, and the terrain, more adventurous.

The ranges described in this book are only a few that can be skied in Utah. The Deep Creeks, the Skyline Plateau, Monroe Mountain, Mount Dutton, Boulder Mountain, and others most certainly can be explored on skis or splitboard if you have the motivation. Grab a topo map, call the US Forest Service to talk with district rangers, and see what's out there!

Exploring the variety of mountains that we have in Utah on skis or snowboard requires advanced knowledge and skill. A good rule is that anyone venturing into the backcountry must be an expert rider at the resorts. The backcountry is untamed, hazardous, and often deadly. It can take decades of learning about avalanche safety and self-rescue to become an "expert," and even then, Mother Nature may scoff and swipe you off the mountain without conscience. Education is of paramount importance. This introduction is a general overview of the tools, mountain skills, and avalanche training you will need to enjoy a lifetime of safe backcountry travels.

EDUCATION

The best way to learn about the backcountry is to get into the backcountry. However, there are steps you should take before jumping right in.

- **Take an avalanche course:** In fact, take two, or three. I recommend taking a refresher every year just to stay up to date on the latest information and techniques. At a minimum, you should take a Level 1 avalanche course. Providers like the American Institute for Avalanche Research and Education (AIARE), the American Avalanche Institute, and local guide services offer classroom and on-mountain instruction during three-day sessions.

Opposite: *Weaving through the aspen trees above the Boundary Creek Yurt, Uinta Mountains*

Boot packing the final push to the summit ridge on Haystack Mountain, La Sal Mountains

- **Take a Backcountry 101 course:** If you've never skied the backcountry, there are basic skills you should know. A Backcountry 101 course will teach you about avalanche characteristics, snowpack fundamentals, clues to instability, terrain assessment, safe travel techniques, rescue techniques, and good decision making.
- **Learn wilderness first aid:** Mountains are dangerous places, and if the unexpected should happen, you need to be prepared. If anyone in your party is hurt, help can be many miles and hours (even days) away. Wilderness first-aid courses will give you the know-how to deal with emergency situations.
- **Do your research:** Mountaineers Books has several resources for further reading. *Backcountry Skiing: Skills for Ski Touring and Ski Mountaineering* by Martin Volken, Scott Schell, and Margaret Wheeler details the skills you need, like trip planning, terrain navigation, avalanche safety, and specialized backcountry ski techniques. *Staying Alive in Avalanche Terrain* by Bruce Tremper is essential reading. This book covers the avalanche gamut with safe travel techniques, how to perform snow stability tests, and rescue strategies.
- **Practice what you have learned:** Perform beacon drills, practice snow shoveling techniques, religiously read avalanche forecasts, study the weather, keep track of the local snowpack, and log your ski tours for future

reference. If you polish your skills, you won't be rusty when it's suddenly time to put them to the test.

EQUIPMENT

Backcountry skiing and snowboarding requires specialized equipment. Since Utah doesn't have glaciers or crevasses to worry about, a basic backcountry kit is all you will need for most day tours. There is a lot to pack, however, so I keep a checklist by my gear closet.

Ski Gear

- **Skis or splitboard:** Almost any skis can be used for backcountry skiing, but lightweight powder skis are generally best for Utah tours. For ski mountaineering, skinnier, lighter skis are best.
- **Bindings:** You need specialty bindings for backcountry touring. AT (or alpine touring) bindings are most popular. They allow the heel to be free for hiking up and locked down for the descent. Telemark bindings are always free heel and require special telemark skiing skills. Splitboard bindings are removable so they can be used for both ascents and descents. A variety of splitboard binding options are available.
- **Boots:** AT boots are much like alpine skiing boots, but they have a walk mode switch that gives the upper cuff range of motion when hiking. Some boots have embedded tech toe and heel pieces that are used with tech bindings like Dynafits. Telemark boots can only be used with telemark bindings. They have a soft flex at the toe to allow range of motion in the telemark turn. For snowboarders, any soft boot can be used when splitboarding, though a hard boot might be a better choice when mountaineering with crampons in steep terrain.
- **Ski poles:** In the backcountry, it's best to invest in adjustable ski poles. By changing the length of the poles, you can adapt to terrain changes, especially when boot packing up steep slopes or for prolonged sidehilling.
- **Climbing skins:** These are fabric straps made from nylon or mohair that have an adhesive on one side that is attached to the ski or snowboard base to allow for uphill travel.
- **Backpack:** There are a multitude of backcountry-specific packs with pockets for avalanche safety gear. Some have added features like Black Diamond's Avalung. Avalanche air bag packs are becoming commonplace and can increase your chances for survival in a slide.
- **Avalanche transceiver:** Also called a beacon, the transceiver is the only reliable way to locate a completely buried victim in time to save their life. The best transceivers have three antennas with multiple-burial-marking capability.
- **Probe:** A long, collapsible pole, the probe is used to pinpoint an exact location of a buried avalanche victim.

- **Shovel:** Avalanche shovels are small and lightweight and are used to dig out avalanche victims and to dig snow pits for snowpack stability tests. Purchase a strong aluminum version.
- **Slope meter:** This tool measures the slope angle, which is critical knowledge for assessing avalanche terrain.
- **Ski helmet:** Choose a lightweight, ski-specific helmet for the backcountry. Some touring packs feature an external helmet-carry system for storing your helmet when it's not in use.

Personal Gear and the Ten Essentials

Bring proper technical clothing: base layer, mid-layer, outer layer, an extra warm emergency layer, hat, gloves, and wool socks. In addition, don't forget your cell phone and the 10 essentials:

- Navigation (map, compass, altimeter, and GPS receiver)
- Sun protection (sunglasses, sunscreen, and goggles)
- Insulation (extra clothing)
- Illumination (headlamp or flashlight, plus extra batteries)
- First-aid kit
- Fire (firestarter and matches/lighter)
- Repair kit (including multitool)
- Nutrition (extra food)
- Hydration (extra water)
- Emergency shelter

Extras

- **Crampons and ski crampons:** These metal traction devices attach to your boots or ski bindings and may be needed in firm snow for steep ascents.
- **Ice ax and Whippet:** An ice ax is used for self-arrest if you start uncontrollably sliding down steep slopes. Whippets are ski poles made by Black Diamond with a metal pick built into the pole's grip.
- **Harness, belay device, rope, and slings:** All are used for mandatory rappels.
- **Personal tracker:** An emergency electronic unit sends an SOS signal via satellite when activated in an emergency. Some versions transmit GPS coordinates and even text messages through a locating messenger service so a friend or family member can track your progress from a website.
- **Voile straps:** Rubber straps used to keep skis together when you strap them to your backpack. Also used for multiple backcountry applications and temporary gear repair. Throw a couple in your pack.

Perhaps the most important thing to bring into the backcountry is a friend. Good, reliable partners are invaluable in the mountains. It is never wise to travel alone in the backcountry. If you're by yourself and get buried in an avalanche or suffer major trauma, your chances of getting out alive are slim to none.

Looking down into Mud Bowl, Northern Wasatch

This is a very general list of gear that you should own. On short day tours you'll only need the basics, but you may want to bring the entire list on longer routes or mountaineering expeditions. Assess the day's objective beforehand, and pack accordingly.

ROAD CONDITIONS AND FEES

Road closures are common in Utah's mountains after big snowstorms. Little Cottonwood Canyon in the Central Wasatch has the highest highway avalanche hazard index of any major road in the United States, with more than thirty-five avalanche paths. Needless to say, it closes frequently for control work. It's always a good idea to check in with Utah Department of Transportation (UDOT) for current road conditions (www.udot.utah.gov). In addition, authorities may enact 4x4 or chain restrictions on certain roads, especially in the Wasatch Mountains.

Some areas require a recreation fee, such as the Mirror Lake Highway (State Route 150) in the Uinta Mountains, Mill Creek Canyon in the Central Wasatch, and American Fork Canyon in the Southern Wasatch. The cost is minimal, and you can usually pay it at staffed booths located at canyon entrances or at trailhead fee boxes.

MOUNTAIN SAFETY

The very first thing you must do before heading out the door on a ski tour is check the avalanche report. The Utah Avalanche Center (www.utahavalanchecenter.org) posts daily advisories for each of the eight Utah forecast zones. The advisory provides detailed information about snowpack conditions, current weather, upcoming forecasts, and an avalanche danger level that rates from "low" to "extreme." Forecasters even go in depth about the day's avalanche problems, so you can know what to watch out for. This information is essential for planning the day's goals and route selections.

Knowing the weather is also important when you are in the backcountry. You could set out when the avalanche danger is moderate, but an approaching storm with high wind can overload avalanche slopes within hours. Be prepared for dropping temperatures and possible precipitation, and pack accordingly. There are numerous sites to gather weather info. For general statewide forecasts, visit the National Weather Service (www .weather.gov). For Wasatch tours, the Salt Lake City National Weather Service Forecast Office (www.wrh.noaa.gov/slc) is one-stop shopping for forecasts and current weather. They even post a detailed forecast specifically produced for the Cottonwood Canyons (www.wrh.noaa.gov/slc/snow/mtnwx/mtnforecast.php). Another good site is Wasatch Snow Info (www.wasatchsnowinfo.com). This website is a clearinghouse of information with links to resort snow reports, avalanche forecasts, weather station observations, and webcams. It's not just for the Wasatch but for the entire mountain west.

If you do trigger an avalanche in the backcountry, and you are near a ski resort, call the appropriate resort dispatch center to alert them about the slide. Give all the information you have, especially whether anyone is missing, because rescue teams don't need to be called out and exposed to avalanche hazard needlessly.

Salt Lake and Park City–Alta Central, (801) 742-2033

Canyons Resort Dispatch, (435) 615-3322

Snowbasin Resort Dispatch, (801) 620-1017

Powder Mountain Dispatch, (801) 745-3772, ext. 123

Sundance Dispatch, (801) 223-4150

Always check your avalanche beacons before heading up the mountain.

BACKCOUNTRY SKIING ETIQUETTE

As with everything in life, there are rules, even when you go into the backcountry. The whole point of escaping into the backcountry is to get away from the strict boundaries of civilization, but backcountry skiers and snowboarders should still follow certain ethics that keep themselves and others safe, as well as keeping wildlands pristine so future access isn't threatened.

Utah is unique because access is so easy and backcountry skier numbers have exploded, especially in the Central Wasatch. As a result, user conflicts have become a common occurrence in recent years, particularly concerning the safety of drivers on canyon roads below avalanche paths. Utah Avalanche Center forecaster Drew Hardesty has partnered with the Access Fund, Black Diamond, American Avalanche Institute, American Institute for Avalanche Research and Education (AIARE), UDOT, and others to propose a backcountry code of conduct. The latest iteration, called "The Pact," suggests backcountry users think about the following before heading into the mountains:

- Do you know current avalanche conditions? What type of avalanche might you trigger today? Find your forecast at www.avalanche.org.
- Will your ski cut, cornice drop, or ski line trigger an avalanche onto the road or others below? What is your plan in case of an accident?
- Do you know the current avalanche control plans for the highways, ski areas, or heli guides? Are there other parties above or below you?

These commonsense questions could help make the backcountry a safer place by creating a culture of avalanche awareness, respect for others, and self-reliance that will hopefully prevent people being hurt or killed due to the negligence of others. If we don't work together as stewards of the backcountry, we may be subject to permanent terrain closures or a backcountry permit system like what is found at Rogers Pass in British Columbia.

Ethics pertain to the land as well. Much of the terrain described in these pages is within wilderness borders. Use Leave No Trace principles and make the backcountry better than you found it. Pack it in, pack it out. Travel in small groups. Camp at least 200 feet from lakes and streams. Respect wildlife. Be considerate of others. These rules should be applied to all areas of backcountry travel, whether wilderness, Bureau of Land Management (BLM), or publicly accessed private property.

HOW TO USE THIS BOOK
Chapters

For this book, I have grouped the routes into twelve geographic sections, or chapters. I chose the Central Wasatch (which includes the Salt Lake Canyons, Big Cottonwood Canyon, and Little Cottonwood Canyon) to come first, rather than choosing a more standard north-to-south orientation. I did this because the Central Wasatch is unarguably the hub of Utah backcountry skiing and where the vast majority of us go for powder turns.

Scoping out lines on Duke from the summit of Castle Peak, Uinta Mountains

Since the Central Wasatch is the "hub," the chapters that follow radiate out geographically from Salt Lake City based on driving distance. Therefore, the Southern Wasatch comes next, followed by the Northern Wasatch, West Desert, Uintas, and finally the Bear Rivers near Logan. From there, the southern Utah chapters begin with the Tushar Mountains near Beaver, then head east to the Henry Mountains, the La Sal Mountains, and finally the Abajo Mountains in the far southeast corner of the state.

Each chapter begins with an area overview that contains general information about the mountains, ski terrain, weather, access, land management, roads, fees, and other pertinent information you need to know.

Route Information

The tours described in this book are appropriate for both skiers and snowboarders. However, these approach routes are only appropriate for snowboarders who use a splitboard with skins for the ascent. In addition, many longer tours require flat-tracking or skate-skiing on low-angle terrain on the return, which can be problematic for snowboarders. Pair your routes with the appropriate gear.

In writing this book, I decided to focus only on day tours. Even the longest routes here can conceivably be completed from dawn to dusk. However, I have also included many of Utah's excellent backcountry yurts, some of which require a multiday trip. In these cases, the day tours begin from the yurts and not the trailheads.

Each route begins with a list of general information and then moves into a more detailed description, divided into several sections including an introduction, trailhead directions, route description, and map, which are detailed below.

Start Point: The elevation of the trailhead, plowed pullout, or parking lot where the tour begins.

High Point: The highest elevation of the tour—usually a mountain summit or terrain feature where you begin your descent.

Trail Distance: The approximate roundtrip mileage from the trailhead to the top and back. In some cases, this includes roundtrip mileage from backcountry yurts.

Trail Time: The average time it should take to complete the tour, roundtrip, starting and ending at the trailhead or yurt. A lot of variables can change this estimate: speed of the group, rest stops, snow conditions, weather, equipment issues, and so on. It also represents the time it takes to do only one run. If you find awesome powder and choose to make multiple laps, the time will increase accordingly.

I came up with these time estimates based on my own experience as an average backcountry skier in decent shape, taking into account short rests and lunch breaks. I then rounded up the time to the nearest hour for an even number. In general, travel time in skin tracks averaged out to between 1 and 2 miles per hour, give or take, depending on slope steepness and terrain challenges. Less experienced backcountry skiers may need more time, while speed goats will be able to hammer out the routes in half the time. Judge your own physical ability and goals for the day to determine how long it may take you to complete each route, using these time estimates as a base to work from.

Skill Level: This is another category that is very subjective and hard to qualify. It's a basic recommendation for the ability level required to safely and successfully complete a route. The difficulty of both the ascent and descent is taken into account. Factors in a difficulty rating include steepness of terrain, distance, avalanche hazards, routefinding, and technical knowledge required. The tours in this book range from lazy days on low-angle meadows to extreme mountaineering trips that require ice axes, crampons, and even rappels. Difficulty ratings are defined by four categories: Beginner, Intermediate, Advanced, and Expert. Some tours have dual ratings, like Advanced/ Expert. These routes fall between categories because they include multiple ascents and descents of varying difficulty.

Beginner routes are shorter tours near roads that generally stay on low-angle, mellow terrain. These are good choices for those just starting out in the backcountry or anyone learning basic skills like skinning. Don't be fooled, however, because beginner routes in this book would still be considered advanced terrain at a ski resort. Variable snow conditions, trees, rock gardens, cliffs, and other backcountry hazards exist in even the easiest of tours. Also, avalanche danger exists everywhere, so don't assume a "beginner" difficulty rating means that the tour is safe.

Skinning up a west-facing snowfield on Hayden Peak, Uinta Mountains

Intermediate routes represent the vast majority of ski tours in Utah. The ascents are a little longer and involve some routefinding and can be exposed to avalanche zones. The descents are on steeper terrain with moderate slope angles and increased avalanche risk. In fact, all of the intermediate routes included are in the sweet spot for avalanche danger (slope angles above thirty degrees).

Advanced routes up the ante as far as slope steepness, approach distance, and technical skill required. Many of these tours are in remote, upper-elevation terrain above tree line and reach the summits of Utah's highest peaks. Exposure to avalanche hazard is significant. Mountaineering skills using crampons and ice axes may be required. Descents may be on steep faces and bowls, in tight couloirs, and on slopes with cliff exposure. Only attempt these routes if you have significant backcountry experience, are well-versed in avalanche knowledge, and are confident about your search-and-rescue skills if an avalanche does occur.

Expert routes represent tours that require special mountaineering skills like rappeling, belaying, and scrambling; feature descents on very steep, high-consequence terrain; or are exposed to extreme avalanche slopes that should only be attempted during periods of very stable snowpack. Some routes may also have very long, physically demanding approaches. If you want to tick off one of these gems, but don't have the chops, consider hiring a guide.

Best Season: Generally all routes can be skied from fall to summer, even through July in some epic years. But every route has a certain season when it's best to visit. Obviously, most tours are good in the winter months due to snow depth and quality, and the vast majority in this book are recommended winter tours. Routes that are best in the fall are based on road access. For example, tours around Tony Grove in the Bear Rivers and Wolf Creek Pass in the Uintas are accessible only in the fall until access roads become snowed in. Many tours, especially big lines in avalanche terrain, are best skied in the spring when snowpack is more stable and a good melt-freeze cycle creates excellent corn skiing. Also, some areas are only accessible in late spring after roads are plowed and reopened for the summer.

Map: For the most part, I reference the USGS 7.5-minute topographic maps where the route is located. Key labels used in the route description, along with other important information, are found in these maps, and it is highly recommended you carry one on your tours. In the Central Wasatch, many other maps are available, including the Alpentech Wasatch Touring maps and the Wasatch Backcountry Skiing Map. These specialty maps show specific, named descents and point out localized hazards and places where avalanche deaths have occurred.

Introduction: Each route begins with a short intro that gives you a general flavor of the tour. It includes elements like history, best snow locations, oddities, and overall mountain information that will help you in selecting a route for the day and to hopefully get stoked for the tour.

Getting There: Driving directions to the trailhead are from the nearest city or town. The directions generally start at a given intersection within the town and mileage starts from there. There's also information about where to park, which can include actual parking lots or plowed shoulders alongside highways.

The Route: This section is a basic and very general description of a specific route from the beginning of a tour to its end. Mileage and elevation are given at certain landmarks or intersections. Be aware that conditions constantly change in the winter, so landmarks like trail signs may be buried or removed. Only use this guide as a supplement to basic routefinding with a map and compass or GPS, especially when traveling in complex, varied terrain or for long distances. Also, backcountry skiing is all about freedom, and the routes described here are just a few among countless variations you can find. Get creative and explore.

In addition to the ascent route, I point out a few descent options. Some tours have only one way down, while others have dozens. The descents in this book are well-known runs that you'll want to try. But there are many different ways you can ski or snowboard down from a route's high point, and it would be impossible to include them all in detail. In addition, I try to note major hazards, such as notorious avalanche paths and terrain traps that should be avoided, as well as areas with cliff exposure. Although the tours I've outlined generally follow safe and efficient routes (aside from the more advanced and expert tours), nothing is foolproof, and avalanches can occur where you least expect them. Observe current conditions on the mountain, and use those observations to make wise terrain choices.

Tour Map: The map included with each tour is intended to guide you along the route and should be cross-referenced with the route description. The map highlights terrain features, landmarks, start and end of the tour, place names, and ascent and descent recommendations. While maps included with this book are helpful, you should rely on the high-quality 7.5-minute USGS topographic maps and a compass for routefinding, especially if you wish to explore beyond the specific routes described here.

A NOTE ABOUT SKI RESORT EXPANSION

Utah is experiencing a huge surge in population growth, and user pressure on the mountains is greater than ever before. The routes described in this book may change dramatically in the coming years, especially in the Central Wasatch. For decades, there have been efforts to link the seven ski resorts of Park City, Big Cottonwood Canyon, and Little Cottonwood Canyon using a European-style system of lifts and gondolas. The latest iteration is called One Wasatch, and the idea is gaining serious traction. If an interconnect plan ever comes to pass, access to the backcountry in the upper Cottonwood Canyons would either be lift served with boundary gates or swallowed into expanded resort boundaries. Keep that in mind when using this book as a guide in those threatened areas.

A NOTE ABOUT SAFETY

Please use common sense. This book is not intended as a substitute for careful planning, professional training, or your own good judgment. It is incumbent upon any user of this guide to assess his or her own skills, experience, fitness, and equipment. Readers will recognize the inherent dangers in skiing, snowboarding, and backcountry terrain and assume responsibility for their own actions and safety.

Changing or unfavorable conditions in weather, roads, trails, waterways, etc., cannot be anticipated by the author or publisher but should be considered by any outdoor participants, as routes may become dangerous or slopes unstable due to such altered conditions. Likewise, be aware of any changes in public jurisdiction, and do not access private property without permission. The publisher and author are not responsible for any adverse consequences resulting directly or indirectly from information contained in this book.

—*Mountaineers Books*

Opposite: *The protected powder in Porter Fork's evergreen trees lasts for days after a storm.*

NORTHERN SALT LAKE CANYONS

THE NORTH CANYONS OF THE SALT LAKE VALLEY, which include Parleys Canyon, Lambs Canyon, Neffs Canyon, and Mill Creek Canyon, are Utah's true urban backcountry zones. Some tours, like Neffs Canyon and Salt Lake City Foothills, even begin right in the city. In fact, there's a history of skiing in the hills above downtown: back in the 1920s, spectators would gather to watch competitive skiers fly off jumps above the University of Utah. Unfortunately, skiing the low-elevation foothills nowadays is extremely dependent on snowfall. So if you happen to see a weather report that calls for powder to dump in the valley that's measured in feet, not inches, drop everything and ski these routes. You'll never forget the surreal feeling of making powder turns above the downtown skyline.

Parleys Canyon is home to Mount Aire, Millvue Peak, and Summit Park Peak. These are the premier backcountry ski areas for Park City residents, as most backcountry access above the town is either lift served or blocked entirely by private property. Quick access from I-80 makes these routes excellent options for those who seek a short tour from Salt Lake or Park City. The mountainsides in this area are typically sun exposed and brushy, and this side of the Central Wasatch gets less snow than points south. But protected powder can usually be found on north-facing tree shots, especially in Lambs Canyon. Also, Mount Aire's east face is a must-ski tour on a powder day when avalanche danger is low.

Mill Creek Canyon is massively popular for cross-country skiers and dog walkers who park at the winter closure gate and continue up the snow-covered road. While many routes are found in Mill Creek, access is best from the Big Cottonwood side for bi-canyon tours. Porter Fork is the exception. You can find adventure by tree skiing through old-growth forests and making steep turns on avalanche-prone faces just minutes from the city.

Neffs Canyon is a seldom-skied pocket above the Olympus Hills neighborhood on Salt Lake City's east side. Most winter users snowshoe or ride the summer trail down on sleds. But if you endure the long approach to Thomas Fork or the upper reaches of Neffs Canyon, you'll be rewarded with untracked skiing and little competition for freshies.

Of course there are more touring opportunities in these canyons that aren't covered here, such as Killyon Canyon in the upper reaches of Emigration Canyon and City Creek Canyon, where good skiing is found on Grandview Peak. Grab a topo map and go explore!

NOTES

Land Management. Tours in the Northern Salt Lake Canyons are located in Uinta-Wasatch-Cache National Forest, while sections of Porter Fork and Neffs Canyon are within the Mount Olympus Wilderness boundary. Follow all wilderness regulations and practice Leave No Trace principles. If you're winter camping, you must camp at least 200 feet from streams and lakes. Contact information for the Salt Lake Ranger District is located in Resources.

Road Conditions and Fees. Mill Creek Canyon is operated by the US Forest Service. The user fee is $3 per car, or you can purchase a $40 annual pass. Dogs are

Skinning through the brush in the Salt Lake City foothills after a major snowstorm

allowed off leash on odd-numbered days only and must be on leash in all developed areas. If you're planning to do a bi-canyon tour with your pooch, keep in mind that dogs are not allowed in Big Cottonwood Canyon. The winter gate at the Maple Grove parking area closes November 1 and reopens July 1. For an overnight stay, rent the Big Water Yurt, operated by Salt Lake County Parks and Recreation. The yurt is located at 7520 feet in the upper Big Water parking lot. See Resources for more information.

Weather. Check the Utah Avalanche Center's Salt Lake advisory and the National Weather Service website for current conditions. See the Resources page for web addresses and phone numbers.

 Salt Lake City Foothills

Start Point	Terrace Hills Drive trailhead, 5300 feet
High Point	Twin Peaks summit, 6291 feet
Trail Distance	3 miles
Trail Time	2 hours
Skill Level	Intermediate
Best Season	Winter
Maps	USGS Salt Lake City North, Fort Douglas

Multiple tracks in the Salt Lake City foothills after a huge storm dumped several feet of powder

Lake-effect snow is a strange and wonderful thing. It usually hammers the Cottonwood Canyons, but sometimes the valleys are blessed with a storm that buries Salt Lake City in snowfall measured in feet, not inches. When that happens, the foothills above the city become crowded with a plethora of skiers and snowboarders who swarm the rolling terrain around the Bonneville Shoreline Trail to make turns in their own backyard. It's a surreal experience to ski deep powder above the state capitol and downtown skyscrapers, and it's an opportunity not to be missed. While it's possible to tour from any access point in the city, the Terrace Hills Drive trailhead in the Avenues neighborhood is among the highest and provides quick access to thousands of acres of terrain. The following describes one such tour, but the route possibilities are too numerous to include in this book. So just skin up and ski down wherever you like!

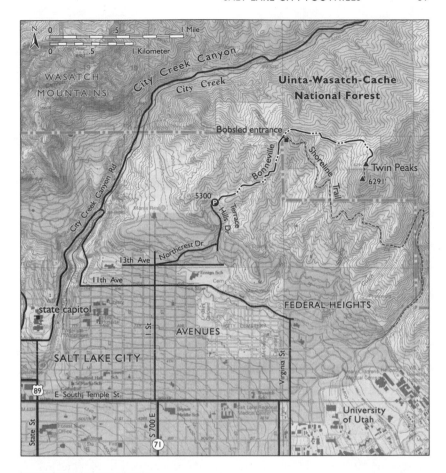

GETTING THERE

From the intersection of State Street and South Temple in Salt Lake City, drive east on South Temple for 1 mile to I Street. Turn left uphill (north) and drive into the Avenues neighborhood. Follow I Street for 1 mile to 13th Avenue, go right, and then hang an immediate left on Northcrest Drive. Continue up the hill for 0.5 mile and turn left on Terrace Hills Drive. Follow it for another 0.4 mile until it dead-ends at a cul-de-sac. Park here, being careful not to block any driveways. There are two trailheads for the Bonneville Shoreline Trail at the west and east sides of the street.

THE ROUTE

While you can skin or hike up anywhere from the Bonneville Shoreline Trail and start making turns, a good option is to climb Twin Peaks, a double summit above the Federal Heights neighborhood. From the east trailhead, follow the trail up into the scrub brush forest. In 0.75 mile, you'll reach a flat area where the popular Bobsled mountain biking trail begins at 5780 feet.

Leave the trail here and climb north up the mountain. After gaining the ridge that overlooks City Creek Canyon at 5950 feet, head east, staying on the ridgeline. It's only 1 mile on the ridge as it curves to the south and then climbs to Twin Peaks at 6291 feet.

Both peaks are somewhat rocky and peppered with scrub oak patches, so use them to take in a view of the city below, and then choose a more wide-open, gentle line on the east or west side of the mountains, where short runs fall to small side-gullies that lead back down to the Bonneville Shoreline Trail. Instead of skiing too far into this bushwhacking territory, skin back up and follow your ascent track on a return to the Bobsled entrance, where you can also pretty much ski or snowboard anywhere in the area that allows enough vertical to make some turns back to the car.

2 Mount Aire

Start Point	Lambs Canyon exit on I-80, 6200 feet
High Point	Mount Aire summit, 8621 feet
Trail Distance	5 miles
Trail Time	4 hours
Skill Level	Intermediate
Best Season	Winter
Map	USGS Mount Aire

Mount Aire, the most prominent peak in Parleys Canyon, is a moderate tour with a straightforward approach and numerous options for a fun descent. The climb up is long but generally mellow, though you won't find peaceful nature with the constant drone of cars and semitrucks on the interstate below. Despite Mount Aire being among the more urban tours in Utah, the mountain is worth climbing for excellent views of Parleys and Mill Creek canyons. Of course, you're there to ski or snowboard, and the east face has got the goods. But be prepared for some serious bushwhacking.

GETTING THERE

From the I-215 interchange on the east side of Salt Lake City, drive east on I-80 for 8 miles up Parleys Canyon, and take the Lambs Canyon exit. Immediately after exiting, park at one of several plowed pullouts near the entrance to Lambs Canyon. If you're coming from Park City, drive west on I-80 and leave the interstate at the same exit.

THE ROUTE

On the west side of the parking area, locate a swath cut into the mountainside. This is an old jeep road. Follow this track northwest as it parallels the interstate for 0.35 mile. At this point, leave the main road and go south up the hillside on a smaller,

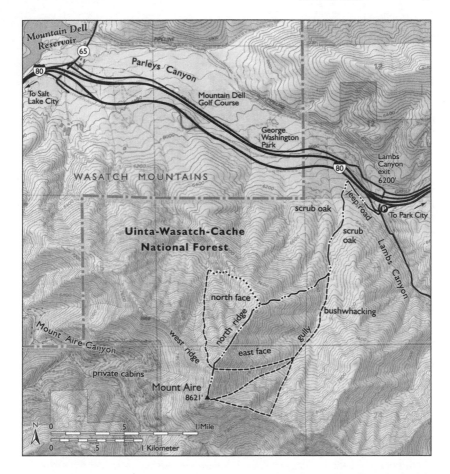

lesser-used track. You won't see it under the snow, but there is usually a skin track in place, and it's the only opening into the thick grove of scrub oak. Keep following the trail as best as you can, because if you get off course, you'll end up bushwhacking through a tangle of jacket-tearing branches.

About a mile from the trailhead, the trees thin out and you'll be skinning through more brushy terrain at around 6900 feet. As you climb, follow a broad, low-angle ridge, southwest that connects to Mount Aire's north summit ridge at 7600 feet. From here, keep trending south by traversing the ridge for another mile and 1000 vertical feet to the top.

The summit of Mount Aire is the start point for several choice ski lines. You may find skiable lines on the west face, but snow quality is questionable, and you'll end up skiing into private property. For cold snow on the north face, ski back down the summit ridge to about 8575 feet where the north ridge connects in a triangle with the west ridge. This triangle is what you want to descend. Wide slopes give way to well-spaced aspen trees, which eventually become too thick for making turns. Skin

Ascent ridge and skin track to the summit of Mount Aire

east back up to the north summit ridge for a quick run back to the car, or retrace your ascent to regain Mount Aire's summit.

The prize line is the east face. Three distinct, steep runs come down from at or near the top. The middle run has the most vertical and sustained fall line at a 40-degree pitch. At the bottom, you'll have to exit through a frozen creek bed choked with brush and trees.

As far as atrocious bushwhacks go, this is probably in Utah's top three. Carefully ski through the pole-tangling trees to a bobsled-type descent in the main gully until it meets up with your skin track in the scrub oak. Follow this back to the car.

3 Millvue Peak

Start Point : Lambs Canyon trailhead, 6630 feet
High Point : Millvue Peak summit, 8926 feet
Trail Distance : 5 miles
Trail Time : 3 hours
Skill Level : Intermediate
Best Season : Winter
Map : USGS Mount Aire

Millvue Peak, an unassuming mountain that lies along the Mill Creek–Lambs Canyon Divide, is a favorite secret for local skiers, splitboarders, and snowshoers. It's easily reached from Lambs Canyon on a well-worn summer trail that cuts through enormous old-growth pine forests and aspen groves. Excellent skiing through perfectly spaced trees that are well protected from wind and sun can be found all over the north-, east-, and west-facing aspects of ridges that surround the peak. An especially good tour can be found in the fir trees on the east side of the canyon on the flanks of Millvue Peak.

GETTING THERE

From the I-215 interchange on the east side of Salt Lake City, drive east on I-80 for 8 miles up Parleys Canyon, and take the Lambs Canyon exit. Drive south on Lambs Canyon Road for 1.5 miles to the Lambs Canyon trailhead. There is a small parking area next to a restroom. If you're coming from Park City, drive west on I-80 and leave the interstate at the same exit.

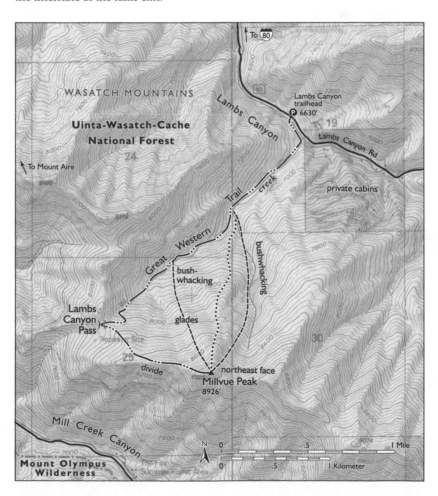

THE ROUTE

Walk southwest across the road to a well-signed trailhead. The path immediately goes down to a creek bottom and crosses a bridge. Beyond the bridge, skin up a couple of switchbacks and generally follow the Great Western Trail route through a forest of quaking aspens and evergreens directly up the canyon. In about 1.4 miles, the route steepens as it leaves the canyon bottom and heads straight up the mountainside on long switchbacks to the top of Lambs Canyon Pass at 8170 feet. It's just over 1400 vertical feet and 1.7 miles from the trailhead to this point.

The views of Mill Creek Canyon and the Salt Lake Valley far below are spectacular from the pass and provide a splendid backdrop for a traverse of the ridge to the top of Millvue Peak. Simply go left (southeast) and follow the undulating Mill Creek–Lambs Canyon Divide for 0.5 mile to the top of Millvue Peak, which is marked by a communications tower just below the summit.

Alternatively, Millvue's north ridge is a faster but steeper way to ascend, but it lacks the dramatic views of the ridge traverse from the pass. Just over a half mile from the trailhead, you'll reach a side-drainage on your left. Cross the snow-covered creek and head straight up the fall line as it follows the ridge 0.8 mile to the summit. This is a good option if you're short on time.

Skiing and snowboarding lines are plentiful here, as you can weave through the pine glades on north-facing slopes from the ridge, or make turns straight from the summit. The northwest glades are a safer choice just after a storm, but if avalanche conditions are low, then the open northeast face is the king line. Both shots return to the bottom of Lambs Canyon, but prepare for some bushwhacking. Private cabins are located on the hillsides east of the trail, so take care not to trespass.

Gladed evergreens with ample turning space on Millvue Peak's north side

Summit Park Peak features some of the most accessible tree skiing in the Park City backcountry.

Summit Park Peak

Start Point	Summit Park Peak trailhead, 7286 feet
High Point	Summit Park Peak summit, 8618 feet
Trail Distance	3 miles
Trail Time	2 hours
Skill Level	Beginner/Intermediate
Best Season	Winter
Map	USGS Park City West

If you're a backcountry skier living in Park City, you know access options are severely limited. With ski resort expansion swallowing up the entire Park City ridgeline, touring from one of America's most famous ski towns can be disheartening. So it's no wonder that Summit Park Peak is so dang popular. This small mountain at the top of Parleys Summit is one of the few places to make backcountry turns in the area, is easy to reach, and boasts one of the best 360-degree views in the county. Plus, the skiing isn't bad either.

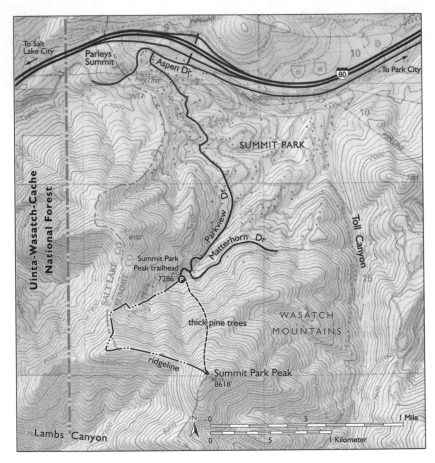

GETTING THERE

From Salt Lake City or Park City, take I-80 east or west (depending on your starting point) to Parleys Canyon and take the Parleys Summit exit. Turn right (west) onto Aspen Drive, and take your first left (south) onto Parkview Drive. Stay on Parkview Drive as it winds through the Summit Park neighborhood until it dead-ends at a T intersection with Matterhorn Drive. This intersection is the trailhead.

THE ROUTE

From the well-signed Summit Park Peak trailhead, skin southwest and up into the evergreen forest. The ascent route roughly follows summer mountain biking and hiking trails that switchback to the top, but a well-established skin track that will likely be in place makes more efficient work of the climb by taking shortcuts. In about a quarter mile, you'll gain the ridge separating Parleys Canyon from Lambs Canyon at about 8070 feet. To top out on Summit Park Peak, follow the ridge east another 0.5 mile to the top of the mountain.

Descent routes are plentiful. You can drop in anywhere along the Summit Park Peak ridgeline, where you'll find open glades. You can also ski from the summit, though the trees are steeper and thicker here. A good rule of thumb in Summit Park is if you ski into thick trees, traverse left or right until you reach another open glade. You can link open tree skiing in this way until you reach the trailhead or Matterhorn Drive for a short walk back to the car.

There's a lot of private property in the area, so be very careful not to ski into someone's backyard.

 Porter Fork

Start Point	Porter Fork trailhead, 6000 feet
High Points	Point 9661, 9661 feet; Point 9776, 9776 feet
Trail Distance	8 miles
Trail Time	5 hours
Skill Level	Advanced
Best Season	Winter
Maps	USGS Mount Aire; Wasatch Backcountry Skiing; Alpentech Wasatch Touring 1

Backcountry skiing in Mill Creek Canyon doesn't get much more accessible than Porter Fork. Sure, many classic tours in Mill Creek exist at higher elevations, but those ascents usually start in Big Cottonwood Canyon. Along with the main drainage, Porter Fork contains several side-canyons that have skiable terrain, but this route focuses on Main Porter Fork. Around Porter Fork Pass and Point 9661, you can find powder-protecting evergreens, low-angle meadows, and steep headwalls. The western cirque below Point 9776 has challenging steeps in avalanche terrain. Overall, you can expect to see fewer people in the skin track than at other Wasatch backcountry zones, but all this comes at a price as the approach is a bit long from Mill Creek Canyon Road.

GETTING THERE

From east Salt Lake City, take I-215 south and exit at 3300 South. Go left over the overpass and turn right on Wasatch Boulevard. Drive south for about a mile and turn left (east) onto 3800 South, which becomes Mill Creek Canyon Road. Drive up the canyon for 4.2 miles to the Porter Fork trailhead, just 0.2 mile beyond the Log Haven restaurant. A sign on the south side of the road marks the trailhead, where a tiny parking area sits in front of a closed winter gate. If this lot is full, additional parking can be found at the Burch Hollow trailhead just 500 feet up the road.

THE ROUTE

Lower Porter Fork is filled with cabins and summer homes, so the tour starts on a wide summer road that is covered in snow in the winter. Go around the gate and head

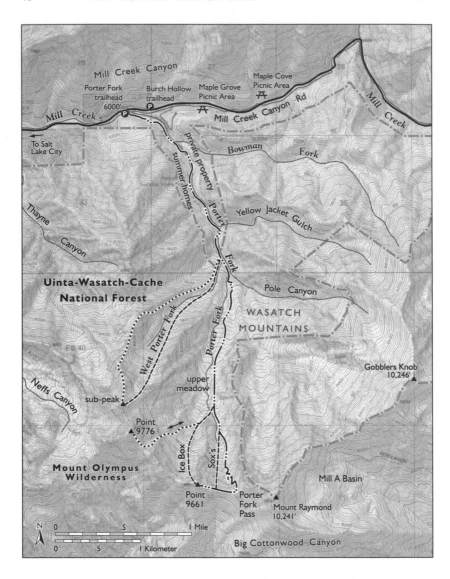

south on the road, being careful not to stray into private property. The skinning here is easy as the road is usually packed and well-traveled.

The cabin area and road ends about 1.5 miles in, at the Mount Olympus Wilderness boundary. From here, you may find tracks on your left heading east into Pole Canyon, and on your right leading into West Porter Fork. Ignore these and keep going straight up the main canyon. From the wilderness boundary, the trail narrows as it switchbacks a couple times up the canyon. Soon after the switchbacks, the trail mellows out and meanders through aspen and fir, with the occasional small meadow in between.

After skinning for about 2.7 miles, you'll come to the upper meadow at around 8200 feet, which is also the bottom of a major avalanche path, evidenced by small trees and new growth. There are a few branches of the trail that lead into the upper headwalls and high points, but the safest ascent is Porter Fork Pass. To get there, stay left at the toe of a heavily wooded ridge that splits the upper canyon and follow the standard summer trail route an additional 0.75 mile on low-angle terrain to the pass, where you'll be treated to expansive views of Big Cottonwood Canyon and beyond.

From the pass, you can meadow-skip back the way you came. This is a good option if avalanche danger is high. If you're up for steeper skiing and snowboarding, follow the Big Cottonwood–Mill Creek Divide west toward Point 9661. Along this ridge are steep, north-facing tree shots called Sox's. West of the point, there are more steep trees and an open bowl called the Ice Box. This is a big avalanche area, so tread carefully.

Other skiing options are on steep faces below Point 9776 on the west side of Porter Fork. From the upper meadow, go right and stay out of avalanche terrain by following a sub-ridge for about 0.7 mile and nearly 1500 vertical feet to the divide or the summit. This point is also where tours from Neffs Canyon (Tour 6) connect to Porter Fork. Again, descents from this western cirque are very dangerous when snow stability is in question.

Playtime in Sox's, a tree run at the head of Porter Fork

For a shorter tour, West Porter Fork offers up good skiing and splitboarding with reasonably safe ascent routes. Immediately after the summer cabin area where you pass the wilderness boundary, look for a tree-covered ridge to your right (west). Ascend this ridge for approximately 1.5 miles as it goes west then curves south to a sub-peak north of Point 9776. Descend the northeast-facing upper face into the West Porter Fork drainage. This is a major slide path, so evaluate snow stability before dropping in.

To return to the trailhead, simply follow your ascent route down Porter Fork. Some sections may be challenging in low snow, and the road in the cabin area is sometimes crowded with hikers and their dogs, so watch your speed around corners.

6 Neffs Canyon

Start Point : Neffs Canyon trailhead, 5610 feet
High Point : Point 9776, 9776 feet
Trail Distance : 8 miles
Trail Time : 5 hours
Skill Level : Advanced
Best Season : Winter
Maps : USGS Sugar House, Mount Aire; Wasatch Backcountry Skiing; Alpentech Wasatch Touring 1

Neffs Canyon is perhaps the closest trailhead for backcountry skiing in the Salt Lake City area. This drainage is very popular with hikers and dogs, even in the winter months, but it sees little love from backcountry skiers and splitboarders due to its

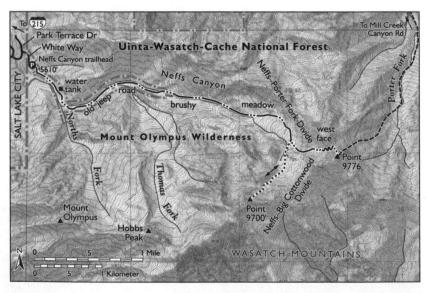

Skiing low-angle meadows in upper Neffs Canyon

low elevation, brushy slopes, and long approach to the upper basin where you can find some actual skiable slopes. But if you put in the effort to skin to the top, you'll reap the benefit of empty aspects, massive views from rocky summits, and a chance to make turns where most skiers never think to go. Neffs is also a good alternate approach for shuttle tours into Mill Creek Canyon via Porter Fork.

GETTING THERE

From east Salt Lake City, take I-215 south and exit at 3300 South. Go left over the overpass and turn right on Wasatch Boulevard. Drive south for about a mile to 3800 South and turn left as if you're driving to Mill Creek Canyon. At the first stop sign turn right onto Parkview Drive and drive 1.1 miles through the Olympus Cove neighborhood to Park Terrace Drive. Turn left and continue to White Way, where a sign points the way to Neffs Canyon. Go right and head uphill to the end of the road, where there is a large parking area at the trailhead.

THE ROUTE

The trail begins at the northeast corner of the parking lot. At this low elevation, you may have to hike on dirt for a bit early or late in the season. Otherwise, skin up the wide old jeep road into the canyon. In a quarter mile, you'll pass a large water tank on your left. In 0.5 mile, the path becomes much narrower as the foliage closes in. Cross a stream and veer left into a dense scrub oak forest.

You'll come to a sign marking the boundary of the Mount Olympus Wilderness 1.6 miles up the canyon. Soon after the wilderness boundary, the canyon becomes very narrow and the streambed falls away from the trail. This spot can be rocky and treacherous, especially if ice forms on the packed trail. Avoid this section by going right about 20 yards past the wilderness sign. You'll come to a bench. Follow it up the canyon for 0.2 mile until it rejoins the trail.

Reach the large, open meadow in the upper portion of Neffs Canyon 2.5 miles from the trailhead. Most snowshoers and hikers turn around here, as the terrain gets steeper from this point. It's also a good place for lunch while you scope out lines on the jagged upper peaks.

To get to the top of Point 9776, the highest peak in Neffs, keep going directly east toward the most obvious peak at the head of the canyon. After 0.5 mile, at the end of the meadow, the terrain rises up onto small sub-ridges covered in aspen trees. Aim for the saddle between Point 9776 and a small peak to the north, and switchback up the ridge. Once you gain the saddle, it's a quick jaunt south to the summit. In total, it's about 1 mile from the meadow to the top.

From here, you can make laps on the broad west face, or drop east into Porter Fork in Mill Creek Canyon. This is a popular option for ski tours as the north- to east-facing slopes hold better snow. To return, you'll have to skin back up to the Mill Creek Divide, or leave a shuttle car at the Porter Fork trailhead (see Porter Fork, Tour 5).

Another good option for skiing and snowboarding is to skin to the Neffs–Big Cottonwood Canyon Divide. From the meadow, tour into the aspen trees as described above, but keep right as the canyon contours south. Stay along the edge of the woods and large rock formations that form the western boundary of the drainage. At the divide around 9700 feet, you'll be treated to splendid views of the Wasatch Mountains and the Salt Lake Valley far below. It's about 3.7 miles and 3600 vertical feet from the trailhead to this point. You'll find good, moderate, north-facing tree skiing here.

When you're ready to retrace your ascent route to the trailhead, be careful in the narrow parts of the canyon, as it is brushy and challenging to slow down. Also, Neffs Canyon is very popular with hikers and their dogs, so stay in control.

 **7   Thomas Fork**

Start Point	Neffs Canyon trailhead, 5610 feet
High Points	Point 9773, 9773 feet; Point 9750, 9750 feet
Trail Distance	7 miles
Trail Time	5 hours
Skill Level	Advanced
Best Season	Winter
Maps	USGS Sugar House, Mount Aire; Wasatch Backcountry Skiing; Alpentech Wasatch Touring 1

Thomas Fork, an offshoot drainage of Neffs Canyon, is a steep, wooded, long tour that pays big with expansive views on top. With an elevation gain of 4200 feet over 3.5 miles, Thomas Fork is no small undertaking, despite its proximity to Salt Lake's suburbs. The tour arguably has better skiing and snowboarding options than Neffs Canyon, such as moderate tree skiing through the rolling drainage bottom and steep chutes on Hobbs Peak. Plus, the head of Thomas Fork is home to the elusive Whipple Couloir entrance.

GETTING THERE

From east Salt Lake City, take I-215 south and exit at 3300 South. Go left over the overpass and turn right on Wasatch Boulevard. Drive south for about a mile to 3800 South and turn left as if you're driving to Mill Creek Canyon. At the first stop sign turn right on Parkview Drive and drive 1.1 miles through the Olympus Cove neighborhood to Park Terrace Drive. Turn left and continue to White Way, where a sign

Hobbs Peak is a triangular mountain split by Hobbs Chute—the marquee ski line in Thomas Fork.

points the way to Neffs Canyon. Go right and head uphill to the end of the road, where there is a large parking area at the trailhead.

THE ROUTE

The trail begins at the northeast corner of the parking lot. At this low elevation, you may have to hike on dirt for a bit early or late in the season. Otherwise, use skis and skins to go up the wide old jeep road into the canyon. In a quarter mile, you'll pass a large water tank on your left. In 0.5 mile, the path becomes much narrower as the foliage closes in. Cross a stream and veer left into a dense scrub oak forest.

Approximately 1.1 miles in, leave the canyon bottom and skin into the thick scrub oak to your right (south). There may be a skin track already in place to lead you into this "secret entrance." If you reach the sign marking the Mount Olympus Wilderness, you've gone way too far.

Skinning up through scrub oak is a hateful bushwhacking experience, and there's about a half mile of it before you ascend into more open terrain. When you get a view of what's ahead, stay generally left, as it's safer from avalanches that can come down from above but is still technically an avy path and should be ascended carefully. At the top of the slide path, near 7700 feet, the terrain levels. Stay left of a small, craggy hill by staying in the trees, and skirt around the steep lower slopes of Point 9750. Here, you'll be treated to a fine view of Hobbs Peak (also known as Triangle Peak for obvious reasons) and the tasty-looking Hobbs Chute that splits the mountain down the middle.

The primary tour leads to the top of Point 9750. Switchback up the mountain's steep, sparsely wooded, west-facing slope to the summit. If you want to ski the Whipple Couloir, traverse south just below the summit to a cleft between the mountain and a rock outcrop. The entrance is hidden here. Many touring parties who ski the couloir hike back up it for a return descent down Neffs, as the exit into Big Cottonwood Canyon is a long, heinous bushwhack.

From the top of Point 9750, ski the patches of open snow down your ascent route. Another skiable option is from Point 9773. Gain the ridge by circumnavigating the rock outcrop at the top of Whipple Couloir, and traverse southwest for 0.25 mile to the top. The descent is on a small, open bowl below and to the west of the summit. Ski the open face for 400 vertical feet, then traverse skier's left above small cliffs. Enter the trees and ski them down into the bottom of Thomas Fork. This tree run is known locally as the Abyss. You can also ski this by skinning up the run from the base of Hobbs Peak to the top of a small sub-peak between Hobbs and Point 9773.

Of course the most visually stunning line is Hobbs Chute. To ski it, strap skis or snowboard to your pack and kick steps straight up the thing. It's around 500 vertical feet of hiking. While that doesn't translate much for ski turns, this aesthetic line is a must-do for any Thomas Fork tour, especially in the spring when the snowpack is stable corn.

To exit Thomas Fork, make turns through the rolling slopes down your ascent route (skier's right) or go down a large slide path on the west side of the canyon (skier's left).

The latter option is steeper and exposed, so only attempt this exit if you're confident in the snowpack's stability.

As you ski down the bottom of Neffs Canyon, be very careful on the narrow trail, as it is brushy and challenging to scrub your speed. Also, the canyon is popular with hikers, even in winter, so stay in control on the way down.

Bonus points go to the fact that Thomas Fork is one of the few areas in the Wasatch where dogs are allowed, so it's an ideal, uncrowded place to take your best friend on a ski tour.

Opposite: *All smiles on a bluebird powder day in the Silver Fork Meadow Chutes* (Mike DeBernardo)

BIG COTTONWOOD CANYON

DEEP POWDER, PERFECTLY SPACED ASPEN TREES, big lines with high consequences, and mellow tours can all be found in Big Cottonwood Canyon. Nowhere else in Utah can you find a better variety of terrain for all skill levels. Beginners can cut their teeth on the low-angle bowls of Powder Park or Toms Hill. Short Swing, Beartrap Fork, and Willow Fork hold some of the best intermediate tree skiing in the state, while steep runs on Kessler Peak or Broads Fork will challenge advanced ski parties. There are even tours long enough to warrant overnight camping to maximize exploration time, such as Mill B South Fork.

In general, tours on the north side of the canyon are easier (with the exceptions of Gobblers Knob and Mount Raymond). Glades, gentle faces, and good skiing are found on all aspects. However, this side is also more sun exposed, which means snow quality goes down during long high-pressure systems. Bi-canyon tours into Mill Creek Canyon generally begin from trailheads on the north side of State Route 190.

The south side is Big Cottonwood's gnar zone, with massive avalanche paths and steep chutes. Cold, north-facing evergreen trees, like those found in Greens Basin, are common and keep powder soft and dry long after a storm. Tours linking with Little Cottonwood Canyon are possible, especially from Silver Fork and Cardiff Fork. The former is home to the Meadow Chutes, which is a very popular area after a powder dump. The latter is a patchwork of private property, so touring access up Cardiff is always an issue.

The backcountry in upper Big Cottonwood Canyon is always under threat from ski resort expansion, especially a long-sought-after interconnect plan to link all seven ski resorts in the Central Wasatch. Routes near Solitude and Brighton, such as Silver Fork Meadow Chutes and Brighton Hill, are current as of this writing, but they may change dramatically in the future.

NOTES

Land Management. Tours in Big Cottonwood Canyon are located in Uinta-Wasatch-Cache National Forest, while parts of the canyon's north side, mostly from the Butler Fork trailhead, fall within the Mount Olympus Wilderness boundary. Follow all wilderness regulations and practice Leave No Trace principles. If you tour on Kessler Peak, know that much of Cardiff Fork is a patchwork of private property, but a special-use agreement between the Cardiff Canyon Owners Association and the US Forest Service allows right-of-way for backcountry skiers and hikers. If you're winter camping in the Big Cottonwood Canyon backcountry, you must camp at least 200 feet from streams and lakes. Contact information for the Salt Lake Ranger District is located in Resources.

Road Conditions. SR 190, also called Big Cottonwood Canyon Scenic Byway, sees the occasional closure for avalanche control work, especially on Kessler Peak. Check the UDOT website (see Resources) before heading up the morning after a big storm, and follow all backcountry closure signs during control work. On the plus side, Big Cottonwood has far fewer avalanche paths than Little Cottonwood and closes much less often. So if Little is shut down, get the goods in Big. Also, a 4x4 vehicle or tire chains are usually required for canyon entry on snow days.

Weather. Big Cottonwood Canyon is blessed with an annual average of 400–500 inches of snowfall in the upper canyon. The Brighton and Solitude snow reports are good sources for new snow totals. Before heading out, check the Utah Avalanche Center's Salt Lake advisory and the National Weather Service website for current weather and snowpack conditions. See the Resources page for web addresses and phone numbers.

 8 Bonkers

Start Point : Broads Fork trailhead, 6200 feet
High Point : Broads Fork–Stairs Gulch Saddle, 10,200 feet
Trail Distance : 8 miles
Trail Time : 6 hours
Skill Level : Advanced/Expert
Best Season : Winter
Maps : USGS Mount Aire, Dromedary Peak; Wasatch Backcountry
: Skiing; Alpentech Wasatch Touring 1

Bonkers, a massive ski line in upper Broads Fork, absolutely belongs on the list of classic descents in the Wasatch. A steep 4000-foot climb in four miles gets you to

Salt Lake City buzzes in the valley far below the upper slopes of Broads Fork.

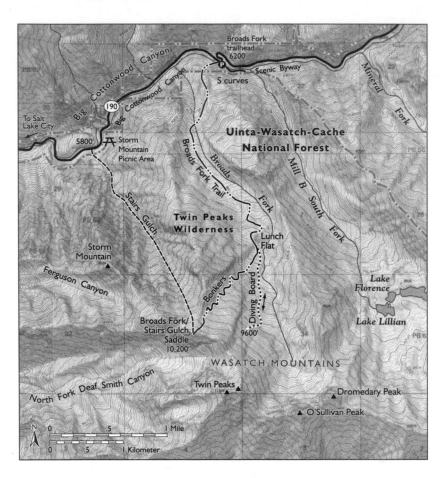

the top, where you'll be rewarded with a nearly 2000-foot descent on a wide-open, northeast-facing ramp. The run is so long you can feasibly make a hundred turns from top to bottom. Just try to ski this thigh-burner without stopping. The saddle atop Bonkers also allows easy access into the expert-only Stairs Gulch, an enormous, glacier-carved gully that drops 5000 feet to the highway below. Both runs are pretty much snow-covered rock slabs, making for unusual avalanche danger (think glide cracks). Ski here only when the snowpack is highly stable.

GETTING THERE

From east Salt Lake City, take I-215 south and exit at 6200 South. Go south on Wasatch Boulevard to Big Cottonwood Canyon Scenic Byway (State Route 190). Drive up the canyon road for 4.2 miles to the S curves, where the Broads Fork Trail shares a trailhead with Mill B South Fork. In winter, park along the road in the vicinity of the first S curve.

THE ROUTE

From the S curves, pick up the Broads Fork summer trail on your right as it heads west above Big Cottonwood Canyon Scenic Byway. In spring, you may have to walk on dirt to the snow level. The trail quickly rises into a fir and aspen forest until it levels out at a hanging valley in Broads Fork proper. In 2 miles, you'll reach a flat meadow at 8300 feet that reveals the whole massive terrain of upper Broads Fork. I call it the Lunch Flat as it's a sweet place for a bite to eat while scoping out skiable lines. From this vantage, Bonkers is the wide snowfield directly to the southwest.

From the flat, switchback straight up the line for nearly 2000 feet to a saddle. Most touring parties drop in here, descending alongside the up track for a run of epic proportions. You can also start the descent on the terrain above Bonkers below Twin Peaks, but it is fraught with cliffs and rock slabs and must be avoided if there are any doubts about snow stability.

From the saddle, another option is Stairs Gulch, a north-facing slide path that will make your palms sweat just looking at it. This is a serious, expert-only descent. But during a window of perfect weather and snow safety, this gulch can be the run of a lifetime. Leave a car near the Storm Mountain Picnic Area for a shuttle, or hitchhike back to your car at the Broads Fork trailhead.

The Diving Board is another fun run. It's a huge apron just beyond Bonkers that earned its name because of the popular rock in the middle that skiers and snowboarders like to huck. To get there, simply skin a bit farther up canyon from the Lunch Flat, and switchback up the next obvious snowfield southeast of Bonkers. Again, only travel here if you are absolutely sure that avalanche stability exists.

To return, descend Broads Fork, the way you came in. The narrow and rocky lower trail is among the most challenging exits in the Wasatch, especially if the snow is crusty and shallow. You'll want to conjure up your inner child and snowplow.

9 Mill B South Fork

Start Point	Mill B South Fork trailhead, 6200 feet
High Points	Monte Cristo Cirque, 10,500 feet; Atheys Line saddle, 10,650 feet
Trail Distance	9–10 miles
Trail Time	8 hours
Skill Level	Advanced
Best Season	Winter
Maps	USGS Mount Aire, Dromedary Peak; Wasatch Backcountry Skiing; Alpentech Wasatch Touring 1

Mill B South Fork is a massive drainage with tons of quality skiing, from headwalls, cirques, and slide paths. In the summer, the Lake Blanche Trail to the Sundial is one of the most popular hikes in the Central Wasatch as thousands of people ascend to

Skinning toward the Sundial near Lake Blanche in Mill B South Fork

the crystal waters of Lake Blanche. But in winter, upper Mill B South Fork is empty. Skiers and snowboarders simply don't go there. There are reasons for this, the main point being that it's hard to get to. A narrow trail from the Big Cottonwood Canyon side requires a long approach, while getting there from Little Cottonwood Canyon means traversing miles of ridgetops while bypassing world-class ski and snowboard terrain that will assuredly change your destination plans along the way. But if you do venture into this hidden gem, you'll be rewarded with the dramatic sawtooth mountains of Sundial, Dromedary, and Monte Cristo along with a 100 percent chance of scoring fresh tracks in your own personal alpine paradise. Plus, Lake Blanche is an excellent spot for winter camping.

GETTING THERE

From east Salt Lake City, take I-215 south and exit at 6200 South. Go south on Wasatch Boulevard to Big Cottonwood Canyon Scenic Byway (State Route 190). The Mill B South Fork trailhead is 4.2 miles up the canyon road, just below the S curves, where you can park along the road in the vicinity of the first curve.

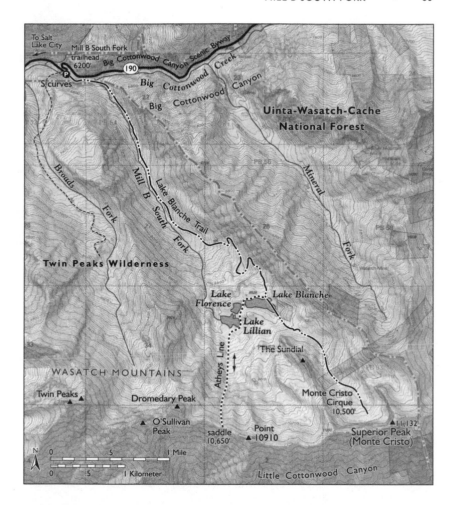

THE ROUTE

From the parking area, skin east along the summer trail adjacent to Big Cottonwood Creek. In less than a half mile, go right at a sign that reads, "Lake Blanche Trail" and follow the path all the way up Mill B South Fork to Lake Blanche. It's about 2700 feet of elevation gain over 3 miles from the trailhead to the lake at 8920 feet. Many skiers choose to camp here or at Blanche's sister lakes, Lake Florence and Lake Lillian, to the west. Winter camping is recommended as it is the only way you'll have time to explore the massive amount of terrain above the lakes.

From Lake Blanche, you have two options. First, you can climb left around the Sundial and skin for 1.5 miles up the open snowfields to access Monte Cristo Cirque at about 10,500 feet. Ski back down the way you came.

Your second option is to trend right from the lake for the open headwalls beneath Dromedary Peak, one of which is the legendary Atheys Line, named after Bob Athey, the Wizard of the Wasatch, who pioneered the route. It's a beautiful series of short couloirs that link together open snowfields that spill down to the flats above Lake Lillian. To get there from Lake Blanche, go southwest to Lake Lillian, then skin south for about a mile toward a saddle between Dromedary Peak and Point 10910. Climb directly up the line by switchbacking or boot packing until you top out on the saddle at about 10,650 feet. Ski the gloriously aesthetic run back down the way you came.

These two featured routes are just a couple examples of skiing and snowboarding that can be found in the upper areas of Mill B South Fork. There's much more scenic, high-alpine touring in open bowls, chutes, and very rocky terrain. You'll just have to explore it! But remember, exposure is high here, which means the snow may be either sun crusted or wind scoured. New snowfall creates avalanche danger, and the upper cirques have plenty of that. Hang fire lurks everywhere beneath cliffs and rock bands that pepper the slopes in all directions, with frightening avalanche crowns dozens of feet deep. Plus, glide avalanches are common in the spring. Travel carefully!

Returning to the car can be sketchy when you ski back down the summer trail to Big Cottonwood Creek. The thin, often icy trail winds through scrub oak, aspen, and brush, and descending can be a challenging, thigh-burning experience, especially when wearing a heavy pack.

10 Mineral Fork

Start Point : Mineral Fork trailhead, 7000 feet
High Point : Point 10481, 10,481 feet
Trail Distance : 8 miles
Trail Time : 5 hours
Skill Level : Advanced
Best Season : Winter
Maps : USGS Mount Aire, Dromedary Peak; Wasatch Backcountry Skiing; Alpentech Wasatch Touring 1

Mineral Fork is historically famous for the once-bustling Wasatch and Regulator Johnson mines, whose crumbling infrastructure are popular sites for summer hikers and mountain bikers. But winter belongs to backcountry skiers and splitboarders, and that's when the canyon becomes a playground for those looking to escape crowds found in the upper Cottonwood Canyons. The approach from the highway is long, but it rewards touring parties with steep terrain and relentless views. Upper Mineral Fork (a.k.a. the Room of Doom) is fraught with dangerous avalanche potential, but lower reaches have anchored, wooded glades that can be skied during unstable periods.

GETTING THERE

From east Salt Lake City, take I-215 south and exit at 6200 South. Go south on Wasatch Boulevard to Big Cottonwood Canyon Scenic Byway (State Route 190).

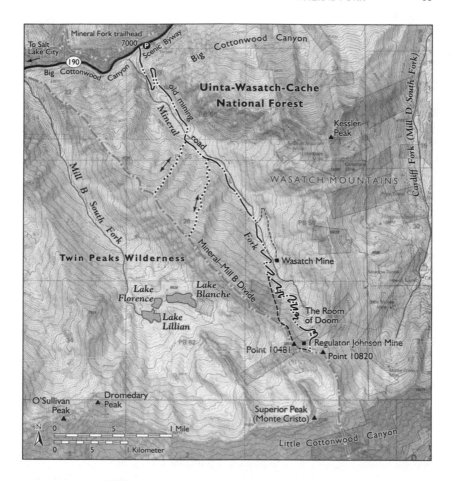

Drive 6 miles up the canyon road, and watch for the Mineral Fork trailhead on the right. There is a small pullout next to the highway shoulder and a brown metal gate across the start of the trail.

THE ROUTE

From the trailhead, follow the old mining road as it parallels a streambed. The route starts out with a few switchbacks, and then becomes more level when it reaches the canyon proper. You'll skin through thick aspen forest for about 2 miles until the foliage opens up, offering your first glimpse of the huge terrain you can ski in Mineral Fork. It is here that you will reach a fork in the trail at 8200 feet. Left crosses the creek and switchbacks up to the Wasatch Mine, where the trail dead-ends. Instead, stay right, where there is probably a set skin track along the east-facing aspect as this route accesses good east-facing shots off the west ridge.

Approaching upper Mineral Fork in the vicinity of the old Wasatch Mine

A mile beyond the Wasatch Mine turnoff, the terrain gets really steep. Switchback up and around a large shelf of cliffs into the upper bowl, called the Room of Doom. It's best to tour here only if the snowpack is stable since huge slides are common, as evidenced by the giant swaths of avalanche paths that run all the way to the creek.

From the trailhead it's about 3.75 miles to the upper bowl, but you can continue farther by boot packing up from the Regulator Johnson Mine to the Mineral–Mill B South Fork Divide to a saddle between Point 10481 and Point 10820.

To return, ski down the Room of Doom and retrace your skin track back on the old mining road to the trailhead. You can also ski steep shots off the Mineral–Mill B Divide by following the ridge northwest of Point 10481 and descending the lineup of slide paths that fall to the bottom of Mineral Fork.

For a shorter tour, the east-facing slopes of lower Mineral Fork have good powder shots that alternate from trees to open faces. From the 7600- to 7700-foot elevations in the bottom of Mineral Fork, choose one of the obvious sub-ridges that go up to the Mineral–Mill B Divide. These ridges provide a somewhat safer haven from avalanches than skinning directly up the face. Ski or snowboard one of the many east-facing shots back down to the canyon bottom.

11 Kessler Peak

Start Point : Argenta trailhead, 7000 feet
High Point : Kessler Peak summit, 10,403 feet
Trail Distance : 3 miles
Trail Time : 4 hours
Skill Level : Advanced/Expert
Best Season : Winter
Maps : USGS Mount Aire, Dromedary Peak; Wasatch Backcountry
: Skiing; Alpentech Wasatch Touring 1

Kessler Peak is one of the most visible mountains in the Wasatch, with tasty back-country ski runs that can be spied right from the road in Big Cottonwood Canyon. Gods Lawnmower (Tour 15) and the massive Argenta Slide Path, a 3000-foot vertical descent that's a siren song for endurance-fueled backcountry skiers and snowboarders, are testament to the massive destruction an avalanche can cause. The mountain is also home to steep and technical tours like the East and West couloirs and can be linked with other popular runs in Cardiff Fork. The area is a favorite with dawn patrollers, and, as a result, there always seems to be a skin track in place. Of course,

The apron below Kessler Peak's East Couloir is a great place to make wide, fast turns.

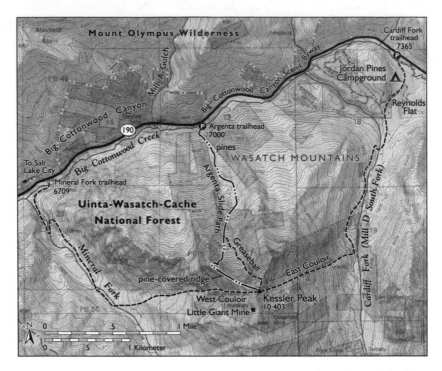

the slide paths and chutes are always avalanche prone, so Kessler Peak should only be skied when the snowpack is stable.

GETTING THERE

From east Salt Lake City, take I-215 south and exit at 6200 South. Go south on Wasatch Boulevard to Big Cottonwood Canyon Scenic Byway (State Route 190). After 7 miles up the canyon road, watch for the Argenta Slide Path to the south. Park here at a large, plowed turnoff next to a historical interpretative marker.

THE ROUTE

From the parking turnout, skin south toward Big Cottonwood Creek and cross a small bridge. Contour west around a stand of pine trees, and then pick up the skin track to the south as it immediately switchbacks up the massive Argenta Slide Path. The climb is steep and sustained as it hugs the trees on the sides of the path, where it is generally safer to ascend. The trail alternates between dark forest and open slopes with nice views of Mount Raymond and Gobblers Knob to the north. Occasionally, the track crosses the slide path to the other side. Practice safe avalanche techniques and cross one at a time. Also, constantly assess avalanche danger with hand shear, pole, and shovel tests.

After about 3000 feet of climbing, you'll top out at around 9800 feet on the pine-covered ridge with nice views of Mineral Fork to the west. This is a good place to rip skins and prepare for a ski down the Argenta Slide Path if that is your objective. Steep tree skiing marks the start before the terrain opens into the massively fun slide path where you can carve fast and playful turns all the way to your car.

To reach the summit of Kessler Peak, continue up the ridge to the 10,403-foot top. The best descents from here are the East and West couloirs, or look for the entrance to Argenta's upper chute (known locally as Greaseball) to the north.

If you descend the excellent and classic East Couloir, be sure to have a car waiting at the Cardiff Fork (Mill D South Fork) trailhead or be prepared to hitch a ride down canyon to the Argenta trailhead. Same goes for the West Couloir, which falls into Mineral Fork, so stash a car at the appropriate trailhead.

12 Circle All Peak

Start Point : Butler Fork trailhead, 7140 feet
High Point : Circle All Peak summit, 8707 feet
Trail Distance : 4 miles
Trail Time : 2 hours
Skill Level : Intermediate
Best Season : Winter
Maps : USGS Mount Aire; Wasatch Backcountry Skiing;
: Alpentech Wasatch Touring 1

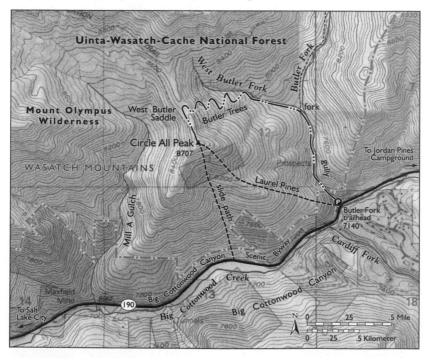

Neck deep, blower pow in the Butler Trees on Circle All Peak
(Mike DeBernardo)

Circle All Peak is a small mountain surrounded on all sides by bigger peaks like Mount Raymond, Gobblers Knob, and Kessler Peak. But what Circle All lacks in stature, it more than makes up for with 360-degree views of Big Cottonwood Canyon and fantastic tree skiing in Butler Fork. When avalanche danger is high, it's a good place to tour as Butler Fork is at a lower elevation and grows large aspen groves that anchor the snowpack. Overall, the whole Butler Fork drainage is an enjoyable tour as you skin up through a quiet forest to ski protected powder that can last for days after a storm. The terrain isn't very steep, but it's the perfect place to go for a short tour with little uphill effort.

GETTING THERE
From east Salt Lake City, take I-215 south and exit at 6200 South. Go south on Wasatch Boulevard to Big Cottonwood Canyon Scenic Byway (State Route 190).

Turn left onto Big Cottonwood Canyon Scenic Byway and drive 8 miles up canyon to the Butler Fork trailhead, located on the north side of the highway. The trail is marked by a small parking area and a sign.

THE ROUTE

Begin skinning up the bottom of the obvious Butler Fork drainage on the north side of the road. There is usually a well-traveled skin track here that crosses over a (sometimes) frozen stream. The path traverses the steep east side of a V-shaped gully, and then levels out in a stand of pines. A half mile into the ascent, there is a fork in the trail. Follow the left fork into West Butler Fork. Continue up a small valley to a series of switchbacks that meander among aspen trees that lead to the top of the West Butler Saddle at 8600 feet.

Once you gain the West Butler Saddle, go left (south) to the top of Circle All Peak at an elevation of 8707 feet. Very good tree skiing can be found in the Butler Trees on the north aspect. You can easily yo-yo through the aspens, and then ski a final run down the Circle All Slide Path that falls south to the road, where you'll have to hike or hitch back to the trailhead.

Alternatively, an awesome way to end the tour by skiing right to your car without having to deal with a bobsled-style descent through the drainage is to descend the southeast ridge through the Laurel Pines.

13 Gobblers Knob

Start Point	Butler Fork trailhead, 7140 feet
High Point	Gobblers Knob summit, 10,246 feet
Trail Distance	8 miles
Trail Time	6 hours
Skill Level	Intermediate/Advanced
Best Season	Winter
Maps	USGS Mount Aire; Wasatch Backcountry Skiing; Alpentech Wasatch Touring 1

Funny name, big mountain. Gobblers Knob supposedly earned its moniker during the Wasatch's mining heyday, when miners raised turkeys on the mountain's slopes. Today, those slopes are the playground of backcountry skiers and snowboarders. Gobblers is the highest mountain on the Big Cottonwood–Mill Creek Canyon Divide, where long, wide runs spill from every aspect. While skinning access is done from both sides, the shortest and most straightforward route is from Butler Fork in Big Cottonwood Canyon. Conversely, the best skiing and snow quality (such as the infamous Alexander Basin) is on the Mill Creek side, so many touring parties use shuttle vehicles for a Gobblers Knob traverse tour. Avalanches are very common in this area, so be mindful of the snowpack before heading out.

GETTING THERE

From east Salt Lake City, take I-215 south and exit at 6200 South. Go south on Wasatch Boulevard to Big Cottonwood Canyon Scenic Byway (State Route 190). Turn left onto Big Cottonwood Canyon Scenic Byway and drive 8 miles up canyon to the Butler Fork trailhead, located on the north side of the highway. The trail is marked by a small parking area and a sign.

To leave a shuttle vehicle in Mill Creek Canyon for a bi-canyon tour, take I-215 south and exit at 3300 South. Go left over the overpass and turn right on Wasatch Boulevard. Drive south for about a mile and turn left (east) onto 3800 South, which becomes Mill Creek Canyon Road. Drive up the canyon for 5 miles to the closed winter gate at Maple Grove and leave a car here before proceeding to the start of the tour in Big Cottonwood Canyon.

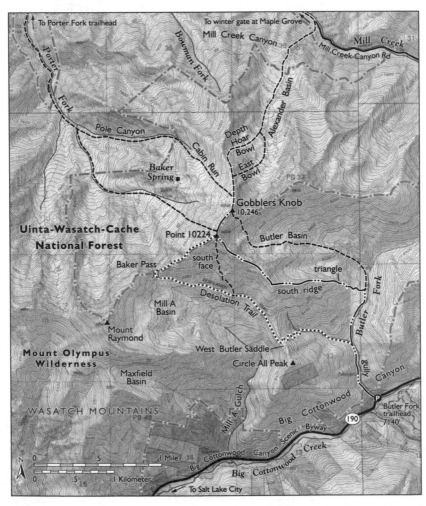

Northside view of Gobblers Knob, with Alexander Basin on the left and Cabin Run on the right

THE ROUTE

Begin skinning up the bottom of the obvious Butler Fork drainage on the north side of the road. There is usually a well-traveled skin track here that crosses over a (sometimes) frozen stream. The path traverses the steep east side of a V-shaped gully, and then levels out in a stand of pines. At the fork in the trail a half mile into the ascent, go right into Butler Fork.

As you skin up Butler Fork, the canyon narrows in the drainage bottom. Small avalanches from the creekside are possible here and can bury you in the terrain trap. Tread here only if you're confident in the snowpack's stability. A half mile from the fork, the drainage opens up a bit at the foot of Gobblers south ridge. Leave the canyon bottom and go left (west) up the east-facing slope.

After climbing about 1000 vertical feet, the slope constricts considerably like the top of a triangle (this is a good place to turn around and ski down for a short tour).

At the top of the triangle, traverse west on the ridge proper, which is quite narrow and may be difficult skinning, especially if wind has left behind undulating, collapsible pillows. But this is a good trade-off as the ridge is safe from avalanches. Continue following the ridge west for 1 mile, which will put you at the Big Cottonwood–Mill Creek Divide at Point 10224. Go right (north) on the summit ridge for a quarter-mile climb to the top of Gobblers Knob.

An alternate route from the Butler Fork trailhead is via the more avalanche-prone Mill A Basin by way of Baker Pass. Skin to the fork in the trail as described above, but instead of going right into Butler Fork, go left toward Mill A Basin. Climb a small, low-angle valley that becomes a series of switchbacks meandering among aspen trees that lead to the top of the West Butler Saddle at 8600 feet. It is 0.75 mile from the fork to the saddle.

From here, generally follow the summer Desolation Trail on the aspen-covered south slope of Gobblers Knob for 0.8 mile to a wide bowl below Baker Pass. Switchback up the bowl about 400 vertical feet to the pass at an elevation of 9340 feet, and go right (northeast) following the west ridge another 0.8 mile and 900 vertical feet to the top of Gobblers Knob (by way of Point 10224).

Descent options are numerous and sometimes very dangerous on Gobblers Knob. To return to your car in Big Cottonwood, ski or snowboard south off the summit into Butler Basin. The runs are wide-open but short until you reach the basin bottom for an eastward, low-angle exit to Butler Fork, where you can follow your ascent route back to the trailhead. During times of deep snow or immediately after a storm, good skiing is found on the south face of Gobblers Knob, otherwise it's sun affected. Retreat from the summit south on the ridge to Point 10224 and make turns down to the bottom of Mill A Basin.

The best skiing and snow is north into Mill Creek Canyon, but you'll need a shuttle vehicle parked at the closed winter gate at Maple Grove. The most avalanche-prone (and as a result the most fun) descent is in Alexander Basin. Cliffs guard this area from the summit, so descend the north ridge beyond the cliff line to either East Bowl or Depth Hoar Bowl. Both are notorious for slides (hence the Depth Hoar name), so be aware. At the bottom of the bowls, ski the old-growth evergreen forest down to the snow-covered Mill Creek Canyon Road and skate-ski west to your stashed vehicle at the closed winter gate at Maple Grove.

Another option is the broad west side of Gobblers Knob. Again, avalanches attack here on a frequent basis. Perhaps the longest and most consistent run is locally known as the Cabin Run. From the summit, make turns on the wide-open, west-facing slope. At around 8700 feet, the run constricts into Pole Canyon, which then becomes Porter Fork. Ski down both of these drainages to Mill Creek Canyon Road. Other west-facing shots off Point 10224 go to the same return via Porter Fork, which will take you to the Porter Fork trailhead, about a half mile down canyon from Maple Grove.

If you choose to exit through Mill Creek Canyon, you'll have to pay the small recreation fee at the mouth of the canyon.

14 Mount Raymond

Start Point : Butler Fork trailhead, 7140 feet
High Point : Mount Raymond summit, 10,241 feet
Trail Distance : 8 miles
Trail Time : 5 hours
Skill Level : Advanced
Best Season : Winter/Spring
Maps : USGS Mount Aire; Wasatch Backcountry Skiing;
: Alpentech Wasatch Touring 1

Mount Raymond is the second-highest mountain along the Big Cottonwood–Mill Creek Divide, standing a mere five feet lower than its neighbor, Gobblers Knob. But Raymond is no slouch, as extreme ski terrain is found off the summit. An approach that's longer than most for the Cottonwood Canyons plus a knife-edge ridge on the ascent can add up to a tour that is pretty spicy. If you're not up for a heart-pounding ascent and descent, don't be dissuaded. A shorter tour on the Raymond shoulder

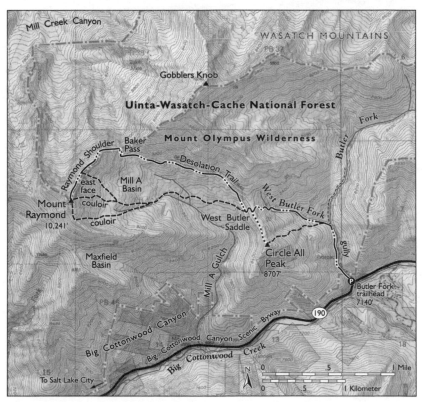

View of Mount Raymond from the top of Circle All Peak

above Baker Pass into Mill A Basin is an ideal place to make intermediate powder laps after a storm.

GETTING THERE

From east Salt Lake City, take I-215 south and exit at 6200 South. Go south on Wasatch Boulevard to Big Cottonwood Canyon Scenic Byway (State Route 190). Turn left onto Big Cottonwood Canyon Scenic Byway and drive 8 miles up canyon to the Butler Fork trailhead, located on the north side of the highway. The trail is marked by a small parking area and a sign.

THE ROUTE

Begin skinning up the bottom of the obvious Butler Fork drainage on the north side of the road. There is usually a well-traveled skin track here that crosses over a (sometimes) frozen stream. The path traverses the steep east side of a V-shaped gully, and then levels out in a stand of pines. Half a mile into the ascent, you come to a fork in the trail. Follow the left fork into West Butler Fork. Continue up a small valley to a series of switchbacks that meander among aspen trees that lead to the top of West Butler Saddle at 8600 feet.

From the saddle, generally follow the summer Desolation Trail on the aspen-covered south slope of Gobblers Knob for 0.8 mile to a wide, open bowl below Baker Pass. Switchback up the bowl about 400 vertical feet to the pass at an elevation of 9340 feet, and go left (south). Climb up the large Raymond Shoulder ridge for about 0.6 mile and 900 vertical feet to the top. Along the way, the ridge narrows to a knife edge at around 9900 feet. Depending on snow conditions, this section may or may not be easy to cross, and cornices may or may not support your weight. There could even be some rock scrambling that can make the ascent scarier than the descent. Even better, there's exposure on both sides. Expect to boot pack your way up, and bring along an ice ax and crampons, just in case. The ridge stays pretty narrow all the way to the summit.

At the 10,241-foot top, there are no easy ways down. The east face is basically a series of couloirs that are pretty intense from an avalanche standpoint. Even spring corn is unsafe because of rock slabs underneath that can release slides during daytime heating. If conditions (and your skills) are deemed good-to-go, then skiing just off the summit down a dogleg couloir into Mill A Basin is possible. The top of this couloir is often guarded by a large cornice. A wider and somewhat safer option is the couloir that can be accessed just south of the main summit.

If these summit shots are too spooky, you can find many lines off the shoulder north of the summit along the ascent route. These runs have more of an open headwall feel to them, and you can get almost as much vertical as you would otherwise from the summit.

All runs open up onto a sweet apron where the snow quality generally improves as it spills into the bottom of Mill A Basin. I like to traverse east through the aspen forest back to the West Butler Saddle, and skin the few hundred vertical feet to the top of Circle All Peak, followed by a bonus run down the aspens into Butler Fork and back to the trailhead.

Gods Lawnmower

Start Point	Cardiff Fork trailhead, 7365 feet
High Point	Top of Gods Lawnmower slide path, 9700 feet
Trail Distance	4 miles
Trail Time	3 hours
Skill Level	Advanced
Best Season	Winter
Maps	USGS Mount Aire Quad; Wasatch Backcountry Skiing, Alpentech Wasatch Touring 1

Gods Lawnmower is the perfect name for this backcountry tour. It's an enormous slide path on the north side of Kessler Peak that looks like God himself fired up a

View of Gods Lawnmower on Kessler Peak from the approach in Cardiff Fork

tractor mower and plowed up the mountain, leaving a swath of open snow through the forest. Of course, nature made this wide ski run using destructive avalanches that swept the mountainside clean. Because of the disastrous avalanche potential on Gods Lawnmower, UDOT frequently conducts control work here after big snowstorms in order to protect the highway, and the route may be closed to touring traffic in the mornings. Ski Gods Lawnmower only when the snowpack is stable, and approach the run with serious caution.

GETTING THERE

From east Salt Lake City, take I-215 south and exit at 6200 South. Go south on Wasatch Boulevard to Big Cottonwood Canyon Scenic Byway (State Route 190). Drive up the canyon road for 8.8 miles to the Cardiff Fork (Mill D South Fork) trailhead parking lot on the south side of the highway.

THE ROUTE

Skin south on the paved private road into Cardiff Fork for 1 mile until it reaches a fork at the Doughnut Falls trailhead. Go right on the old Cardiff Fork jeep road (left goes to the ever-popular Doughnut Falls). A little over a mile from the parking area, look for a steep skin track to the west that heads into an aspen forest covering the ridge between Cardiff Fork and the Gods Lawnmower slide path. If it recently snowed and there is no track in place, begin breaking trail at the lowest-angled section of slope above the road. Follow the ridge as it snakes up the north side of Kessler Peak. At about 9700 feet, the slope becomes too steep for climbing skins, so traverse west and drop into Gods Lawnmower at this elevation.

The top of the run begins with steep turns that eventually lessen into lower-angle terrain. As you sweep turns down this classic descent, watch for small cliffs and be careful to avoid the terrain traps that litter the slide path. At the bottom of the steep stuff, an almost-flat section holds surprisingly good skiing when the snow is soft and fast. To finish, stop in the flats and skin back up and over the ridge you used to ascend in order to ski back down to Cardiff Fork and the parking lot. Or you can continue down Gods Lawnmower into the steep aspen trees that provide even more vertical down to Big Cottonwood Creek. Located up creek is a water pipe that you can walk across to the road, where you can hitch a ride back to your car.

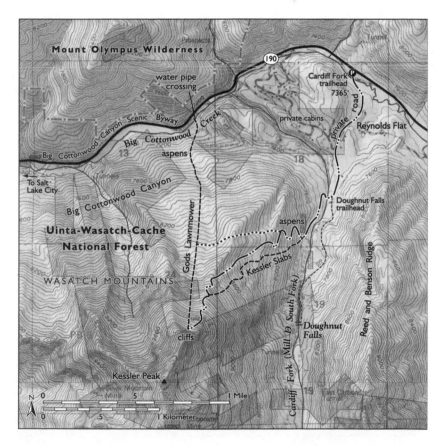

Lastly, you can ski just east of your ascent route on the Kessler Slabs. This wide run between the trees has seen avalanche fatalities and should be skied only in times of bomber snow stability. The slabs are just as they sound: rock slabs that have very little anchoring properties beneath the snow. Small cliffs and rock bands add to the danger.

16 Short Swing

Start Point : Spruces Campground, 7500 feet
High Point : The Cone summit, 9269 feet
Trail Distance : 3 miles
Trail Time : 2 hours
Skill Level : Beginner/Intermediate
Best Season : Winter
Maps : USGS Mount Aire, Park City West; Wasatch Backcountry
: Skiing; Alpentech Wasatch Touring 1

Short Swing in Big Cottonwood Canyon is an ideal spot for a short tour if you can't ski all day long. It consists of the entire ridgeline on the east side of lower Mill D North Fork. The ridge is composed of mini peaks that feature all kinds of ski terrain,

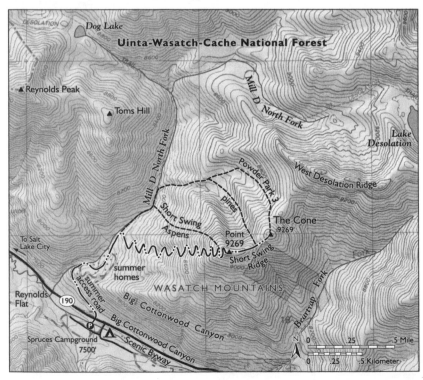

Skinning on the top of the Short Swing ridgeline

such as steep, pine-covered aspects; sunny, east-facing back bowls; and west-facing, perfectly spaced aspen groves that spill down to Mill D for more than a thousand feet. Along with being a convenient spot to bang out a quick tour, it's also a popular area during high-avalanche-danger days as many low-angle, tree-anchored shots can be found here.

GETTING THERE
From east Salt Lake City, take I-215 south and exit at 6200 South. Go south on Wasatch Boulevard to Big Cottonwood Canyon Scenic Byway (State Route 190). Drive 9.5 miles up the canyon road and turn right into the Spruces Campground, where there is a large, plowed parking lot.

THE ROUTE
From the campground, walk north across the highway to the start of the Mill D North Fork drainage. Follow the skin track on a road as it goes up and through a neighborhood of summer cabins. After 0.5 mile, you'll enter the main drainage, where the landscape opens up immediately after leaving the cabin area. Go right (east) into the aspens and switchback up the mountainside. If it hasn't snowed in a while, there will assuredly be a skin track (or seven) already in place. You'll reach the top of Short Swing Ridge at around 9250 feet.

There are a few descent options here, primary among them being the way you skinned up. These west-facing aspen groves are the money shots with perfectly spaced glades on a consistent fall line that drops for more than 1500 feet from the ridge to the canyon floor. You can also drop northeast into steep, shaded pine trees that offer a short run but the possibility of more quality snow.

To reach what is known locally as the Cone, continue northeast by traversing the ridge for 0.3 mile down to a saddle, and then climb up to the summit of the Cone at about 9269 feet. This is the start of Powder Park 3, a low-angle meadow just south of West Desolation Ridge, an excellent terrain choice during periods of high avalanche danger.

To return to your car, ski down your ascent route in Mill D North Fork, back to the highway and the Spruces Campground.

Reynolds Peak and Toms Hill

Start Point : Spruces Campground, 7500 feet
High Points : Toms Hill summit, 9080 feet; Reynolds Peak summit,
: 9422 feet
Trail Distance : 6 miles
Trail Time : 4 hours
Skill Level : Intermediate
Best Season : Winter
Maps : USGS Mount Aire; Wasatch Backcountry Skiing;
: Alpentech Wasatch Touring I

Reynolds Peak and Toms Hill are like mountain siblings with conflicting personalities. Reynolds is big, steep, and slide prone, while Toms is smaller, mellower, and a good place to ride during elevated avalanche danger. But if you put them together, you have a side-by-side pair of peaks with several choice lines to ride for any skill level, season, or snow condition. Both mountains can be linked with full-day tours to Butler Fork (Tours 12, 13, and 14) and Little Water Peak (Tour 18).

GETTING THERE
From east Salt Lake City, take I-215 south and exit at 6200 South. Go south on Wasatch Boulevard to Big Cottonwood Canyon Scenic Byway (State Route 190). Drive 9.5 miles up the canyon road and turn right into the Spruces Campground, where there is a large, plowed parking lot.

THE ROUTE
From the campground, walk north across Big Cottonwood Canyon Scenic Byway to the start of the Mill D North Fork drainage. Follow the skin track on the summer road as it goes up and through a neighborhood of cabins. Continue along the streambed for 1.3 miles, and go left at the signed fork toward Dog Lake.

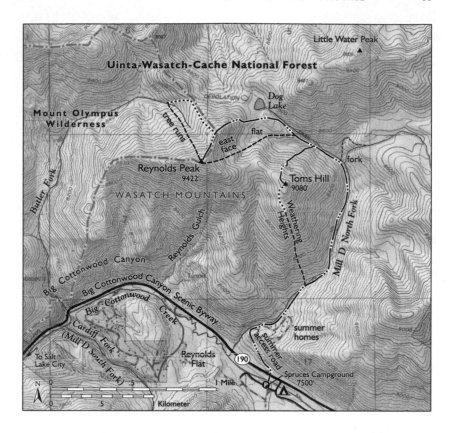

For Toms Hill, split left off the main trail just 0.16 mile after the fork while staying in the main drainage. Follow this up for a quarter mile until you see the open northeast face of Toms Hill. Skin south directly up the mountain by switchbacking outside the slide path along the trees to the top of Toms Hill, which is approximately 9080 feet in elevation. The summit is a knobby rock outcropping that juts from the aspen trees on the ridge. Ski or snowboard the 30-degree shot you just ascended. This short run is great for multiple laps. You can also continue skinning a short distance south along the ridge for a longer and steeper east-facing run called Weathering Heights that takes you back to the bottom of Mill D North Fork. Many touring parties save this for a home run back to the trailhead, but the aspect is often covered in crusty, sunbaked snow.

For Reynolds Peak, stay on the main trail; Dog Lake at 8750 feet is 0.65 mile from the fork. From here, go southwest and ascend to a large, flat area above the south shore of the lake. You'll then contour west around the flat to the aspen-covered north ridge of Reynolds Peak. This ridge provides a safe route to the summit in only 0.5 mile and 670 vertical feet from the lake. Descent options include the dangerous, avalanche-prone east face, which takes you back to the flat above Dog Lake, or money shots in the treed

The east face of Reynolds Peak is the most popular run in the area and is usually the first to be tracked out.

north face into Butler Fork. From the bottom of Butler, skin east up through aspen and evergreens to regain the Reynolds Peak north ridge.

To return, go back the way you came down Mill D North Fork to the Spruces Campground.

18 Little Water Peak

Start Point : Spruces Campground, 7500 feet
High Point : Little Water Peak summit, 9605 feet
Trail Distance : 6 miles
Trail Time : 4 hours
Skill Level : Intermediate
Best Season : Winter
Maps : USGS Mount Aire, Park City West; Wasatch Backcountry
: Skiing; Alpentech Wasatch Touring I

Little Water Peak is a nondescript summit between Mill Creek and Big Cottonwood canyons that rises to an elevation of 9605 feet. But this rounded hump hides steep, avalanche-prone skiing on her cold north face that offers killer powder turns into Mill Creek Canyon. Other honest-to-goodness backcountry ski lines exist on the rest of the compass as well, if your timing is right. You can ski or snowboard Little Water as an out-and-back from Mill D North Fork in Big Cottonwood Canyon, or do a bi-canyon tour with a shuttle car stashed in Mill Creek Canyon. Either way, you can make tracks off the summit of Little Water until your heart's content.

GETTING THERE

From east Salt Lake City, take I-215 south and exit at 6200 South. Go south on Wasatch Boulevard to Big Cottonwood Canyon Scenic Byway (State Route 190). Drive 9.5 miles up the canyon road and turn right into the Spruces Campground, where there is a large, plowed parking lot.

To leave a shuttle vehicle in Mill Creek Canyon, take I-215 south and exit at 3300 South. Go left over the overpass and turn right on Wasatch Boulevard. Drive south for about a mile and turn left (east) on 3800 South, which becomes Mill Creek Canyon Road. Drive up the canyon for 5 miles to the closed winter gate at Maple Grove and leave a car here.

THE ROUTE

From the campground, walk north across Big Cottonwood Canyon Scenic Byway to the start of the Mill D North Fork drainage. Follow the skin track on the summer road as it goes up and through a neighborhood of cabins. Continue along the streambed for 1.3 miles, and go left at the signed fork toward Dog Lake.

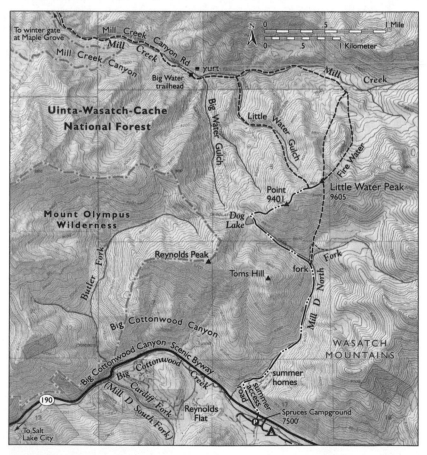

View of Little Water Peak from the top of Reynolds Peak

From the fork, the skinning becomes a bit steeper as the canyon climbs for 0.65 mile to Dog Lake at 8750 feet. Circumnavigate the shore halfway around its east side, and skin northeast up an aspen-covered sub-ridge of Little Water Peak, through alternating aspen woods and brushy meadows on the south- and west-facing aspects. A small meadow at Point 9401 (a false summit that will have you cursing if you're exhausted from a long day) is a good place to rest before the final push up the low-angle summit ridge. From the lake, it is approximately 0.75 mile and 850 vertical feet to the wide summit

As far as the skiing goes, if you like open spaces paired with aspen groves and semi-low-angle slopes, Little Water can provide. If it snowed recently, make turns down the south aspect for a safe intermediate run back into Mill D North Fork, which will spit you out at the signed fork where you can follow the skin track back to your car at the Spruces Campground.

If you're looking for something steep and risky the north face awaits. Approach the Mill Creek side of the mountain with care; ski the slide-prone incline only when avalanche danger is low. Northeast from the summit is a wide, steep bowl locally known as Fire Water. This line goes down into the pine trees that fill upper Mill Creek Canyon. When you reach the bottom, skate-ski or skin west down to the Big Water Yurt at the Big Water trailhead, and follow the closed Mill Creek Canyon Road to where you stashed a car at the winter gate at Maple Grove.

Another, somewhat safer, line is down Little Water Gulch. Face skiing holds good powder turns on the mountain's northwest side, but it soon turns into tree skiing all the way down the gulch to upper Mill Creek Canyon. Follow the road west from the Big Water trailhead as described above.

If you choose to exit through Mill Creek Canyon, you'll have to pay the small recreation fee at the mouth of the canyon.

19 Lake Desolation Area

Start Point : Spruces Campground, 7500 feet
High Point : Point 9990, 9990 feet
Trail Distance : 8 miles
Trail Time : 5 hours
Skill Level : Intermediate
Best Season : Winter
Maps : USGS Mount Aire; Wasatch Backcountry Skiing;
: Alpentech Wasatch Touring 1

Lake Desolation is surrounded by quality backcountry skiing, from south-facing open glades to tree skiing on north and east aspects. The area draws all kinds of backcountry

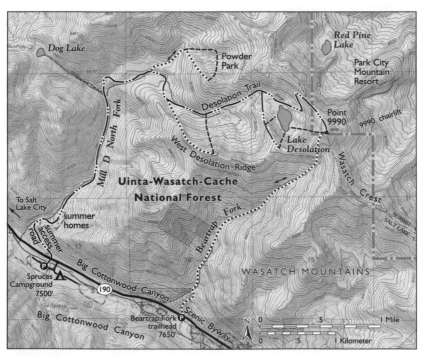

Working it on soft snow in Powder Park

types—from weathered telemarkers out for a long tour to modern twin-tippers barreling down from Park City Mountain Resort (in what used to be Canyons Resort) next door. They all come to this tiny lake nestled in a box canyon deep in the Wasatch Mountains to farm powder that is well protected from wind and sun.

GETTING THERE

From east Salt Lake City, take I-215 south and exit at 6200 South. Go south on Wasatch Boulevard to Big Cottonwood Canyon Scenic Byway (State Route 190). Drive 9.5 miles up the canyon road and turn right into the Spruces Campground, where there is a large, plowed parking lot.

THE ROUTE

Getting to Lake Desolation can be either hard or easy, depending on where you're coming from. If you have a pass to Park City Mountain Resort, a descent into the

Lake Desolation backcountry is as easy as riding the 9990 chairlift and skiing down the short, west-facing slopes to the lake at 9200 feet.

If you're a backcountry purist, start at the Spruces Campground in Big Cottonwood Canyon. Cross the highway north to the summer access road into Mill D North Fork, and follow the trail through an area of summer homes into the main drainage. Continue up the trail for 1.3 miles until you reach a signed fork. Go right (east) on Desolation Trail (left goes to Dog Lake). Follow the trail another 2 miles to Lake Desolation. From the lake, ascend the west ridge that curves like a cauldron around the lake. Here you can ski or snowboard mellow meadows where powder farming is the thing, or continue up to the high point of the ridge for steep, north-facing runs filled with evergreens. If conditions are favorable, the west face below Point 9990 offers a longer descent, but it gets tracked out quickly from the slackcountry skiers.

Alternatively, you can skin up Beartrap Fork from the Beartrap Fork trailhead, located 1 mile up canyon from Spruces Campground. Follow the Beartrap Fork route to the highest west ridge and ski down to Lake Desolation (see Beartrap Fork, Tour 21).

Another exciting zone is West Desolation Ridge, a sparsely treed, open shoulder that separates Mill D North Fork from Beartrap Fork. To get to the ridge, leave Desolation Trail 0.8 mile from the signed fork and head south toward an obvious, prominent ridge. Skin up this ridge as it curves east to the highest point at 9660 feet. The good skiing is found on shaded, north-facing slopes that attract with their siren song of powder and small cliffs, but the whole area is avalanche prone and claimed a victim in 1979.

For a mellower tour, try Powder Park. This protected, north-facing, low-angle meadow is popular with Wasatch Mountain Club touring trips and is a safe place to ski when avalanche danger is high. About a half mile from the fork, head north through the trees. You'll soon exit into a meadow at 8700 feet. To the east is a small mountain. Cross the meadow and go around the mountain for 0.3 mile to the base of its west ridge. Ascend the ridge southeast for approximately 600 vertical feet to the top. Powder Park is the north-facing, open slope between the trees.

20 Greens Basin

Start Point : Spruces Campground, 7500 feet
High Point : Point 9699, 9699 feet
Trail Distance : 5 miles
Trail Time : 3 hours
Skill Level : Intermediate
Best Season : Winter
Maps : USGS Mount Aire; Wasatch Backcountry Skiing; Alpentech Wasatch Touring 1

Greens Basin is a lovely meadow beneath slopes of huge evergreens that rise up from the canyon floor between Days Fork and Silver Fork. Driving up Big Cottonwood

Canyon, you can see these well-spaced, powder-filled trees above the Spruces Campground. It is among this blanket of evergreens where good powder can be found long after a storm, thanks to ample shade and protection from the wind. A ski tour in Greens Basin makes for a fairly mellow day even though the basin rises 2200 vertical feet in 2.5 miles from the Spruces parking lot. This may sound like a big ascent, but the trail to the top is mostly low-grade and is protected from avalanche terrain.

GETTING THERE

From east Salt Lake City, take I-215 south and exit at 6200 South. Go south on Wasatch Boulevard to Big Cottonwood Canyon Scenic Byway (State Route 190). Drive 9.5 miles up the canyon road and turn right into the Spruces Campground, where there is a large, plowed parking lot.

THE ROUTE

Locate the skin track in the southwest corner of the parking lot and skin through the Spruces Campground to enter Days Fork. Take the path that hugs the east side of the canyon. In about a half mile, leave the bottom of Days Fork and begin climbing east up a series of steep switchbacks that take you 300 feet up to the top of a small

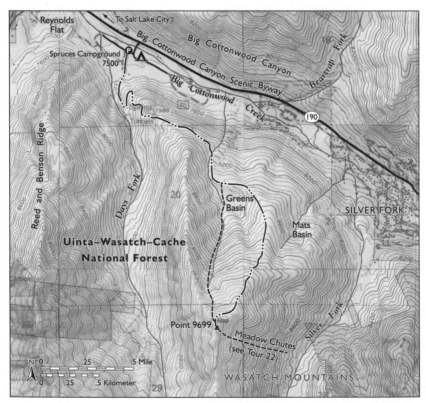

*Cold powder in shady evergreens assures soft turns days after a storm in
Greens Basin.*

sub-ridge. From here, the skin track becomes less steep and traverses east through the
pines up to a lovely meadow at 8300 feet. This is Greens Basin, and it will make you
dream of building a little ski cabin where you can shred laps all day, every day.

Skin across Greens Basin to the southeast side and start making switchbacks on
a shoulder that stands between Greens Basin and Mats Basin. Climb south up the
shoulder through evergreen and aspen forests to the top of a 9699-foot unnamed peak
that overlooks Silver Fork Canyon.

Descend straight north into the evergreens where excellent, protected tree skiing
leads to a narrow gully that returns to Greens Basin meadow. Return to the Spruces
Campground the way you came up.

You can also create a longer tour by skiing from Point 9699 east into the Meadow
Chutes in Silver Fork Canyon. Do laps on these low-angle, east-facing slopes, but stop
before the steep rollovers near the canyon bottom during times of high avalanche
danger. People have died in slides on these rollers.

To access Silver Fork Meadow Chutes from Solitude Mountain Resort, see Tour 22.

21 Beartrap Fork

Start Point : Beartrap Fork trailhead, 7650 feet
High Point : Point 9990, 9990 feet
Trail Distance : 4 miles
Trail Time : 3 hours
Skill Level : Intermediate
Best Season : Winter
Maps : USGS Park City West; Wasatch Backcountry Skiing;
: Alpentech Wasatch Touring 1

Beartrap Fork is one of the best places to ski on a powder day in the Wasatch. This hidden drainage harbors excellent low-angle slopes and an 800-vertical-foot run of perfectly spaced aspen trees that would make Billy Kidd leave Steamboat Springs in a hop turn. With tree-anchored slopes and wind-protected aspects, Beartrap is the place to be when the snow is deep and the avalanche danger is considerable. There is also good touring in the upper canyon among low-angle evergreen trees. This area

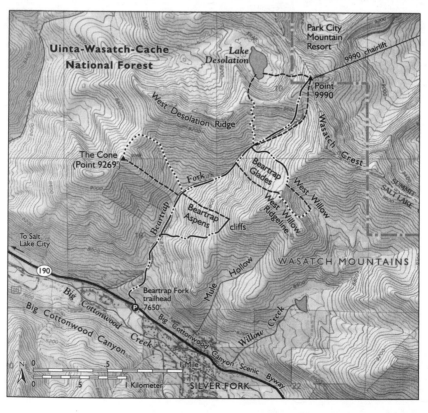

The Beartrap Aspens have some of the most consistent, backcountry tree skiing in the Wasatch.

is easily accessed by the 9990 lift at Park City Mountain Resort (formerly Canyons Resort) as well.

GETTING THERE

From east Salt Lake City, take I-215 south and exit at 6200 South. Drive south on Wasatch Boulevard to Big Cottonwood Canyon Scenic Byway (State Route 190). Drive 10.7 miles up the canyon road to the Beartrap Fork trailhead, located on the north side of the road. There is no good parking so you have to find a wide spot on the south shoulder of the highway just east of the Spruces Campground and west of Silver Fork.

THE ROUTE

Begin at the unmarked Beartrap Fork trailhead and locate the skin track above a private road on the north side of the highway. The trail winds through a tight grove of aspen trees before entering Beartrap Fork proper, marked by a narrow gully. There are a few homes here, so be careful not to trespass onto private property.

At the narrow gully, many skin tracks may be going in different directions, but it's best to trend right onto a shoulder that offers a safe route and avoids the terrain trap at the canyon bottom.

Continue up the shoulder through the aspens for a mile from the trailhead as it becomes the ridge between Beartrap Fork and Mule Hollow. You will come to a small cliff band at around 9200 feet, where the aspens give way to evergreen trees. Cut north across the slope to avoid avalanche-prone areas below the cliff band. Staying in the trees, scope out your line, de-skin, and descend west down the Beartrap Aspens, which is some of the best backcountry tree skiing in the Wasatch. This 800-foot run is a classic because of its perfectly spaced aspen trees.

Alternatively, from about 8300 feet up the canyon, skin northwest into the aspens for 0.5 mile to a saddle between the Cone and West Desolation Ridge. You can ski Short Swing and Powder Park 3 from here (Tour 16) and return to Beartrap by skiing the southeast faces of the Cone.

For a longer tour, go farther up the bottom of Beartrap Fork as it curves northeast. Stay climber's right of the gully, following the summer trail route. At around 8900 feet, head east for another climb to the ridge for more low-angle skiing and meadow-skipping among evergreen trees on the west face called the Beartrap Glades. You can also ski east into West Willow, a less-traveled area with a few open runs that terminate at a nice meadow. Return to Beartrap Fork by skinning up West Willow Ridgeline.

In the upper canyon, you can easily access the Lake Desolation area (Tour 19). From the bottom of the Beartrap Glades, go north and switchback up the south-facing slope for around 600 vertical feet to the ridge above the lake, where you can ski the short, north-facing trees to the shore. Also from upper Beartrap Fork, another 0.6-mile skin will get you to the top of Point 9990 in Park City Mountain Resort. Descend back the way you came, or make turns down the west-facing slope to Lake Desolation.

Another alternative is to enter the canyon from the top of the 9990 lift at Park City Mountain Resort to ski laps from the Wasatch Crest. Just ski or snowboard south from the lift terminus and pick up the skin track at the canyon bottom.

22 Silver Fork Meadow Chutes

Start Point	Solitude Mountain Resort, 8000 feet
High Point	Point 9699, 9699 feet
Trail Distance	4 miles
Trail Time	3 hours
Skill Level	Intermediate
Best Season	Winter
Maps	USGS Park City West, Brighton, Dromedary Peak; Wasatch Backcountry Skiing; Alpentech Wasatch Touring 1

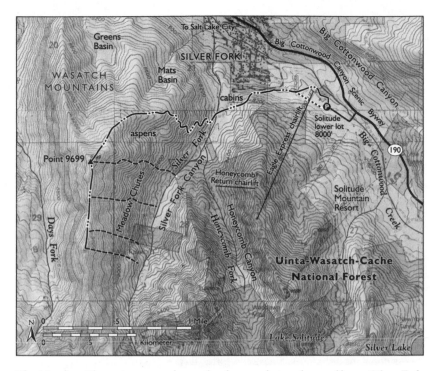

The Meadow Chutes is a general term for the east-facing slopes of lower Silver Fork Canyon. The proximity of this backcountry terrain to Solitude Mountain Resort places it among the most popular spots for day tours, especially since the wide, powder-filled meadows are easy to salivate over from the Eagle Express and Honeycomb Return chairlifts. While the terrain may seem benign from a distance, fatal avalanches have occurred here, and it's not uncommon to see huge crown-lines on the upper slopes. Steep rollovers closer to the canyon bottom also hold extreme avalanche danger. When the snowpack is questionable, tree skiing in the low-angle aspens is a good option.

GETTING THERE

From east Salt Lake City, take I-215 south and exit at 6200 South. Go south on Wasatch Boulevard to Big Cottonwood Canyon Scenic Byway (State Route 190). Go left (east) and drive 12 miles up the canyon road to the first entrance for Solitude Mountain Resort on the right. Park on the west side of the large lower lot near the Eagle Express chairlift.

THE ROUTE

At the northwest corner of the parking lot, locate a road that goes west behind the bottom of the Eagle Express chairlift. Skin or skate-ski for 0.75 mile through the evergreen forest to the mouth of Silver Fork Canyon. At this point, you've entered

Skiing down the Meadow Chutes on a spring day

the Silver Fork community of homes and cabins. Respect private property and stay on the road.

Alternatively, many touring parties choose to reach the road by ski-traversing across the lower runs of Solitude, passing beneath the Eagle Express chairlift. You'll come to the road on the other side of the ski run. This shortcut will save a little time and mileage.

When you reach the mouth of Silver Fork Canyon, go left (south) and follow the summer trail route on the canyon bottom. There are many ways you can skin up to the top, but the safest route is by staying in the aspen trees on the ridge that separates Silver Fork from Mats Basin. To get there, leave the canyon bottom in less than a quarter mile from the mouth of the canyon and switchback straight up into the trees. It's a steep climb that can be icy in the mornings when it hasn't snowed in a while. In about a half mile, you'll reach the top of Mats Basin, which falls away to the north. Continue skinning up the ridge another half mile to the top of Point 9699 at the head of Greens Basin. It's around 1600 vertical feet from the Solitude Mountain Resort base to this high point.

The safest skiing is on the low-angle meadow adjacent to the aspen trees just below Point 9699. As you skin south along the ridge, the runs get steeper and wider as the east-facing slopes open up into wide bowls. Pick your poison all along the ridge, and get there early on a powder day, because this place gets tracked out fast.

Avalanche fatalities are known to happen here, as the bowls above constrict into narrow gullies below. On top of these terrain traps, the runs have steep rollovers halfway down that are notorious for slides. Only tour here on stable days, or lap the less steep upper bowls and make your final run through the aspen trees to the canyon bottom. Return to Solitude via the road you skinned in on.

23 Willow Fork and USA Bowl

Start Point	Willow Fork trailhead, 8000 feet
High Points	Point 10009, 10,009 feet; Scott Hill, 10,116 feet
Trail Distance	4 miles
Trail Time	3 hours
Skill Level	Beginner/Intermediate
Best Season	Winter
Maps	USGS Park City West; Wasatch Backcountry Skiing; Alpentech Wasatch Touring 1

Willow Fork, or "the Willows," is a generally low-angle and avy-safe backcountry ski area across the highway from Solitude Mountain Resort in Big Cottonwood Canyon. It's a lesser known but awesome place for either a short tour or an all-day yo-yo fest where you can find open, low-angle bowls next to steep tree runs covered in well-spaced pines. Willow Fork also provides easy access to the Wasatch Crest, where you can ski into the north-facing and avalanche-prone West and South Monitor bowls. To the east of Willow Fork is USA Bowl, a marquee line where skiers at Solitude can look upon your backcountry powder tracks with jealousy.

GETTING THERE

From east Salt Lake City, take I-215 south and exit at 6200 South. Go south on Wasatch Boulevard to Big Cottonwood Canyon Scenic Byway (State Route 190). Drive 11.5 miles up the canyon road just past Silver Fork to the Willow Fork trailhead, located on the north side of the road. There is no good parking so you have to find a wide spot on the highway shoulder. The trailhead is marked by a large sign. If necessary, you can also park at Solitude Mountain Resort across the highway. For USA Bowl, it's closer to park along the road by the upper Solitude lot or in the small lot if you can find a spot.

THE ROUTE

To begin, skin north from the Willow Fork trailhead into a stand of aspens. In a half mile, you'll reach Willow Lake (a.k.a. Willow Heights) at 8500 feet. This small pond is a popular destination for summer picnickers but is frozen over during the winter, so it will probably just look like a large, flat, snow-covered meadow.

Go right around the lake and head southeast toward Willow Knob, a small, 9475-foot peak at the end of the ridgeline between Willow Fork and USA Bowl. To get to the knob, you'll have to switchback up a steep pine forest for 0.75 mile to the top. At the Willow Knob summit, you can ski short, steep tree shots back the way you came. For a longer tour, continue 0.5 mile east to the Wasatch Crest. If avalanche conditions are stable, ski or snowboard the Monitor Bowls into the Park City side of the crest using best safety practices as these bowls are notorious for big slides. Skin up the adjacent ridge to regain the Wasatch Crest.

Safer skiing and snowboarding is in Willow Fork. Go north on the ridge 0.4 mile from the point where you reached the Wasatch Crest, to the unnamed high point of 10,009 feet and descend the low-angle, west-facing Main Willow Bowl, or go just beyond to ski Wills Hill.

To return to the Willow Fork trailhead, ski or snowboard back down to Willow Lake and follow your ascent route.

If you only want to ski USA Bowl, it's better to begin at the cabins across the highway from Solitude's upper entrance. Follow the snow-covered summer road 0.25 mile until it turns to the east. Leave the road here on an old jeep road–grade that heads north. About a half mile after leaving the road, turn right and skin up into the aspen forest along an indistinct ridge. Climb the ridge east for 1 mile to the Wasatch Crest as described above.

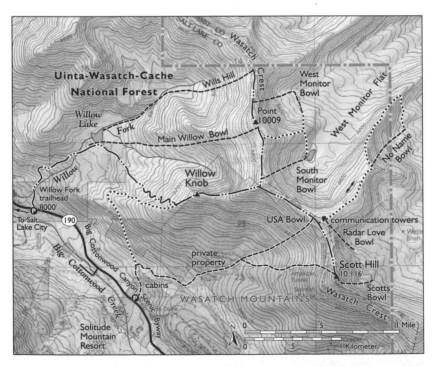

Buried on one of the deepest powder days of the year

Once you reach the crest, traverse the ridge southeast 0.5 mile to the tall radio and communication towers. The huge south- and west-facing bowl that goes back down to Big Cottonwood Canyon Scenic Byway is USA Bowl. Ski this after it snows because the southerly aspect gets crusty in the sun.

From the communication towers, you can also ski No Name Bowl. Ski down the ridge that heads northeast from the towers to its terminus, where No Name Bowl awaits below. Carefully assess the avalanche dangers here before dropping in. Return to the communication towers via the tree-covered ridge north of the bowl.

Just east of the towers is the start of Radar Love Bowl. This east-facing bowl is a short but fun shot that is also avalanche prone and has no safe return route. Enter here only when snowpack is stable.

The high point of the ridge is Scott Hill at 10,116 feet. From the top, ski the west-facing aspect of USA Bowl, or drop in on the east face, also called Scotts Bowl. Avalanches are of concern here, so use the trees south of the bowl to minimize risk on your return route.

To return to Solitude from any of these descents, ski down USA Bowl. At the bottom, follow the summer road through the cabin area back to Solitude. Be careful to stay on the road, as much of the land here is private property.

24 Brighton Hill and Point 10420

Start Point : Guardsman Pass winter closure, 8900 feet
High Point : Point 10420, 10,420 feet
Trail Distance : 3 miles
Trail Time : 2 hours
Skill Level : Beginner/Intermediate
Best Season : Winter
Maps : USGS Brighton; Wasatch Backcountry Skiing;
: Alpentech Wasatch Touring 1

Brighton Hill to Point 10420 is the closest you can backcountry ski near Brighton Ski Resort without having to ride any chairlifts to get there. The ridge and lower slopes can be a good place to take beginner backcountry skiers and splitboarders who are comfortable with riding in the trees. A low-angle ridge from the Guardsman Pass

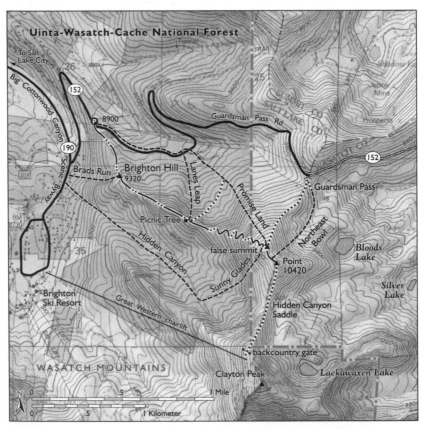

Picnic Tree on the ridge to Point 10420

winter closure leads to the base of Point 10420, where more advanced riding can be found on steep, treed slopes. The ridge is also a safe haven from snowmobiles, which are always buzzing on Guardsman Pass Road but aren't allowed anywhere else in upper Big Cottonwood Canyon.

GETTING THERE

From east Salt Lake City, take I-215 south and exit at 6200 South. Go south on Wasatch Boulevard to Big Cottonwood Canyon Scenic Byway (State Route 190). Drive 13.8 miles up the canyon road to the turnoff on Guardsman Pass Road, located on the north side of the road. Drive up the plowed road past houses and a large switchback for about a mile until the plowing ends. There is ample parking along the road near a large pit toilet.

THE ROUTE

The skin track begins at the end of the large, plowed turnaround at the base of the ridge. Climb southeast through the trees for 0.25 mile to the top of Brighton Hill at 9320 feet. From here, you can ski a short hit on the west-facing Brads Run down to the highway near the base of Brighton Ski Resort. Otherwise, continue up the ridge as it flattens out and goes east toward Point 10420.

Almost a mile from the trailhead, you'll reach an area called Picnic Tree, which is a humongous, toppled-over dead tree that makes a good seat with a view. It's also the start of a north-facing tree shot called Lanes Leap. This run is only 500 vertical feet though, so to get to the real goods, continue up the ridge. You will soon notice the terrain getting steep as the skin track begins to climb toward Point 10420. Stay near the pines on the left for protection. In 0.5 mile from Picnic Tree, you'll crest a false summit at 10,370 feet. Ski the northwest pines, called Promise Land, or the southwest-facing Sunny Glades into Hidden Canyon when snow conditions are ripe. If bagging the actual peak is your goal, ski east onto a saddle, and climb up the remaining 50 vertical feet to the true summit.

To return, ski the tree-filled north-facing runs on Promise Land, and skin back up to regain the ridge at Picnic Tree to ski Brighton Hill to the trailhead. You can also ski down to Guardsman Pass Road and pole back to the car. Another favorite run is the Northeast Bowl. This shot dumps you at the east side of Guardsman Pass, where it's a mere 200-vertical-foot skin west to the pass. Ski the road back to your car, or skin south up the ridge back to the top of Point 10420. If you ski the southwest-facing Sunny Glades, you'll end up in Hidden Canyon, which will empty you near the base of Brighton Ski Resort. Use a shuttle car or skin up Brighton Hill to return to the trailhead.

Of course the easiest way to reach the summit of Point 10420 is via the Great Western chairlift at Brighton Ski Resort. At the top of the chairlift, go north to the backcountry access gate and ski or snowboard down the ridge to the Hidden Canyon Saddle. From here, skin up the remainder of the ridge for almost 300 vertical feet to the top. This ridge is very rocky, however, so a deep snowpack may be required. Descend the routes described above and ski down Hidden Canyon for the return to the Brighton base.

Opposite: *Sweeping turns on Red Top in Little Cottonwood Canyon*

LITTLE COTTONWOOD
CANYON

"WASANGELES" IS A DEROGATORY TERM most often used to describe traffic jams on skin tracks of the Central Wasatch, and it is especially true for Little Cottonwood Canyon. On any given day—snow or sun, powder or crust—expect to join a horde of ski-touring parties getting after it, especially around Alta and Snowbird. There's good reason for Little Cottonwood's popularity: it's arguably the center of backcountry skiing in North America, if not the world. Huge amounts of "The Greatest Snow on Earth" drop in the upper canyon. The terrain is vast and steep. People gravitate to Alta to work for one ski season but then never leave. This place is skiing's holy land.

Tours in Little Cottonwood are generally more difficult and higher consequence than tours in Big Cottonwood. Mount Superior, Cardiac Ridge, White Pine, and the Pfeifferhorn are prime examples of big, photo-worthy lines. But moderate skiing and snowboarding does exist. Grizzly Gulch, Catherine Pass, and Pink Pine are great routes for intermediates and are prime locations for beginners to learn the craft. Backcountry access gates at both Alta and Snowbird allow for endless touring opportunities where you can ski the resort for a few hours then easily seek fresh lines farther afield.

Despite the length of Little Cottonwood Canyon, there are only three main trailheads where ski tours start: Alta's upper parking lot, the Cardiff Pass trailhead by the Alta Guard weather station, and the White Pine trailhead just down canyon from Snowbird. This lack of feasible starting points (mostly due to parking issues in avalanche run-out zones) means you'll generally have to endure longer approaches to get to the goods. This is especially true for tours that originate from White Pine. Many of the ski and snowboard descents described here are actually in Big Cottonwood Canyon, such as upper Silver Fork and upper Cardiff Fork, but they appear in this chapter because the trailheads and ascent routes are in Little Cottonwood.

The backcountry in upper Little Cottonwood Canyon is always under threat from ski resort expansion, especially a long-sought-after interconnect plan to link all seven ski resorts in the Central Wasatch. Routes near Alta, particularly those surrounding and accessed from Grizzly Gulch, are current as of this writing but may change dramatically in the future.

NOTES

Land Management. Tours in Little Cottonwood Canyon are located in Uinta-Wasatch-Cache National Forest. The Pfeifferhorn and Red Pine Trees are located entirely within the Lone Peak Wilderness. Pink Pine, Lake Peak, and White Baldy are right on the wilderness border. Follow all wilderness regulations and practice Leave No Trace principles. Much of upper Cardiff Fork is a patchwork of private property, but a special-use agreement between the Cardiff Canyon Owners Association and the US Forest Service allows right-of-way for backcountry skiers. If you're winter camping in the Little Cottonwood Canyon backcountry, you must camp at least 200 feet from streams and lakes. Contact information for the Salt Lake Ranger District is located in Resources.

Road Conditions. State Route 210, also called Little Cottonwood Canyon Scenic Byway, is frequently closed for avalanche control work after big storms. It has the highest highway avalanche hazard index of any major road in the United States, with more than thirty-five avalanche paths. Check the UDOT website (see Resources) before heading up the morning after a big storm, and follow all backcountry closure signs during control work.

Weather. Upper Little Cottonwood Canyon is a microclimate that gets bombarded with snow. In fact, Alta is among the snowiest resorts in the world with a seasonal average of 510 inches per year. Alta and Snowbird have up-to-date snow totals on their websites. Before heading out, check the Utah Avalanche Center's Salt Lake advisory and the National Weather Service website for current conditions. See the Resources page for web addresses and phone numbers.

25 The Pfeifferhorn

Start Point : White Pine trailhead, 7700 feet
High Point : The Pfeifferhorn summit, 11,326 feet
Trail Distance : 10 miles
Trail Time : 9 hours
Skill Level : Expert
Best Season : Winter/Spring
Maps : USGS Dromedary Peak; Wasatch Backcountry Skiing; Alpentech Wasatch Touring 2

The Pfeifferhorn is perhaps the most iconic peak in the Central Wasatch. It used to be called the Little Matterhorn due to its similar appearance to the Matterhorn in the Alps. But everyone has been calling this aesthetic peak the Pfeifferhorn, named after Charles Pfeiffer, who headed the Wasatch Mountain Club in the 1930s. In 2013 the US Board on Geographic Names officially changed the name to the Pfeifferhorn. As for skiing? This mountain is a beast and one of the most sought-after ski-mountaineering experiences in Utah. A long approach from the White Pine trailhead, steep climbing below the summit, and expert-only descents, including the rappel-with-your-skis-on Northwest Couloir, await. Crampons and an ice ax are essential gear, as well as a harness, two to three full-length slings, carabiners, and a rope.

GETTING THERE

From east Salt Lake City, take I-215 south and exit at 6200 South. Go south on Wasatch Boulevard to Little Cottonwood Canyon Scenic Byway (State Route 210), and follow it east up Little Cottonwood Canyon for 5 miles to the White Pine trailhead on the south side of the road. There is a large parking area with an outhouse.

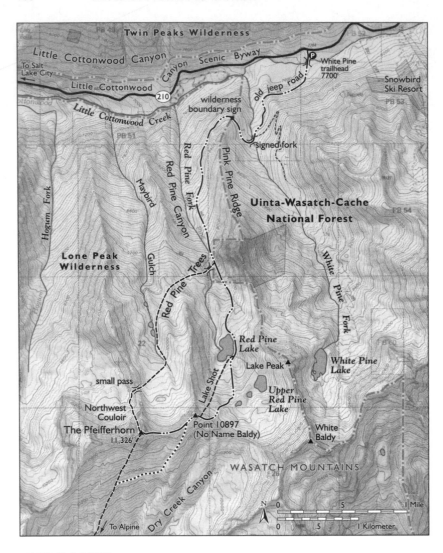

THE ROUTE

From the White Pine parking area just down canyon from Snowbird, locate the trail behind the outhouse on the west side of the lot. Follow it 60 vertical feet down to Little Cottonwood Creek and cross the large wooden footbridge. At the other end, the trail widens into a jeep road and rises west for 0.75 mile before coming to a signed fork next to the creek at 8070 feet. Go right across the creek and continue west. At the toe of Pink Pine Ridge you'll pass a sign at the boundary of Lone Peak Wilderness as the trail curves south into Red Pine Fork.

Continue following the summer trail route south through forests of aspen, spruce, and fir while staying on the east side of Red Pine Fork. About 1.25 miles beyond the wilderness boundary, you'll come to a fork in the skin track at 9170 feet where the summer trail intersects Red Pine Fork at a small bridge. Instead of crossing the creek, stay left and continue up Red Pine Fork another 0.65 mile and 600 vertical feet to Red Pine Lake.

To gain the Little Cottonwood–Dry Creek Divide, skin across or around the lake to a stand of evergreens on a small ridge that rises up from the south side of the shore. Climb this ridge as it breaks above the trees near Upper Red Pine Lake and curves southwest. At about 10,400 feet, the ridge sort of melds into an upper headwall. This east-facing aspect can be icy in the mornings, especially in the spring, so be prepared to climb with ice ax and crampons if needed.

Once you gain the divide, you'll stand on Point 10897. This unnamed peak is known locally as No Name Baldy, though some backcountry skiers call it Red Bird Point. Whatever the name, the view here will suck the breath right out of you, especially when you first glimpse Box Elder Peak to the south. Also, an excellent ski run called Lake Shot is found here. Make turns down the wide, northeast-facing shot back to the shore of Red Pine Lake.

To reach the Pfeifferhorn, traverse west along the divide from No Name Baldy. The ridge can get narrow at times, and if the snow is icy, then it's best to crampon up and boot across instead of risking a slide-off above exposure. In 0.5 mile from No Name, you'll reach the base of the Pfeifferhorn's summit cone, where another good ski or snowboard descent falls north into Maybird Gulch.

If you insist on summiting and skiing some wild terrain, keep those crampons on and get out the ice ax, because you might need them to complete the climb. From the

View of the Pfeifferhorn from Lake Peak on the White Pine/Red Pine Divide

base of the Pfeifferhorn's summit cone to the top, the climbing gets real steep. It's a 300-vertical-foot boot pack up the east ridge to the summit.

At the top, the marquee line is the Northwest Couloir: steep skiing on a wide chute that narrows down to a 50-foot cliff right in the middle of the couloir. There is no going around it. Locate climbing bolts skier's right on the rock wall, set up your rappel anchor with slings, throw your rope, and rappel down. Sometimes old slings and such are left behind on the bolts, but bring your own in case they don't look trustworthy.

After the heart-pounding rappel, you can open up some speed and make turns down the wide apron that spills into upper Hogum Fork. To return, traverse east across the snowfields and climb the short but steep wall to a small pass that separates Hogum from Maybird Gulch. Ski the east face a measly 200 vertical feet down into Maybird, and ski north while working your way skier's right beneath the ridge that separates Maybird from Red Pine. At the toe of this ridge, where the Maybird and Red Pine canyons merge, ski the east-facing Red Pine Trees down to the creek. Cross the creek and follow the summer trail route back down to the White Pine trailhead.

If you summit the Pfeifferhorn, you can also ski the easier run on the mountain's southwest face. This run drops thousands of feet on a southerly aspect into Dry Creek Canyon, which eventually ends up at the Dry Creek trailhead at 5700 feet in the town of Alpine. These lower-angle runs can be perfect corn skiing in the spring. Of course you'll need a ride back to the White Pine trailhead from Alpine. Otherwise, ski the upper section of the south face, then traverse east and skin back up to No Name Baldy, where Lake Shot will get you back down to Little Cottonwood Canyon.

26 Red Pine Trees

Start Point	White Pine trailhead, 7700 feet
High Point	Red Pine–Maybird Divide, 9700 feet
Trail Distance	6 miles
Trail Time	4 hours
Skill Level	Intermediate
Best Season	Winter
Maps	USGS Dromedary Peak; Wasatch Backcountry Skiing; Alpentech Wasatch Touring 2

Red Pine Fork is filled with big descents that require stamina, bravery, and mountaineering skill. But despite the imposing mountains above Red Pine Lake, there are in fact intermediate routes in the lower canyon, like the Red Pine Trees, where touring parties can find powder stashes and enjoy a mellow day. This is a pleasant, low-angle tour that mostly follows the summer trail up Red Pine Fork before veering off to the Red Pine–Maybird Divide, where a makeshift log shelter (assuming it's still there) provides an ideal spot to picnic before skiing or snowboarding down.

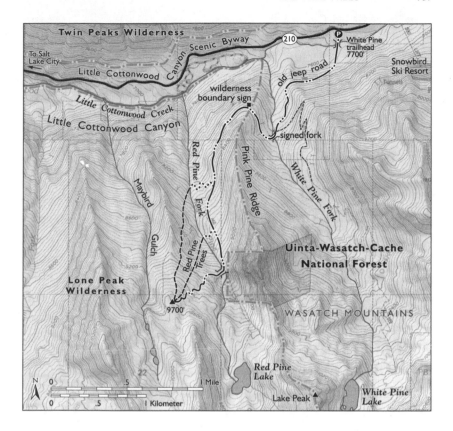

GETTING THERE

From east Salt Lake City, take I-215 south and exit at 6200 South. Go south on Wasatch Boulevard to Little Cottonwood Canyon Scenic Byway (State Route 210), and follow it east up Little Cottonwood Canyon for 5 miles to the White Pine trailhead on the south side of the road. There is a large parking area with an outhouse.

THE ROUTE

From the White Pine parking area just down canyon from Snowbird, locate the trail behind the outhouse on the west side of the lot. Follow it 60 vertical feet down to Little Cottonwood Creek and cross the large wooden footbridge. At the other end, the trail widens into a jeep road and rises west for 0.75 mile before coming to a signed fork next to the creek at 8070 feet. Go right across the creek and continue west. At the toe of Pink Pine Ridge you'll pass a sign at the boundary of Lone Peak Wilderness as the trail curves south into Red Pine Fork.

Continue following the summer trail route through evergreen forests while staying on the east side of Red Pine Fork. About 1.25 miles beyond the wilderness boundary, you'll come to a fork in the skin track at 9170 feet. Left continues up the bottom of Red Pine

Taking a break inside a makeshift shelter in the Red Pine Trees

Fork to Red Pine Lake. To get to Red Pine Trees, hang a right and cross the creek on a small bridge. This tiny wooden bridge may be buried under the snow, but a skin track is usually in place to signal its location, unless you get there immediately after a snowstorm. In times of deep snowpack, the creek may not even be visible under the snow anyway.

Once you cross the creek, the ascent steepens as you switchback up to the Red Pine–Maybird Divide. The grade isn't difficult as the route climbs over small terraces with very short, steep sections followed by flat meadows. Just over a quarter mile from the bridge, you might come across a makeshift log shelter at 9600 feet, just below the divide. It's a good spot to have lunch, stop for a hot drink, or just relax before preparing for the descent.

To return, ski alongside your ascent route on low-angle, gladed terrain back to the Red Pine Fork Trail. You can also stay far left of your skin track for a longer descent in similar terrain to a lower part of the creek. Be very careful here as unstable snow bridges exist above the water where it's easy to fall in. If you go this route, you'll have to skin east back up to the trail for the return route to the parking area.

27 Pink Pine Ridge

Start Point : White Pine trailhead, 7700 feet
High Point : Pink Pine Ridge, 9600 feet
Trail Distance : 4 miles
Trail Time : 3 hours
Skill Level : Intermediate
Best Season : Winter
Maps : USGS Dromedary Peak; Wasatch Backcountry Skiing;
: Alpentech Wasatch Touring 2

A little bit of white and a little bit of red makes pink. Anyone who remembers their preschool lessons knows this simple fact, so it is that Pink Pine Ridge is a moniker given to the spine that separates the White Pine and Red Pine drainages. It's an excellent, quick tour for those skiers and snowboarders who are short on time. One run can be done car-to-car in fewer than three hours, maybe two if you're a spandex-clad rando dude. Pink Pine is also a relatively safe place to ski, as low-angle shots spill from the east-northeast slopes with a snowpack anchored by aspen and evergreen trees.

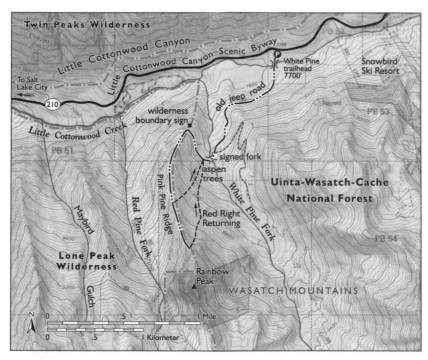

Skiing down from Pink Pine Ridge below Red Right Returning

GETTING THERE

From east Salt Lake City, take I-215 south and exit at 6200 South. Go south on Wasatch Boulevard to Little Cottonwood Canyon Scenic Byway (State Route 210), and follow it east up Little Cottonwood Canyon for 5 miles to the White Pine trailhead on the south side of the road. There is a large parking area with an outhouse.

THE ROUTE

From the White Pine parking area just down canyon from Snowbird, locate the trail behind the outhouse on the west side of the lot. Follow it 60 vertical feet down to Little Cottonwood Creek and cross the large wooden footbridge. At the other end, the trail widens into a jeep road and rises west for 0.75 mile before coming to a signed fork next to the creek at 8070 feet. Go right across the creek and continue west toward Red Pine Fork. As soon as you pass the Lone Peak Wilderness sign at the toe of the wooded ridge, begin skinning left (south) up the mountain. Due to the popularity of this route, there is usually a skin track already in place.

Skin up while staying on the safety of the ridge for about a quarter mile to an elevation of around 9600 feet. From here, east-facing lines open up on the left. You can choose to descend any of several short lines from the ridge, which vary from open shots to tight trees. Perhaps the most popular run is near the top of the ridge below 9947-foot Rainbow Peak, where the skin track ends underneath a series of small cliffs. A short, narrow chute holds quality tree skiing that flows into an open bowl known locally as Red Right Returning. At the bottom of this run, it's quick and easy to regain Pink Pine Ridge to do multiple laps.

To return, descend through the aspen forest below Red Right Returning while angling skier's left back to the bottom of White Pine Fork near the creek crossing, then simply follow the White Pine Trail back to your car.

28 Lake Peak (No Name Peak)

Start Point : White Pine trailhead, 7700 feet
High Point : Lake Peak summit, 10,718 feet
Trail Distance : 7 miles
Trail Time : 5 hours
Skill Level : Advanced
Best Season : Winter/Spring
Maps : USGS Dromedary Peak; Wasatch Backcountry Skiing;
: Alpentech Wasatch Touring 2

Lake Peak is a mountain with many names. The USGS map marks it as Thunder Mountain, while the Wasatch Backcountry Skiing Map refers to it as No Name Peak. But these days many backcountry skiers and guides prefer the term Lake Peak due to its proximity to both White Pine and Red Pine lakes, so that is the name I use here. This 10,718-foot high point is actually part of the Pink Pine Ridge that connects to White Baldy. While not a true summit in itself, Lake Peak looks impressive enough from afar to be a magnet for powder seekers. Excellent skiing and snowboarding is found on the north side into Boulder Basin, while the signature line is a descent down Lake Chute that goes from the top all the way to White Pine Lake. Touring access starts from the White Pine trailhead, while Snowbird skiers can easily traverse from the resort's Gad Valley.

GETTING THERE

From east Salt Lake City, take I-215 and exit at 6200 South. Go south on Wasatch Boulevard to Little Cottonwood Canyon Scenic Byway (State Route 210), and follow it east up Little Cottonwood Canyon for 5 miles to the White Pine trailhead on the south side of the road. There is a large parking area with an outhouse. To reach Snowbird, continue up canyon another mile. If you access Lake Peak from Snowbird, it's a good idea to leave a shuttle vehicle at the White Pine trailhead for the exit.

THE ROUTE

From the White Pine parking area, locate the trail behind the outhouse on the west side of the lot. Follow it 60 vertical feet down to Little Cottonwood Creek and cross the large wooden footbridge. The trail widens into a jeep road and rises west for 0.75 mile before coming to a signed fork next to a creek, White Pine Fork, at 8070 feet. Go

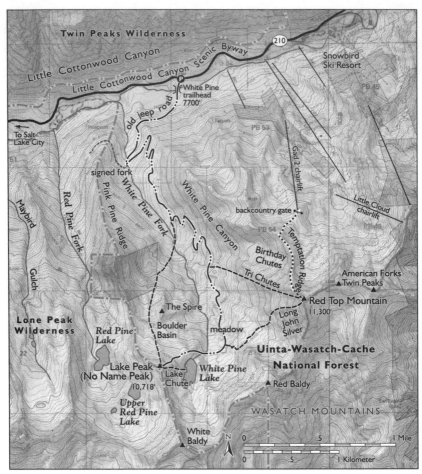

left (east) and ascend the road through a series of switchbacks as it rises into White Pine Canyon. In 1.25 miles, the trail levels out at around 8500 feet. Keep following the jeep track, which may be difficult to decipher when the snow is deep, but the canyon's popularity assures there will likely be a skin track to follow.

Three miles from the trailhead, you'll find yourself in a large meadow beneath the slopes of Red Baldy at around 9850 feet. To the west is Lake Peak. Head in that direction. You first have to skin up a small ridge that splits down the center of White Pine. It's just over 150 feet of vertical that takes you to White Pine Lake at the foot of Lake Peak at 10,000 feet.

For an alternate approach from Snowbird, check in with ski patrol at the top of the Gad 2 chairlift, and exit at the backcountry gate (which is only open when avalanche danger is low). Boot pack 400 vertical feet to the top of Temptation Ridge, and follow the ridge south past the Birthday Chutes to either the Tri Chutes or Long John Silver on Red Top Mountain. Descend either of these runs during stable avalanche

Fast and wide turns in the Lake Chute entrance

conditions, but as you go down, stay skier's left to avoid ending up too low in White Pine Canyon. When you reach the meadow below Red Baldy, skin west to White Pine Lake as described above.

To reach the top of Lake Peak from White Pine Lake, you'll have to boot pack up the mountain's steep slopes. Depending on the season, your ascent route may vary. The ridges are always safer from avalanches but are also prone to exposed rock. If the snowpack is stable, I like to boot up what I want to ski in order to check the snowpack layers on that particular aspect. In general, the north face and Lake Chute are both viable ascent routes. An ice ax, Whippet, and crampons are good to bring along.

Once you've climbed the 700 vertical to the summit of Lake Peak, you have a few killer descent options. First, you can make turns through the east-facing Lake Chute. The entrance is located just south of the main summit, and the line—a wide couloir that falls all the way to White Pine Lake—is a must-do. The other fine lines are the north-facing runs into Boulder Basin. A ridge splits the north face in two, and both sides can be rocky at the top. Once you're below the upper elevations, where the two runs converge into the massive open bowl of Boulder Basin, the skiing becomes more moderate.

To return, you can simply retrace your ascent route down the jeep road to the White Pine trailhead. Another option is to stay skier's left at the bottom of Boulder Basin, and descend through the trees located west of the Spire. This large fin of rock is one of the more prominent features in White Pine, and its west side harbors low-angle tree skiing for a nice alternative to the summer road. If you choose this option, rejoin the road at around 8500 feet where White Pine Fork emerges from a narrow gully into an open meadow.

(29) Red and White Baldy

Start Point : White Pine trailhead, 7700 feet
High Points : Red Baldy, 11,171 feet; White Baldy, 11,321 feet
Trail Distance : 8 miles
Trail Time : 6 hours
Skill Level : Advanced/Expert
Best Season : Winter/Spring
Maps : USGS Dromedary Peak; Wasatch Backcountry Skiing;
: Alpentech Wasatch Touring 2

Red Baldy and White Baldy are the two major peaks that crouch at the head of White Pine Canyon. Both are large mountains with exposed, rocky terrain and avalanche-prone slopes that offer some of the most adventurous skiing in the Wasatch, mostly due to variable snow and a long approach from the White Pine trailhead. You can cut your ascent time in half with a lift ticket at Snowbird, but the backcountry gates in the resort's Gad Valley are rarely open until late spring. Periods of stable powder or late-season corn are the best times to visit.

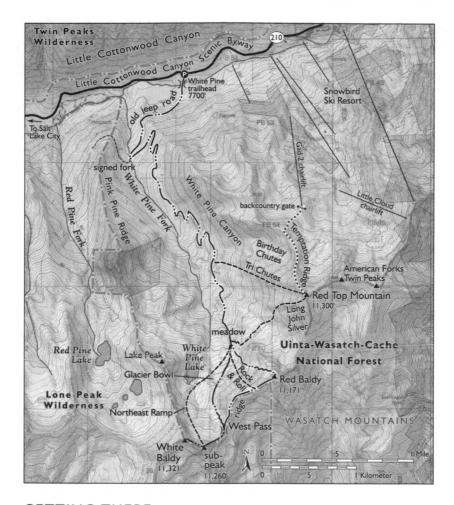

GETTING THERE

From Salt Lake City, take I-215 and exit at 6200 South. Go south on Wasatch Boulevard to Little Cottonwood Canyon Scenic Byway (State Route 210), and follow it east up Little Cottonwood Canyon for 5 miles to the White Pine trailhead on the south side of the road. There is a large parking area with an outhouse. To reach Snowbird, continue up canyon another mile.

THE ROUTE

From the White Pine parking area, locate the trail behind the outhouse on the west side of the lot. Follow it 60 vertical feet down to Little Cottonwood Creek and cross the large wooden footbridge. The trail widens into a jeep road and rises west for 0.75 mile before coming to a signed fork next to a creek, White Pine Fork at 8070 feet. Go left (east) and ascend the road through a series of switchbacks as it rises into White

Huge, open terrain is found in upper White Pine.

Pine Canyon. In 1.25 miles, the trail levels out at around 8500 feet. Keep following the jeep track, which may be difficult to decipher when the snow is deep, but the canyon's popularity assures there will likely be a skin track to follow.

Three miles from the trailhead, you'll find yourself in a large meadow at around 9850 feet beneath the slopes of Red Top Mountain, Red Baldy, and White Baldy. Red Baldy is the peak in the middle. To ski the northwest-facing Red Baldy run, it's often prudent to simply skin up the large, 1300-vertical-foot wall to the top, assuming the snow stability is good-to-go. During big snow years it may be possible to ski from the summit, but most of the time it is wind scoured and rocky. In that case, start making turns below the top.

For an alternate approach from Snowbird, check in with ski patrol at the top of the Gad 2 chairlift, and exit at the backcountry gate (which is only open when avalanche danger is low). Boot pack 400 vertical feet to the top of Temptation Ridge, and follow the ridge south past the Birthday Chutes to either the Tri Chutes or Long John Silver on Red Top. Descend either of these runs during stable avalanche conditions, but as you go down, stay skier's left to avoid ending up too low in White Pine Canyon. When you reach the meadow, you'll be below Red Baldy's northwest face.

Another good ascent option is from West Pass, a low saddle between Red and White Baldy. To reach it from the large meadow, continue up canyon 0.75 mile by traversing around the bottom of Red Baldy. You'll have to climb up a small headwall for around

200 vertical feet to the pass. Find the easiest and most efficient way through the cliff bands and rocks, which varies depending on wind loading and snow level.

When you reach the pass at 10,700 feet, traverse the ridge northeast for just over a half mile to the top of Red Baldy. Along the way, large rock fins above exposure may have to be negotiated if snow is low. A false summit at around 11,100 feet is the start of Rock & Roll, the best ski run on the West Pass side. The descent starts out wide but soon chokes into a chute that spits you out onto a wide apron on Red Baldy's lower flanks.

The rest of the way to the true summit of Red Baldy is on a sketchy, knife-edge ridge, so it's only necessary if you're desperate to bag the peak and possess good mountaineering skills.

White Baldy is a much more technical beast to climb and ski and should only be attempted under the most stable snowpack conditions. West Pass is the best way to go, so follow the ascent route described above. Once at the pass, go west on White Pine Ridge. At around 10,800 feet, the ridge becomes very steep and is littered with boulders and cliffs. You can ascend this section by boot packing up, but crampons, ice axes, and maybe even ropes and harnesses are recommended. Also, contouring around the cliffs on the north side of the ridge is the best line. Only skilled mountaineers should attempt this ascent.

When you reach a sub-peak at 11,260 feet, you're at the top of the Northeast Ramp. This obvious, skiable line is the only safe way down, but it has big exposure over a gigantic glacial moraine. At the bottom of the ramp, the terrain widens into Glacier Bowl, where you can open up with wider, faster turns back to the bottom of White Pine Canyon.

30 Red Top Mountain

Start Point : White Pine trailhead, 7700 feet
High Point : Red Top Mountain summit, 11,300 feet
Trail Distance : 8 miles
Trail Time : 5 hours
Skill Level : Advanced
Best Season : Winter/Spring
Maps : USGS Dromedary Peak; Wasatch Backcountry Skiing;
: Alpentech Wasatch Touring 2

Red Top Mountain, also known locally as Red Stack, is one of many mountains in White Pine Canyon that's over 11,000 feet. Red Top dominates the skyline with neighbors like American Fork Twin Peaks and Red and White Baldy. As a result, she's a coveted mountain to climb and ski, with a long approach from the White Pine trailhead, or easier access from Snowbird. Many aesthetic lines, like Long John Silver and the Tri Chutes, fall from her crown, but the top is usually too rocky to ski from due to winds that scour her exposed crimson top.

GETTING THERE

From Salt Lake City, take I-215 and exit at 6200 South. Go south on Wasatch Boulevard to Little Cottonwood Canyon Scenic Byway (State Route 210), and follow it east up Little Cottonwood Canyon for 5 miles to the White Pine trailhead on the south side of the road. There is a large parking area with an outhouse.

THE ROUTE

From the White Pine parking area, locate the trail behind the outhouse on the west side of the lot. Follow it 60 vertical feet down to Little Cottonwood Creek and cross the large wooden footbridge. The trail widens into a jeep road and rises west for 0.75 mile before coming to a signed fork next to a creek, White Pine Fork at 8070 feet. Go left, (east) and ascend the road through a series of switchbacks as it rises into White Pine Canyon. In 1.25 miles, the trail levels out at around 8500 feet. Keep following

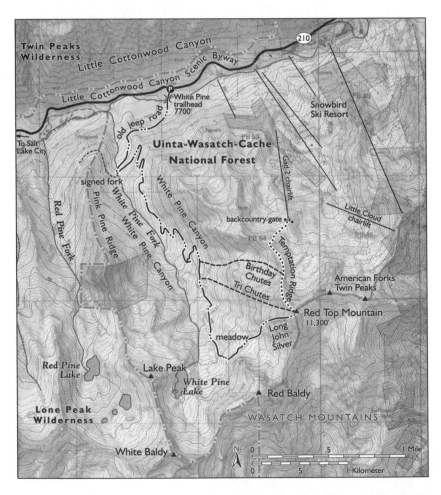

Big, skiable lines are everywhere on Red Top Mountain.

the jeep track, which may be difficult to decipher when the snow is deep, but the canyon's popularity assures there will likely be a skin track to follow.

In just over 3 miles, cut left over a small ridge and enter a large meadow below Red Top Mountain and Red Baldy. Continue left up a bowl, and boot pack up one of the rocky shoulders bisected by a run known as Long John Silver. You can either summit the peak or stop just short of the top and ski one of several long and steep chutes. Go north to access the Tri Chutes, three skinny runs that return to the bottom of White Pine Canyon. You can also continue north to Temptation Ridge, where the Birthday Chutes fall to the northwest. Or you can just ski down where you climbed on Long John Silver, a southwest-facing, spicy shot with a lot of vertical. Return to White Pine trailhead on the jeep road.

For an alternate approach, you can also access Red Top Mountain from the top of the Gad 2 chairlift at Snowbird when ski patrol opens the backcountry gate (which is only open when avalanche danger is low). Boot pack 400 vertical feet to the top of Temptation Ridge and follow the ridgeline all the way to the summit. From here, you can also tour to American Fork Twin Peaks, Red Baldy (Tour 29), and Silver Creek to the south.

31 Scotties Bowl

Start Point	White Pine trailhead, 7700 feet
High Point	Point 10121, 10,121 feet
Trail Distance	3 miles
Trail Time	3 hours
Skill Level	Advanced
Best Season	Winter
Maps	USGS Dromedary Peak; Wasatch Backcountry Skiing; Alpentech Wasatch Touring 2

Scotties Bowl is a classic descent in Little Cottonwood Canyon, just to the west of Snowbird's resort boundary. It's a great tour, much like a five-star rock climb with a hand crack that leads to a face climb that leads to laybacks, stemming, and friction moves. Scotties has variety like that as it starts with a really steep, treed slope, funnels into fast, low-angle terrain, and features a lot of gullies and shoulders to play on. Scotties isn't just about a good, long powder run—it's also like a natural terrain park.

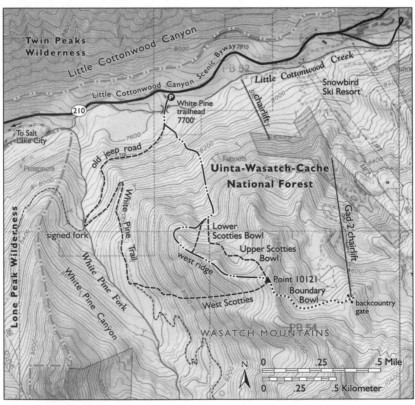

Scotties Bowl hangs far above Highway 210 at the bottom of Little Cottonwood Canyon.

Access to Scotties is very easy from the Bird when the Gad 2 backcountry access gate is open. On those days, Scotties is best avoided if you're looking for solitude, as it gets tracked out really fast from skiers hungry for a quick sidecountry hit. When the resort gate is closed, it's a great tour right from the highway with more than 2000 feet of vertical to shred. But the gate is usually closed when avalanche danger is high, so make a careful snow stability assessment before ascending this massive slide path.

GETTING THERE

From east Salt Lake City, take I-215 south and exit at 6200 South. Go south on Wasatch Boulevard to Little Cottonwood Canyon Scenic Byway (State Route

210), and follow it east up Little Cottonwood Canyon for 5 miles to the White Pine trailhead on the south side of the road. There is a large parking area with an outhouse.

THE ROUTE

From the White Pine trailhead, locate the trail behind the outhouse and follow it 60 vertical feet down to Little Cottonwood Creek. Cross the large wooden bridge and follow the trail as it widens into a jeep road. As soon as you exit the trees, you can see the Scotties Bowl slide path on your left. There will probably be a skin track already in place unless it just snowed. Huff and puff up the slide path while keeping close to or inside the trees on the east side for safety.

About a quarter mile into the climb, at around 9000 feet in elevation, you'll reach Lower Scotties Bowl, which is guarded by cliffs at its head. Safely cross westbound on the bottom of the bowl's snowfield, and switchback up to the west ridge. From here, you can go around the cliffs and have a safe route to follow the rest of the way. If you're short on time, you can ski or snowboard from here down the lower bowl. Otherwise, continue up the ridge another half mile to the top of Point 10121, which stands above Upper Scotties Bowl. The only direction to go from here is down, so point those tips and enjoy the ride back to the car.

You can also find good turns on West Scotties when the snow is soft. From the peak, ski the west slopes down to the bottom of White Pine Fork, and follow the summer trail back to the trailhead. This aspect is often sun crusted, so it's best skied right after a storm.

Of course the easiest way to ski Scotties is from Snowbird. For this alternate approach, check in with ski patrol at the top of the Gad 2 chairlift, and exit the backcountry gate (which is only open when avalanche danger is low). Traverse west for 0.4 mile beneath Boundary Bowl and switchback to the top of Point 10121. From here, you can descend as described above. To ski from the resort, you'll either want to leave a shuttle car at the White Pine trailhead or be prepared to hitchhike (or walk) 0.8 mile back up Little Cottonwood Canyon Scenic Byway to the Snowbird base.

32 Mount Superior

Start Point	Alta Guard weather station, 8650 feet
High Point	Mount Superior summit, 11,050 feet
Trail Distance	5 miles
Trail Time	4 hours
Skill Level	Advanced/Expert
Best Season	Winter/Spring
Maps	USGS Dromedary Peak; Wasatch Backcountry Skiing; Alpentech Wasatch Touring 1

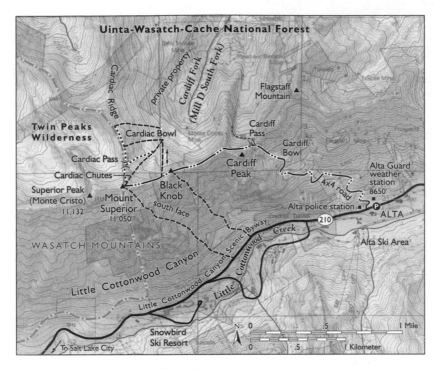

Mount Superior is the monarch of the Central Wasatch. Like a doting mother, she stands watch over Alta, providing a dramatic backdrop for resort photos and an irresistible lure for backcountry skiers attracted to her aesthetic south face that spills like a queen's robe 3000 feet from summit to road. A relatively short approach and a knife-edge ridge to the top makes for an excellent adventure in itself and is a good way to access Cardiac Bowl from her north side via the north chutes. But that steep, cliff-strewn south face is a test piece that demands respect and should only be skied on a stable snowpack.

GETTING THERE

From east Salt Lake City, take I-215 south and exit at 6200 South. Go south on Wasatch Boulevard to Little Cottonwood Canyon Scenic Byway (State Route 210), and follow it east up Little Cottonwood Canyon for 8 miles to Alta. Just after passing the Shallow Shaft restaurant, park on either side of the road at the large pullouts.

THE ROUTE

The skin up starts behind the Alta Guard weather station on the north side of the highway. It basically follows a summer 4x4 road underneath a powerline as it passes the Alta Guard weather station and contours up the mountainside. The climb is not very steep, and if those backcountry skiers who broke trail were smart, the skin track should stay in safe zones that avoid terrain traps and gullies. It's a good place for

The south face of Mount Superior is one of Utah's premier backcountry lines.
(Mike DeBernardo)

beginner backcountry skiers to practice skinning technique, thanks to the low-angle slopes and proximity to Alta.

After 0.6 mile, you'll likely come to a fork in the skin track. Stay left (west), as going right leads to the top of Flagstaff Mountain. From here, the route follows a sub-ridge with sparse pine trees. A mile from the trailhead, you'll reach the bottom of Cardiff Bowl, where a few switchbacks lead to the top of Cardiff Pass at around 10,000 feet.

From the pass, head west on the ridge, contouring around Cardiff Peak on her north side, then keep going either on skins or by boot packing until you get to Little Superior (a.k.a. Black Knob) at around 10,500 feet and about a half mile from the pass. Good runs can be skied here on the north side into Cardiff Fork (Mill D South), or the south side back down to Little Cottonwood Canyon Scenic Byway. Be aware that Cardiff Fork is littered with parcels of private property, and user conflicts have arisen in the past. A special-use permit is in place that allows right-of-way for recreationists, so please be respectful of the landowners.

Continuing from Black Knob to Superior, the going gets steep and sometimes rocky at this point. Follow the thin ridge to the 11,050-foot summit and be sure to hang out to enjoy the massive view before dropping in.

From the top, you can descend the north-facing Cardiac Chutes into Cardiac Bowl, and then skin back up to the ridge by Black Knob to return. Cardiac Bowl is also a good way to access Cardiac Ridge via the pass. Get there by switchbacking west to Cardiac Pass, and traversing north on Cardiac Ridge to access the many sweet chutes and couloirs that line up along the east face, which all spill into the impressive Cardiac Bowl.

The classic descent is to ski or snowboard the absolutely massive south face of Mount Superior. This run is a test piece for backcountry skiers in Utah and is a line you will never forget as you make turns high above Alta for almost 3000 vertical feet to Little Cottonwood Canyon Scenic Byway. However, because it's south-facing, there is a small window of quality snow, so you have to time your trip just right. Also, the south face is home to massive avalanche activity, so only attempt this run when avalanche conditions are stable. You may also want to study a photo of the run taken from across the canyon, because small cliffs and rock bands are strewn about the place, so choosing the correct route is essential. For your first time, find a ski buddy who's done it before. To return from the bottom of the face, hike up the road to Alta or hitch a ride back to your car.

On a side note, there is some confusion here as topographic maps show the true summit of Superior as being farther west and marked as Superior Peak. Locals call this Monte Cristo, and her elevation is 11,132 feet. The mountain that locals refer to as Mount Superior is the smaller summit at 11,050 feet.

33 Cardiff Pass

Start Point : Alta Guard weather station, 8650 feet
High Point : Cardiff Peak summit, 10,277 feet
Trail Distance : 3 miles
Trail Time : 2 hours
Skill Level : Beginner/Intermediate
Best Season : Winter
Maps : USGS Dromedary Peak; Wasatch Backcountry Skiing;
: Alpentech Wasatch Touring 1

Backcountry skiers derisively call the Central Wasatch "Wasangeles," and for good reason. The range's proximity to the Salt Lake metropolis humming in the valley below means skiers and riders are crawling all over the place. Nowhere is this better illustrated than at Cardiff Pass. Located just above the Town of Alta, Cardiff (also known as Pole Line Pass, thanks to the powerline strung above) can feel like an LA traffic jam on the skin track, especially the morning after a storm. While Cardiff Pass is the main ascent route for the expert-only tours on Cardiac Ridge, Mount Superior, and Flagstaff Mountain, this tour describes the beginner-friendly ski and snowboard routes in the area, which is a great place for first-timers to learn the finer aspects of skinning technique.

GETTING THERE

From east Salt Lake City, take I-215 south and exit at 6200 South. Go south on Wasatch Boulevard to Little Cottonwood Canyon Scenic Byway (State Route 210), and follow it east up Little Cottonwood Canyon for 8 miles to Alta. Just after passing the Shallow Shaft restaurant, park on either side of the road at the large pullouts.

THE ROUTE

The skin up starts behind the Alta Guard weather station on the north side of the highway. It basically follows a summer 4x4 road underneath a powerline as it passes the Alta Guard weather station and contours up the mountainside. The climb is not very steep, and if those backcountry skiers who broke trail were smart, the skin track should stay in safe zones that avoid terrain traps and gullies. It's a good place for beginner backcountry skiers to practice skinning technique, thanks to the low-angle slopes and proximity to Alta.

After 0.6 mile, you'll likely come to a fork in the skin track. Stay left (west), as going right leads to the top of Flagstaff Mountain. From here, the route follows a sub-ridge with sparse evergreen trees. A mile from the trailhead, you'll reach the bottom of Cardiff Bowl, where a few switchbacks lead to the top of Cardiff Pass at around 10,000 feet.

There are two options here: ski the south and east faces of Cardiff Bowl back to the car on the Little Cottonwood side, or ski north-facing bowls into Cardiff Fork (Mill D South) in Big Cottonwood Canyon. You can also choose to top out on Cardiff Peak to the west, where a weather station strung with Christmas lights sits.

From Cardiff Peak, the slide-prone north face harbors cold powder and steep skiing down to the old Cardiff Mine in Cardiff Fork, but the steep headwalls are short and require a skin back up in avalanche terrain to regain the ridge. Also, be aware that Cardiff Fork is littered with parcels of private property, and user conflicts have arisen in the past. A special-use permit is in place that allows right-of-way for recreationists, but please be respectful of the landowners.

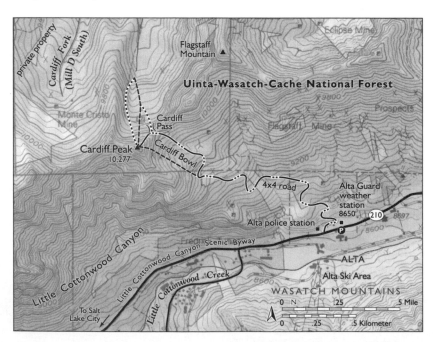

Skiing down to Alta from Cardiff Pass

Skiing or snowboarding south from Cardiff Pass back to Alta is mellow, but the snow quality can be poor unless you hit it during or immediately after a storm. It's also a great place for farming corn on spring-morning tours.

(34) Flagstaff Mountain and Upper Days Fork

Start Point : Alta Guard weather station, 8650 feet
High Point : Flagstaff Mountain summit, 10,530 feet
Trail Distance : 3 miles
Trail Time : 2 hours
Skill Level : Intermediate/Advanced
Best Season : Winter
Maps : USGS Dromedary Peak; Wasatch Backcountry Skiing Map; Alpentech Wasatch Touring 1

Upper Days Fork is the place to see and be seen on a powder day when the snowpack is stable and the sky is blue. The upper cirque of Days Fork is part of the Valhalla that

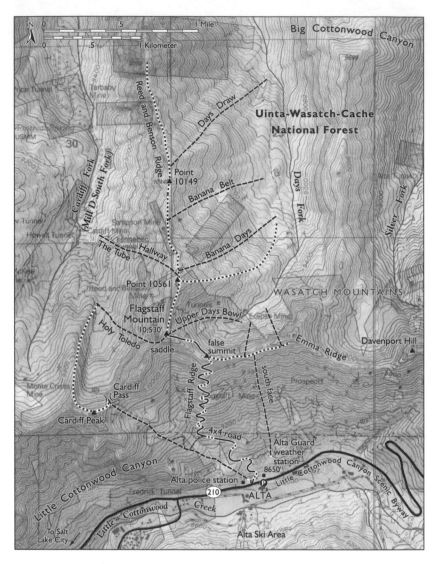

is the Alta backcountry, so it tends to get crowded and tracked out, but it provides some of the best bang for the buck when farming turns. You'll find yourself part of a backcountry scene that includes Alta and Snowbird employees, casual backcountry fiends, the Wasatch Powderbird Guides helicopter flying above, and maybe even a film crew shooting pro skiers for next year's ski movies. Short chutes, wide-open bowls, and tree-covered aspects that provide plenty of descent choices are on the menu in Upper Days. In fact, when standing below the upper cirque, you can scan from east to west and discover dozens of skiable lines in a row stretching from Emma Ridge to Reed and Benson Ridge. But the most popular lines are the ones that fall from Flagstaff Mountain. These shots are the first to be poached in Days Fork, and the lines are steep and tasty.

GETTING THERE

From east Salt Lake City, take I-215 south and exit at 6200 South. Go south on Wasatch Boulevard to Little Cottonwood Canyon Scenic Byway (State Route 210), and follow it east up Little Cottonwood Canyon for 8 miles to Alta. Just after passing the Shallow Shaft restaurant, park on either side of the road at the large pullouts.

THE ROUTE

The skin up starts behind the Alta Guard weather station on the north side of the highway. Follow the skin track past the Alta Guard weather station under the power-lines as if you're heading to Cardiff Pass. It basically follows a summer 4x4 road as it contours up the mountainside. The climb is not very steep, and if those backcountry skiers who broke trail were smart, the skin track should stay in safe zones that avoid terrain traps and gullies. It's a good place for beginner backcountry skiers to practice skinning technique, thanks to the low-angle slopes and proximity to Alta.

After 0.6 mile, you'll likely come to a fork in the skin track. Go right toward Flagstaff Mountain (left goes to Cardiff Pass). It gets steep here as a series of switchbacks goes up Flagstaff Ridge to a false summit at 10,200 feet. From here, touring options are everywhere: You can continue northwest for 0.25 mile to the true Flagstaff summit

The south side of Flagstaff Mountain can be picture perfect the morning after a storm.

at 10,530 feet and ski Upper Days Bowl, or you can traverse east on Emma Ridge and drop in anywhere to hit steep north-facing lines and chutes.

Longer tours are possible by following the top of Reed and Benson Ridge north of Flagstaff Mountain, where dozens of east-facing lines offer more vertical into the bottom of Days Fork. Popular runs include Banana Days and Banana Belt, found just north of Point 10561. Farther along the ridge is Days Draw, a long run that's amazing on a deep powder day. It begins just north of Point 10149.

The west side of Reed and Benson Ridge is mostly cliffs with narrow couloirs, like Holy Toledo. This wide but short chute is found at a saddle just south of and below the Flagstaff summit. Another popular option is Hallway Couloir. This chute is very hard to find from above and is often easier to just boot pack up from the bottom. To find the upper entrance, traverse Reed and Benson Ridge from the Flagstaff summit to just beyond Point 10561. The start is at the bottom of a west-facing gray cliff. You'll likely have to pick your way down through rocks and bushes. The Hallway is a long, 1800-foot run that connects to the Tube, a natural half-pipe that goes to the bottom of Cardiff Fork. It's a playful terrain feature that's epic on a powder day.

To return to Alta from Cardiff Fork, skin south up the sub-ridge that leads to Cardiff Peak and ski the south-facing runs below the powerline back to Alta. From the bottom of Days Fork, skin back up to Reed and Benson Ridge and then to Emma Ridge to ski the open bowls and shoulders of the south face back to Alta.

35 Davenport Hill and Upper Silver Fork

Start Point	Alta upper lot, 8800 feet
High Point	Davenport Hill summit, 10,120 feet
Trail Distance	3 miles
Trail Time	3 hours
Skill Level	Intermediate
Best Season	Winter
Maps	USGS Dromedary Peak, Brighton; Wasatch Backcountry Skiing; Alpentech Wasatch Touring 1

Davenport Hill, one of the high points on Emma Ridge above the Town of Alta, provides many classic ski descents from her summit—most notably in the upper bowls of Silver Fork. The mountain divides the bowls, which makes it like a high-altitude buffet table—you can choose to ski whatever you want from here. Tight chutes, steep, north-facing glades, and open bowls with short approaches are all here for the taking. Backcountry skiing in upper Silver Fork is very similar to tours in neighboring Days and Cardiff forks, where dawn patrollers sneak in powder runs before work. But Silver Fork remains less crowded due to the fact that it's not along the Cardiff Pass skin track, leaving more untouched powder for those willing to traverse the ridge a bit to garner the goods.

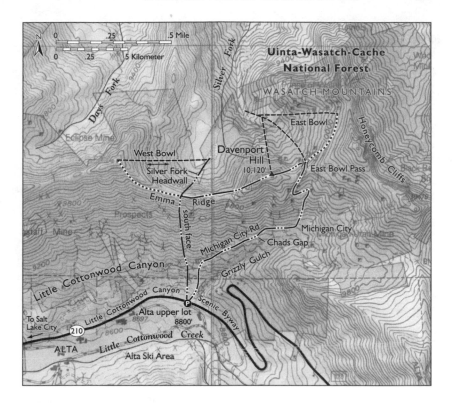

GETTING THERE

From east Salt Lake City, take I-215 south and exit at 6200 South. Go south on Wasatch Boulevard to Little Cottonwood Canyon Scenic Byway (State Route 210), and follow it east up Little Cottonwood Canyon for 8 miles to the Town of Alta. Park at the upper lot before the Albion Basin winter gate.

THE ROUTE

From the closed winter gate, locate a small hill to the west of the narrow Grizzly Gulch entrance. Skin up to the top and continue for less than a quarter mile and 200 vertical feet until you meet up with the 4x4 Michigan City Road. Go right (east) as the road traverses into Grizzly Gulch. You'll walk between the gigantic mine tailing piles of the legendary Chads Gap and enter the old mining area known as Michigan City at around 9400 feet. If the snow level is low, you can sometimes see a bit of Utah's mining past where old equipment and buildings are rusting away.

After about 0.6 mile from the trailhead, leave the road and skin left (north) up a steep shoulder. It's 600 vertical feet in 0.3 mile to East Bowl Pass, and you'll need to avoid terrain traps and gullies along the way. You can ski or snowboard northwest into Silver Fork here, or traverse 0.4 mile northeast along the ridge to find powder in the

Skiing down the Silver Fork Headwall from Emma Ridge

East Bowl. To summit Davenport Hill, go west from East Bowl Pass along the ridge for 0.25 mile until you reach the top.

Several runs can be ridden from the top of Davenport Hill, mostly steep gullies that spill north into Silver Fork and have serious avalanche potential. For a mellower ride, keep traversing west on Emma Ridge for 0.5 mile until you reach the Silver Fork Headwall, a quality run that falls north to the flats below. The West Bowl looms over the scene and can easily be reached from the ridge for an extra 0.3 mile from the top of Silver Fork Headwall. But to maximize vertical, it's best to ski a run into Silver Fork, then skin up to the top of West Bowl through the east-facing trees.

To return from Silver Fork, skin back up to Emma Ridge and ski the south face to Alta and your vehicle.

36 Grizzly Gulch and Patsey Marley

Start Point	Alta upper lot, 8800 feet
High Point	Patsey Marley summit, 10,555 feet
Trail Distance	4 miles
Trail Time	3 hours
Skill Level	Beginner/Intermediate
Best Season	Winter
Maps	USGS Dromedary Peak, Brighton; Wasatch Backcountry Skiing; Alpentech Wasatch Touring 1

Grizzly Gulch is a legend of Alta backcountry skiing. It is the site of the iconic Chads Gap, where pro skiers earn fame and ski movie segments by jumping the 130-foot span between two piles of mine tailings. Grizzly is also a highly developed touring area, with homes at the bottom, powerlines above, and a snowcat track running the length of the gulch, where Nordic skiers get a workout. Despite all this, Grizzly Gulch accesses a vast backcountry area from Twin Lakes Pass between Alta and Brighton, with Patsey Marley at its head. There is a proposal to put a chairlift up Grizzly Gulch to connect Alta to Solitude. If this comes to pass, it will drastically change backcountry skiing in the area.

GETTING THERE

From east Salt Lake City, take I-215 south and exit at 6200 South. Go south on Wasatch Boulevard to Little Cottonwood Canyon Scenic Byway (State Route 210), and follow it east up Little Cottonwood Canyon for 8 miles to the Town of Alta. Park at the upper lot before the Albion Basin winter gate.

THE ROUTE

Follow the groomed road at the Albion winter gate. The road switchbacks to the mouth of Grizzly Gulch, but in 0.2 mile, skin tracks on your left provide shortcuts

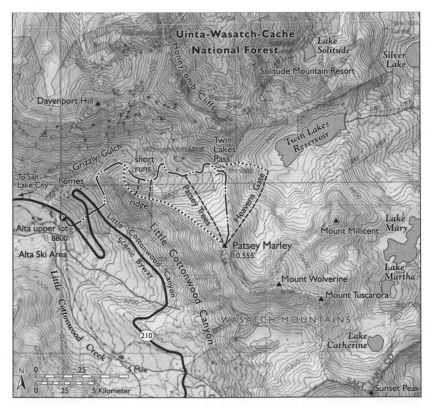

Tree shots below Patsey Marley in Grizzly Gulch are a safe place to be on high avalanche danger days.

between the two main corners. After you shortcut the switchbacks, skin north and contour around the cluster of homes that dot the mountainside. Be sure to keep a wide berth and avoid trespassing into people's yards. A short switchback climbs a south-facing slope above the houses and enters Grizzly Gulch below a string of powerlines at about 9250 feet. Sometimes the trail is groomed here all the way to the Honeycomb Cliffs above Solitude Mountain Resort. As you ascend, note the old mining relics from Alta's past scattered around the gulch.

For an alternate ascent to Patsey Marley, leave the road after 0.75 mile, and switchback right (south) to a small ridge where laps on a steep, open north-facing slope allow easy turns with little uphill effort. Otherwise, traverse the ridge southeast for an additional 0.7 mile to the top of Patsey Marley. This exposed route can be very windy, and the undulating terrain is more difficult for beginning skinners.

For the main route to Patsey Marley, continue up the bottom of Grizzly Gulch another 0.5 mile to Twin Lakes Pass at around 9997 feet. From here, you can enjoy the view of Mount Wolverine above, Twin Lakes below, and Brighton Ski Resort beyond.

To summit Patsey Marley from the pass, climb south on the ridgeline for 0.5 mile. There's usually a cornice at the top that you'll have to traverse under to gain the summit. Be careful here and skin across the face one at a time. After you pass the cornice, it's a short hop to the summit at 10,555 feet. From the top of Patsey Marley, you can ski down her wide north face into the Patsey Trees for a return trip to the car through Grizzly Gulch. You can also ski northeast toward Twin Lakes via Heavens Gate, a steep chute with an appetite for avalanches. From the bottom, skin west back up to the pass to return to Grizzly Gulch.

For beginner backcountry skiers and snowboarders, Twin Lakes Pass is a good place to turn around: the descent down Grizzly Gulch from here features mellow terrain that mostly avoids avalanche terrain, and it is especially easygoing if the road has recently been groomed.

37 Wolverine Cirque

Start Point : Alta upper lot, 8800 feet
High Point : Mount Wolverine summit, 10,795 feet
Trail Distance : 4 miles
Trail Time : 3 hours
Skill Level : Advanced
Best Season : Spring
Maps : USGS Dromedary Peak, Brighton; Wasatch Backcountry
: Skiing; Alpentech Wasatch Touring 1

Split by massive cliffs that fall from the ridge, Wolverine Cirque is a steep skier's wet dream. Dozens of couloirs line up like toy soldiers, ranging from easier descents in

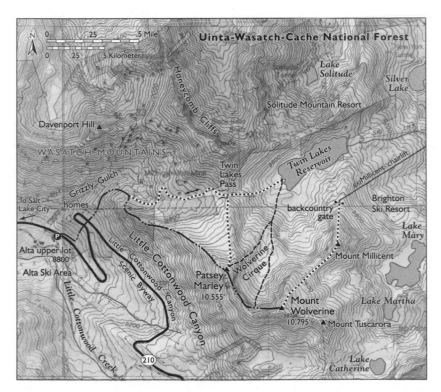

Dropping in on Granny Chute in Wolverine Cirque

wide chutes to pucker-worthy hop-turn fests in super technical hallways. But enjoy-ing this playground of chutes comes at a price, as the cirque is notorious for having a bad, wind-loaded snowpack and high avalanche danger. Giant cornices often guard the entrances of the chutes, and the lower aprons can be choked with avy debris. As a result, spring is often the best time to ski here, when the snow is stable and the weather calms down. While Wolverine Cirque is actually in Big Cottonwood Can-yon, the true touring route starts at Alta in Little Cottonwood Canyon. Sidecountry skiers can also find easy access from the Millicent area at Brighton Ski Resort.

GETTING THERE

From east Salt Lake City, take I-215 south and exit at 6200 South. Go south on Wasatch Boulevard to Little Cottonwood Canyon Scenic Byway (State Route 210), and follow it east up Little Cottonwood Canyon for 8 miles to the Town of Alta. Park at the upper lot before the Albion Basin winter gate.

THE ROUTE

Follow the groomed road at the Albion winter gate. The road switchbacks to the mouth of Grizzly Gulch, but in 0.2 mile, skin tracks on your left provide shortcuts between the two main corners. After you shortcut the switchbacks, skin north and contour around the cluster of homes that dot the mountainside. Be sure to keep a wide berth and avoid trespassing into people's yards. A short switchback climbs a south-facing slope above the houses and enters Grizzly Gulch below a string of pow-erlines at about 9250 feet.

After 0.75 mile, switchback right (south) to a short, steep, open area and onto a ridge and follow it for an additional 0.7 mile to the 10,555-foot summit of Patsey Marley.

You can also get there by staying at the bottom of Grizzly Gulch on the standard route to Twin Lakes Pass, and then turning right onto the north ridge of Patsey Marley and following it south on the ridgeline for 0.5 mile. There's usually a cornice near the top that you'll have to traverse under to gain the summit. Be careful here and skin across the face one at a time. After you pass the cornice, it's a short hop to the summit.

The top of Patsey Marley is the westernmost point of Wolverine Cirque, but to ski into the cirque, you'll want to continue south on the ridge as it curves to the east for just under a half mile to the summit of Mount Wolverine at 10,795 feet.

Along the way, there are several descent routes—simply pick your poison. There are sixteen named chutes from Patsey Marley to the end of the northernmost shoulder of Mount Wolverine. Chutes with names like Tips and Tails, THC, Bronco Couloir, Zoot Chute, the Scythe, and Granny Chute, the widest and most popular, are yours for the taking. They all end at the flats at the bottom of Wolverine Cirque.

To return, ski down to Twin Lakes Reservoir while staying skier's left, and then skin west up to Twin Lakes Pass, where you can descend Grizzly Gulch to the car.

To get to Wolverine Cirque from Brighton, ride the Millicent chairlift. Check in at the ski patrol shack before exiting the backcountry gate, and boot up almost 600 vertical feet to the top of Mount Millicent at 10,452 feet. Traverse southwest 0.5 mile to the summit of Mount Wolverine.

38 Catherine Pass Area

Start Point : Alta upper lot, 8800 feet
High Points : Mount Tuscarora summit, 10,640 feet; Mount Wolverine,
: 10,795 feet
Trail Distance : 5 miles
Trail Time : 3 hours
Skill Level : Intermediate/Advanced
Best Season : Fall/Winter
Maps : USGS Brighton; Wasatch Backcountry Skiing Map;
: Alpentech Wasatch Touring 1 and 2

The Catherine Pass area, just outside the Alta ski area boundary, is one of the
first places of the season you can tour in Utah, thanks to predictable early-season

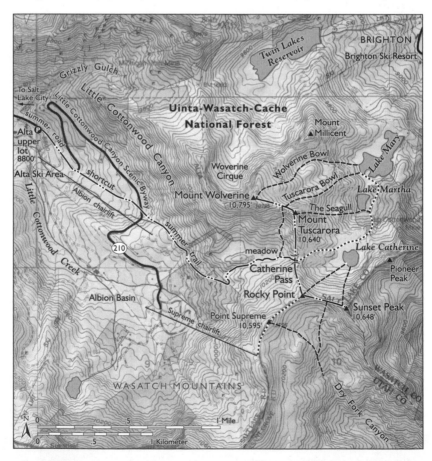

Skinning across a meadow toward Catherine Pass

snowfall in Little Cottonwood Canyon. Autumn is also the best time to visit for first tracks before the Supreme chairlift at Alta starts running, because once it does, the whole place becomes tracked-out sidecountry terrain with easy return runs back to the resort. Even so, it's a popular route between Alta and Brighton and has touring options from easy glades to steep chutes. Much of the "backcountry" terrain here is best accessed using Alta's Supreme chairlift when ski patrol opens the gate.

GETTING THERE
From east Salt Lake City, take I-215 south and exit at 6200 South. Go south on Wasatch Boulevard to Little Cottonwood Canyon Scenic Byway (State Route 210), and follow it east up Little Cottonwood Canyon for 8 miles to the Town of Alta. Park at the upper lot before the Albion Basin winter gate.

THE ROUTE

Skin east up the often-groomed, snow-covered summer road. Follow the road as it heads into Albion Basin alongside the ski resort boundary. In 0.5 mile, leave the road at the first switchback and continue skinning along the resort boundary. This is a good shortcut that saves more than a half mile of skinning. After about a mile from the parking lot you will rejoin the road where it ends near the top of the Albion chairlift. From here, keep left, generally following the summer trail route as you traverse east into a flat meadow at the bottom of Catherine Pass at around 10,000 feet. Check out the view of Mount Wolverine and Mount Tuscarora to the north before continuing east for a short skin up a few switchbacks for just over 200 vertical feet to gain the pass where you can see Lake Catherine below.

There are many touring options with good skiing at all points of the compass. Most people go south along the ridge to Rocky Point, where excellent east-facing chutes hold good snow. Farther along the ridge is Sunset Peak, a 10,648-foot summit that is questionable for ski descents on the north face when avalanche danger is high. Both options end at Lake Catherine and require a skin back up to the pass.

Dry Fork Canyon offers south- and east-facing shots. Ski down from the ridge between Rocky Point and Sunset Peak as far as you want to go. The terrain gets flat and rocky below the upper faces. Return by skinning north back to the ridge.

Alternatively, you can traverse northeast to Point Supreme at 10,595 feet from the Supreme chairlift at Alta after the ski patrol opens the gate. It holds prime low-angle skiing in the fall, but all northwest-facing shots are inbounds once Alta opens for the season. Skiing the short bowls east off Point Supreme into Dry Fork Canyon is always backcountry and is a great place to do laps from the Supreme chairlift. Return to the resort via an adjacent ridge.

For a bigger and truer backcountry experience, use Catherine Pass to access Mount Tuscarora. From the top of the Supreme chairlift, traverse north along the ridge to Catherine Pass. From the pass switchback up Tuscarora's south ridge. From the pass it's 0.3 mile and around 425 vertical feet to the summit.

Descent options from Tuscarora include the south face, which takes you back into Alta. The most advanced line is the Seagull. This 45-degree, east-facing couloir is a 1300-foot line that goes through steep rock walls down into an apron. From the bottom, skin southwest back to Catherine Pass.

West of Tuscarora is Mount Wolverine. Traverse the adjoining ridge to find Tuscarora Bowl and Wolverine Bowl to the north. These low-angle bowls are popular when avalanche danger is high, and both runs end up at Lake Mary, where you can skin back to Catherine Pass.

From Mount Wolverine, you can access Wolverine Cirque and the Twin Lakes Pass area (see Wolverine Cirque, Tour 37, and Grizzly Gulch and Patsey Marley, Tour 36). From Twin Lakes Pass, ski down Grizzly Gulch for a return run to Alta.

Opposite: *Hiking up the west face of Mount Timpanogos*
(Mike DeBernardo)

SOUTHERN WASATCH

BIG TERRAIN AND LONG TOURS—that's what you can expect when you come to ski the backcountry of the Southern Wasatch. This area is home to the tallest peaks in the range, with Mount Nebo awarded top honors with a summit at 11,928 feet. Almost all tours in the Southern Wasatch require approaches that extend for miles. Once you do arrive at skiable slopes, they're huge, open faces with massive avalanche potential. Be wary of snowpack stability and only attempt these tours when avalanche danger is unlikely.

This chapter covers Lone Peak on the north end, down to Mount Nebo in the south. While Lone Peak is more associated with the Central Wasatch, it is included here because the trailhead is located in the town of Alpine in northern Utah County. Mount Timpanogos is a mountain of gargantuan proportions, with the South Summit as her epicenter for epic runs, especially for spring corn. The peaks west of Provo are generally called the Cascades as it's a series of summits that comprise the enormous Cascade massif. The difficult access and long approach makes this spot the domain of the Wasatch Powderbird Guides heli-skiing service. Skiable terrain is everywhere here, and the Big Springs Hollow route is the best jumping-off point for exploratory, on-foot tours farther afield. But beware, this range is notorious for unsurvivable, tree-snapping avalanches.

Mount Nebo is perhaps the most challenging mountain of them all. Access via a steep and rocky jeep road, followed by many miles of skinning and mountaineering in serious alpine terrain, is required. Some parties camp overnight for a two-day affair, but if you can drive up most of the road, a long day tour is possible.

NOTES

Land Management. Tours in the Southern Wasatch are located in Uinta-Wasatch-Cache National Forest. Lone Peak, the Three Temptations, and Box Elder Peak are within the Lone Peak Wilderness boundary. Timpanogos is within the Mount Timpanogos Wilderness, and Nebo is within the Mount Nebo Wilderness. Follow all wilderness regulations and practice Leave No Trace principles. If you're winter camping, you must camp at least 200 feet from streams and lakes. Contact the Pleasant Grove and Spanish Fork ranger districts for more information. Web addresses and phone numbers are found in Resources.

Road Conditions and Fees. American Fork Canyon is a National Recreation Area that requires a recreation fee. As of this writing, a three-day pass is $6 and an annual pass is $45. The highway is plowed to Tibble Fork Reservoir in the winter. If you park at Aspen Grove for Mount Timpanogos, you'll have to pay a $6 recreation fee there as well.

Weather. The Southern Wasatch doesn't get nearly the amount of snow the Central Wasatch is blessed with. The snowpack can often be more fickle as well. Check the Utah Avalanche Center's Provo advisory and the National Weather Service website for current conditions. See the Resources page for web addresses and phone numbers.

The south face of Lone Peak is among the best spring-corn tours in Utah.

39 Lone Peak

Start Point : Schoolhouse Springs trailhead, 5500 feet
High Point : Lone Peak, 11,253 feet
Trail Distance : 9 miles
Trail Time : 7 hours
Skill Level : Advanced/Expert
Best Season : Spring
Maps : USGS Lehi, Draper, Dromedary Peak

Lone Peak is the king of the Central Wasatch Mountains. This iconic peak is best known as a rock-climbing destination, with challenging traditional routes found in the Lone Peak Cirque. But the mountain, which is visible from North Salt Lake to Provo, sees far fewer people in the winter months. Despite her reputation as one of the most difficult Wasatch summits to ascend due to mileage and total elevation gain from the valley floor, the mellow south face allows for a long but nontechnical day of spring corn skiing. In fact, some of the longest south-facing corn runs in all of Utah are found here.

GETTING THERE
From Salt Lake City or Provo, take I-15 to the Alpine exit and head east on State Route 92. At 5300 West, turn left (north). At the roundabout, take the second exit

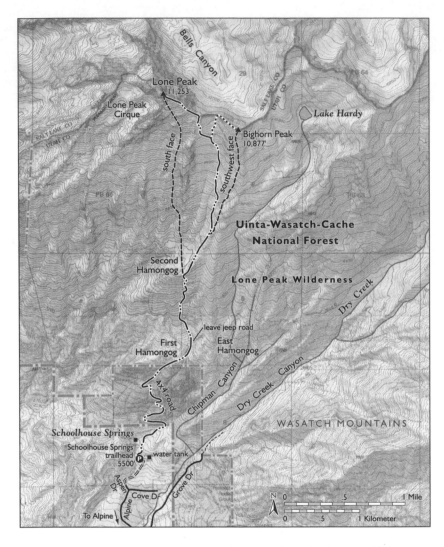

onto Main Street and continue to 200 North. Turn right. Take the second left on 200 East. Eventually this street turns into Grove Drive. Drive for 1.6 miles to the intersection with Alpine Cove Drive and turn left. Then take the next left onto Aspen Drive. It almost immediately becomes a dirt road. Follow it to a dead end at a large metal gate next to a municipal water tank. Park here.

THE ROUTE

The low elevation of this trailhead means you may have to hike for the first portion of the route, especially in the spring. Go around the gate and head up a closed jeep road as it switchbacks past the water tank and up the mountainside.

In 1.8 miles, the road comes to First Hamongog at 7000 feet. What is a Hamongog? Basically it's a meadow, but undoubtedly a Mormon pioneer derived the word from a biblical passage that refers to the "valley of the multitudes of Gog." Here, you'll see a sign marking the boundary of Lone Peak Wilderness. The start of the summer trail is on your left. I recommend ignoring the summer route as the trail is narrow, overgrown, and difficult to follow in the winter, so you'll likely end up bushwhacking through scrub oak. Instead, go across the meadow to its far end where the jeep trail continues straight up a steep slope.

In just 0.4 mile and 600 vertical feet, the road curves sharply to the right (east). Leave the road here and ascend north up the steep but open slope to an evergreen forest on a small ridge. Drop down a short distance to the other side of this ridge into another mountain meadow. This is Second Hamongog, located at 8100 feet.

Cross the meadow to the base of Lone Peak's massive south face. This is where the fun begins. Skin directly up the low-angle slopes between Lone Peak and Bighorn Peak for 1.5 miles and more than 3000 feet to the summit ridge at about 10,700 feet. Along the way, don't forget to look down at the valley for a fantastic view of Utah County and the Southern Wasatch Mountains.

From the ridge, go west another 0.3 mile and 550 vertical feet to Lone Peak's summit. You will actually top out on a small outcrop just south of the true summit. If you insist on standing atop the true summit, it will require a short but extremely exposed traverse on a knife-edge ridge that calls for an ice ax, crampons, rope, and a lot of guts. But for this route, skiing the south face begins from the south summit.

Spring is the best time to ski or snowboard the south face, as it's well known as one of the very best corn descents in the state. From the top, choose one of two low-angle ramps that are separated by a small sub-ridge with cliffs on its west side. Both lines flow down for 3000 vertical feet to Second Hamongog.

If you have the time and energy, you can also ski Bighorn Peak. After taking a run on Lone Peak's south face, ascend your original approach route back to the summit ridge, and then go east for a little less than a half mile above a large cliff band to the 10,877-foot summit of Bighorn. From the top, ski the steep southwest face all the way down to Second Hamongog, and then follow your ascent route back to the trailhead.

40 Box Elder Peak

Start Points	Dry Creek Canyon trailhead, 5700 feet; Tibble Fork trailhead, 6400 feet
High Point	Box Elder Peak summit, 11,101 feet
Trail Distance	9 miles
Trail Time	7 hours
Skill Level	Advanced/Expert
Best Season	Winter/Spring
Maps	USGS Timpanogos Cave, Dromedary Peak

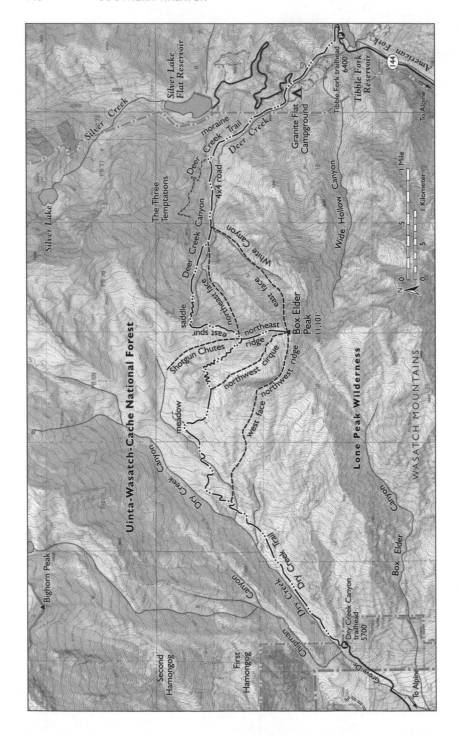

Box Elder is a dramatic, beautiful peak that dominates the skyline around the American Fork, Dry Creek, and Deer Creek canyons. Viewed from the metropolitan sprawl of Utah County to the west, the mountain appears as a common, snow-covered triangle. But to see her from the north and east, you get to witness the terrifying aftermath of geologic time. Massive cliffs warped from seismic energy rise up from a gigantic, horseshoe-shaped bowl, which is the showcase skiable line. Avalanche paths called Shotgun Chutes spill down through swaths of north-facing evergreens for thousands of feet, and wide-open headwalls surround the remaining aspects for tons of vertical, no matter how you choose to ski it.

There are two approaches: one from Tibble Fork and the other from Dry Creek Canyon. Both are equal in mileage and comparable in vertical. Any way you slice it, Box Elder is a big mountain with a big approach that promises an unforgettable adventure.

GETTING THERE

Dry Creek Canyon: From Salt Lake City or Provo take I-15 to the Alpine exit and head east on State Route 92. At 5300 West, turn left (north). At the roundabout, take the second exit onto Main Street and continue to 200 North. Turn right. Take the second left on 200 East. This street becomes Grove Drive. Follow it 2.5 miles all the way to the end, where there is a dirt parking lot at the trailhead.

Tibble Fork: Take the Alpine exit off I-15 and go east on SR 92. In 7 miles you'll enter American Fork Canyon. About 5 miles up canyon, go left at a fork onto SR 144. Continue for 2.5 miles to Tibble Fork Reservoir. Park here in a large maintained lot. You'll have to pay a recreation fee at the ranger shack to park here.

THE ROUTE

Dry Creek Canyon: My preferred route starts at Dry Creek. The route is a bit more direct, and you don't have to pay the recreation fee to park your car. The downside is the lower elevation means you may have to hike up to the snow line for the first couple of miles, especially during spring ascents.

From the trailhead, hike northeast through scrub oak on a steep, old jeep road. The condition of this trail may be severely rutted due to landslides that frequently occur in the area. You'll almost immediately come to a fork. Stay right as the path becomes rocky and goes straight up the mountainside on a bench above the Dry Creek drainage.

As the scrub oak gives way to conifer trees, you will encounter several stream crossings and a couple of trail signs at forks. Stay right on Dry Creek Trail and follow the signs toward Deer Creek. In 2.8 miles, you'll reach a large, open meadow at 8300 feet where you'll get your first glimpse of Box Elder's massive northwest cirque. There are two main ridges that form a horseshoe around the cirque: the northwest ridge and the northeast ridge. I prefer the northeast ridge because it provides access to the famous Shotgun Chutes. To get there, go south across the meadow directly toward the mountain, following the route as it goes up onto a flat plateau beneath the cirque. Switchback up a wide, west-facing wall to the start of the evergreens on the northeast ridge at 9300 feet.

Skiing down Box Elder Peak's legendary northwest cirque

Ascend south right up the ridge as it steeply climbs up through the trees. It takes many switchbacks over a thousand vertical feet before the trees thin and the ridge mellows at around 10,400 feet. Along the way, you can scope out the two Shotgun Chutes that cut through the trees. These double-barrels are classic ski descents that can only be attempted in the most stable of avalanche conditions. For the summit, travel along the low-angle, wind-affected ridge for another 0.5 mile to the top at 11,101 feet.

Tibble Fork: At the reservoir, the route starts at a gated entrance at the east end of the parking lot. A groomed road popular with snowmobilers switchbacks up and to the northwest into Deer Creek Canyon. Follow the road for about 1 mile passing the Granite Flat Campground along the way. At the end of the road, locate a large sign with a posted map that marks the start of the Deer Creek Trail. Follow it northwest toward the mountains, keeping right at any forks you may encounter.

In 1.75 miles from the start, you'll be at the moraine that sits below Silver Lake Flat Reservoir at 7300 feet. Go west by following an old 4x4 road that parallels Deer Creek on the north. In 0.5 mile, the road switchbacks up into the steep triple ridges that make up The Three Temptations. Instead, stay west for another 1.25 miles along the creek and ascend to the saddle at the Deer Creek–Dry Creek Divide at 9400 feet.

From the saddle, go up the east spur of the northeast ridge through evergreens for 0.5 mile and 1000 vertical feet to the top of the Shotgun Chutes and the main summit ridge. Continue to the top as described above.

Ski and snowboard descents are numerous from the summit. You can retrace your ascent route on the ridge and through the steep evergreens alongside the Shotgun Chutes. This is a great option if avalanche hazard is spooky or visibility is low. From the summit, the northwest cirque is the showcase line. It's a nearly 3000-foot, giant bowl that isn't as steep as it looks from below (around 40 degrees), but it does have exposure as you navigate through small cliff bands to the mellow flats below.

A good option for a return to Dry Creek is a descent of the west face. From the summit, ski down the northwest ridge to around 10,600 feet. From here, a continuous fall line sends you down to Dry Creek. Be aware, however, because at 8500 feet, the run enters a narrow gully. Stay skier's left on a sub-ridge to avoid the terrain trap (though be prepared for some bushwhacking). The sub-ridge skier's right is not a good option as it terminates at a large cliff.

If you parked at Tibble Fork Reservoir, the east and northeast faces drop you back into Deer Creek, but both are steep, exposed, and massively dangerous in high avalanche conditions, as both lines funnel into avalanche gullies. The largest descent from the summit on the east face constricts into White Canyon, which eventually intersects with Deer Creek. These shots are best left for spring corn tours when the snowpack is stable.

 The Three Temptations

Start Point : Tibble Fork trailhead, 6400 feet
High Point : Point 11038, 11,038 feet
Trail Distance : 8 miles
Trail Time : 6 hours
Skill Level : Advanced
Best Season : Winter
Maps : USGS Timpanogos Cave, Dromedary Peak

Looking for a backcountry ski zone blessedly devoid of Central Wasatch traffic? The Three Temptations in American Fork Canyon is a safe bet. The "three" refers to triple snowfields that become ravines between four ridges that spill down from the Little Cottonwood Divide for nearly 3500 vertical feet to the bottom of Deer Creek Canyon. The terrain features a huge, tasty-looking face above those tempting spines, where you can find dozens of skiable lines, but watch out for dangerous terrain traps in between. The only problem is timing. The south-facing Three Temptations is often sun crusted, so plan your trip right after it snows. Also, be prepared for a long approach from the trailhead.

GETTING THERE
From Salt Lake City or Provo, take I-15 to the Alpine exit and head east on State Route 92. In 7 miles you'll enter American Fork Canyon. About 5 miles up canyon, go left at a fork onto SR 144. Continue for 2.5 miles to Tibble Fork Reservoir. Park here in a large maintained lot. You'll have to pay a recreation fee at the ranger shack to park here.

THE ROUTE

Start at a gated entrance at the east end of the lot. A groomed road popular with snowmobilers switchbacks up and to the northwest into Deer Creek Canyon. The Three Temptations appear after you come around the second curve. Follow the road for about 1 mile, passing the Granite Flat Campground along the way. At the end of the road, locate a large sign with a posted map that marks the start of the Deer Creek Trail. Follow it northwest toward the mountains, keeping right at any forks you may encounter. It's a 1.25-mile skin through the forest from the campground to the bottom of the steep triple ravines that make up the Three Temptations. Any of the ridges between the ravines are good routes to gain elevation.

The west ridge is best if you want to avoid terrain traps and climb all the way to the top of Point 11038. To get there, switchback up the broad shoulder to the top, where you can descend open bowls that funnel into The Three Temptations. If avalanche

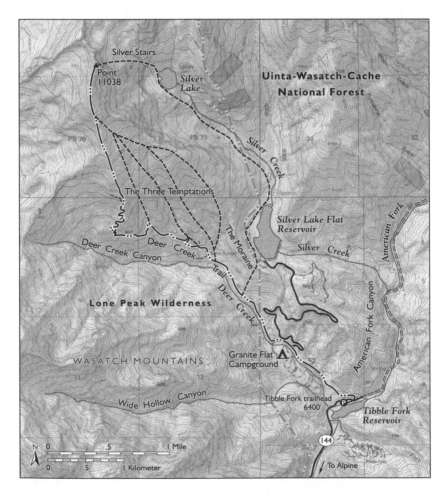

The Three Temptations are a series of ridges and gullies—playful terrain for a big descent. (Mike DeBernardo)

danger is a concern, you may also work the ridgelines for a long and playful 3500-foot vertical drop back to Deer Creek. However, you may be forced to bushwhack at the bottom, and the flat return to the car will be obnoxious for snowboarders.

Alternatively, you can make turns from Point 11038 down the east-facing Silver Stairs, an expert-only descent that ends at Silver Lake. From there, follow Silver Creek down to Silver Lake Flat Reservoir, where you can ski the wide, low-angle run called the Moraine back to the Dry Creek–Deer Creek Trail.

42 Mount Timpanogos South Summit

Start Point	Aspen Grove trailhead, 6900 feet
High Point	Mount Timpanogos South Summit, 11,722 feet
Trail Distance	7 miles
Trail Time	6 hours
Skill Level	Expert
Best Season	Spring
Maps	USGS Aspen Grove, Timpanogos Cave

Mount Timpanogos can be a very intimidating place to backcountry ski or snowboard, and each summit is a serious endeavor to reach no matter the season. While the main summit of "Timp" is the choice destination for summer hiking, this exposed peak offers little for good backcountry skiing and snowboarding. The nearby South

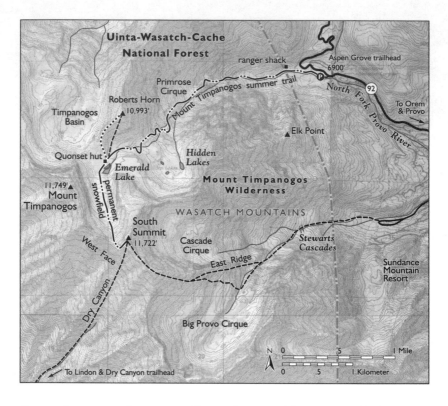

Summit, however, is the jumping-off point for some of the most epic ski descents in all of Utah, including the famed East Ridge and the nearly 5000-vertical-foot West Face. But if you want to ski a peak that doesn't require too much mountaineering skill, head up Roberts Horn. It's lower than the upper summits and can easily be skied as a day tour from the Quonset hut at Emerald Lake.

GETTING THERE

From the intersection of 800 North and State Street in Orem, drive east on 800 North for 2.5 miles to Provo Canyon, and then continue up US Highway 189 for 7 miles. Turn left at the Alpine Scenic Highway (State Route 92), following the signs to Sundance Mountain Resort. Drive past the ski resort, and 4.8 miles after leaving US 189, park at the large, well-signed Aspen Grove Recreation Area. There is a small fee to park here.

THE ROUTE

At the Aspen Grove trailhead on the west side of the parking lot, skin west past a ranger shack and into the bottom of Primrose Cirque. Follow the Mount Timpanogos summer trail route for 1 mile through the brushy flats until the terrain gets really steep. Here, the trail switchbacks up for 0.5 mile through a series of small cliffs to the base of the Primrose Cirque headwall at around 8300 feet. While the summer trail is easy to follow, you can cut travel time by shortcutting between switchbacks when possible.

At the bottom of the headwall, you're in serious avalanche terrain, so make a thorough snowpack assessment before continuing. An early spring morning is the best time to travel here, when the snow is hard and it's too early for wet slides. Make switchbacks up the main face until it becomes really steep, and then boot pack the rest of the way if needed. After climbing 2 miles and 3000 feet from the trailhead, you'll reach a spectacular hanging valley. Traverse west on the flats for 0.5 mile to the old Quonset hut that hunkers down at Emerald Lake at 10,400 feet by the permanent snowfield below the main summit.

Head due south from the hut up and across the permanent snowfield (so named because snow lasts all summer in this amphitheater of rock and can be skied year-round). It's low-angle stuff until the last 300 feet or so to the saddle. From here, you can ski your ascent route down the snowfield and the massive run down Primrose Cirque to Aspen Grove.

For the South Summit, traverse from the top of the snowfield east a short bit on the upper West Face high above the metropolitan Provo-Orem area, and then climb about 200 vertical feet to the top of the South Summit. You may have to boot pack this final climb if the snow is firm, and depending on conditions, ice axes and crampons may be needed.

Massive ski and snowboard terrain on Mount Timpanogos (Mike DeBernardo)

At the top, take in the sweeping view of the Southern Wasatch before your epic descent. The West Face is a nearly 5000-vertical-foot run on open slopes that fall into Dry Canyon, which goes all the way down to the city of Lindon. The West Face is best done as a spring descent, so the lower canyon will probably be dry—be prepared to walk the low elevations to the Dry Canyon trailhead parking lot, where you left a shuttle vehicle or arranged for a pickup.

The East Ridge is another big descent from the South Summit. To get there, traverse southeast and down an additional 0.4 mile to the top of the triangular prow. This "ridge" between Cascade Cirque and Big Provo Cirque is more like a wide face that's broken up by a series of cliff bands high above Sundance. The trick is to find chutes and passageways through the cliffs, usually to the far skier's left or skier's right, depending on snow depth. It would be wise to take a photo of the line from below before skiing it, so you have some idea of where to go. Falling is not an option here as a slide-for-life will surely send you over the rocks. This is expert-only terrain. At the bottom, exit couloirs lead to the brushy lower canyon at Stewarts Cascades, then down to Sundance, where you hopefully left a shuttle vehicle, or you'll have to hitch a ride back to the Aspen Grove trailhead.

For a relatively mellow day tour on Timpanogos, try skiing or snowboarding Roberts Horn. This is a small, pointed peak north of the Quonset hut at Emerald Lake. To reach it, climb 0.5 mile and 600 vertical feet up its south ridge to the top. The climb is exposed to large cliffs on both sides, so you may need crampons and an ice ax or Whippets if the snow is hard. To descend, make turns down the south face back to the hut, and then ski the classic 3000-foot run down Primrose Cirque to the car.

(43) Big Springs Hollow

Start Point	Big Springs trailhead, 5800 feet
High Point	Point 10006, 10,006 feet
Trail Distance	11 miles
Trail Time	9 hours
Skill Level	Advanced
Best Season	Spring
Map	USGS Bridal Veil Falls

Big Springs Hollow is a long approach for some short runs above tree line. However, that's not to say it isn't worth making the arduous skin to the top. Backcountry skiers and splitboarders who brave the miles and elevation gain are treated to some of the most dramatic mountain views in the entire Wasatch Range. Jagged peaks rise from the valley like thorns, surrounded by massive bowls that cause earth-shaking, tree-snapping avalanches. The terrain here is downright spooky when the snowpack is unstable, so the entire South Fork of the Provo River is best left for spring corn skiing. The whole Cascade Mountain massif is also a favorite playground of the Wasatch

High above Provo on the Cascade Mountain Divide

Powderbird Guides heli-skiing operation, so if conditions are ripe, you'll likely have company.

GETTING THERE

From the intersection of 800 North and State Street in Orem, drive east on 800 North for 2.5 miles to Provo Canyon, and continue up US Highway 189 for 5.7 miles. Exit the highway on the right at Vivian Park, and follow South Park Road into the canyon. In 3.3 miles, turn right on Spring Hollow Road. Continue for 0.2 mile as it climbs south to where it dead-ends at Big Springs Park. There is a large parking area surrounded by picnic tables and public restrooms.

THE ROUTE

At the southeast corner of the parking lot, locate the snow-covered Spring Hollow Road and begin climbing here. An adjacent trail that starts on the west side meanders through the forest. Both go to the same place, but the road is more direct. The road and trail intersect after only 0.3 mile. Skin up the road for 1.1 miles, where it forks at a trail sign at 6200 feet. Stay left and keep following the Big Springs Trail summer route deeper into the canyon.

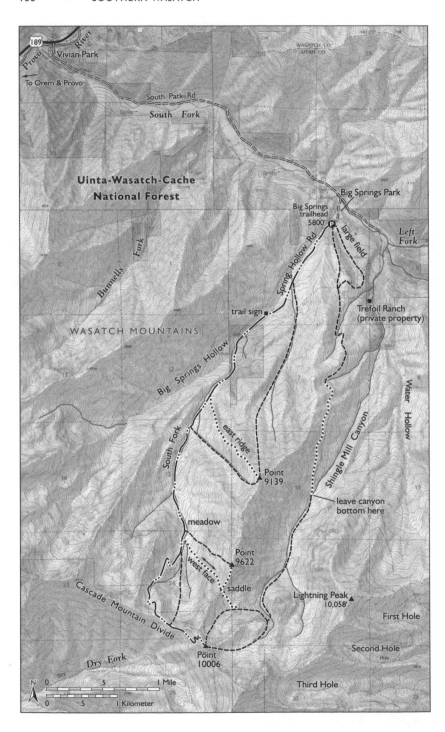

Just over a half mile later, the canyon splits where the trail descends to the creek. Stay left and enter the south fork. Skin alongside the creek, where in another 0.5 mile you'll come to the indistinct, tree-covered east ridge of Point 9139. There is good north- and northwest-facing skiing in evergreen forests and slide paths from this summit that makes for a shorter tour. To get there, leave the trail and climb up the east ridge for 1 mile and more than 2000 vertical feet to the top.

To descend, ski or snowboard down the northwest-facing gulch back to the trail, or descend via the north-facing avalanche paths that spit you out near Big Springs Park at 6100 feet. While these runs and the approach are good in deep snow, late-season skinning can be hampered by brush and bare spots on the ascent ridge.

To ski upper Big Springs Hollow, keep heading up canyon on the summer trail route. In 3.1 miles from the trailhead, the canyon splits again at 7700 feet at the toe of a large and obvious ridge. Once more, stay left and traverse above the narrow gully, which is a major terrain trap. In 0.5 mile, you'll come to a large meadow. To the east, there is a series of northwest-facing avalanche paths that fall from Point 9622. These are also good skiing options and can be reached by leaving the canyon bottom at 8300 feet and aiming for a saddle just south of the highest point. Check for avalanche stability before climbing up or skiing down.

From the saddle at 9300 feet, follow the ridge north for an additional 300 vertical feet to reach the top of Point 9622. Ski down the 1000-foot northwest face back to your ascent route for an easy diversion before trucking on deeper into the canyon.

Beyond the meadow at 8300 feet, you enter the most serious avalanche terrain of the tour. Unavoidable terrain traps, open faces, and cirques litter the upper canyon. If you have any doubts about snow stability, this is a good place to turn around. If you're confident, keep following the summer trail route as it stays west of the creek and switchbacks onto a sub-ridge at 8800 feet. Follow this ridge for 0.4 mile until it terminates at the bottom of a large cirque at 9200 feet. Cross this in a southeast direction one at a time around a small peak that's protected by cliffs on its north end. Enter a sparse pine forest on a low-angle ramp that leads right to the Cascade Mountain Divide.

Take in the spectacular view of Provo and Utah Lake far below to the west, the dramatic sawtooth ridges of Cascade Mountain and Mount Timpanogos to the north, Freedom and Provo peaks to the south, and the Uinta Mountains far in the east. To get to Point 10006, traverse southeast along the ridge for about a half mile. You may have to sidehill on the west face above the manmade terraces to avoid large cornices that often grow here. Along the way, ski descents that may be good fall off the north face of the ridge, but are short options for making turns. These runs also allow you to easily follow your ascent route back to the car.

From the summit of Point 10006 your choice of descents includes the northeast bowls of Shingle Mill Canyon that spill from either side of the summit. These wide faces are, of course, avalanche prone but are fun to ski in spring corn. At the bottom of the bowls at around 8900 feet, climb west for the saddle below Point 9622, where you can ski the west face back to the bottom of Big Springs Hollow and then follow your ascent route back to the trailhead.

This is the best way because I do not recommend skiing down Shingle Mill Canyon as an exit route. Trefoil Ranch Girl Scout Camp owns the canyon entrance and blocks all access to and from the mouth of the drainage. If you do choose this exit, leave the canyon bottom at 7600 feet and traverse on the west side, where the Shingle Mill summer trail heads up the mountainside. Follow this meandering trail north for 3.25 miles all the way back to Big Springs. If you miss the trail turnoff and get trapped at the property line, which is littered with NO TRESPASSING signs in lower Shingle Mill, prepare yourself for a serious bushwhack around the property. Stay on the west side of the canyon and head north along the mountain on the 6200-foot contour line. You'll eventually reach a large, flat field split by a well-traveled path that goes directly back to the parking lot at Big Springs Park.

44 Mount Nebo

Start Point : Mona Pole Road, 6000 to 7000 feet
High Point : Mount Nebo summit, 11,928 feet
Trail Distance : 8 miles (starting at 6000 feet)
Trail Time : 8 hours
Skill Level : Expert
Best Season : Spring
Map : USGS Mona

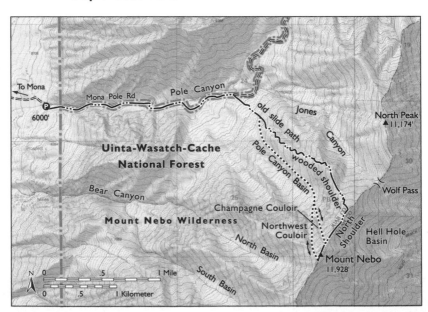

Mount Nebo's northwest couloir is long, steep, and a massively fun spring tour.

Mount Nebo is the highest peak in the Wasatch Range. It's also the southernmost point, so she sees much less traffic than her urban sisters up north in Salt Lake. Winter finds Nebo especially devoid of people as access is difficult and the approach is long. Mount Nebo is named after the biblical overlook in Jordan where Moses was granted a view of the promised land he would never enter. If you have the moxie to make the climb, you'll find a skier's promised land of challenging couloirs, forested gullies, and fantastic views from the highest perch on the Wasatch Front. But be prepared for a strenuous, all-day adventure on expert-only descents through steep couloirs.

GETTING THERE

From Provo, take I-15 south to Mona at exit 233. Go west for 1 mile on State Route 54 to the town center, then turn north on SR 91. In 2 miles, turn east on 1800 North (Canyon Lane). Continue for 1.5 miles as you drive under the interstate to where the main road ends at a gravel pit. From here, stay right (south) on a dirt road that loops around the gravel pit and curves east directly toward Pole Canyon. Park at the Mona Pole Road sign located at the canyon entrance. In spring, you can drive up the canyon on a rocky 4x4 track to the snow line, but it's not recommended unless you have a serious four-wheel-drive vehicle or ATV.

THE ROUTE

From wherever you left your vehicle, skin up Mona Pole Road as it climbs up the canyon. At about 7500 feet, you'll see a huge, open slide path on the right that comes all the way down to the road. Exit the road here and skin up the slide path. It is a steep and brushy ascent, as new growth is beginning to reclaim the avalanche destruction.

To avoid avalanche danger, the safest route is the nearest ridge. To climb it, switchback up the slide path to about 8600 feet, then hop right onto a wooded shoulder that parallels the avalanche path. Continue up the shoulder as it ascends to above tree line at around 10,500 feet. The ridge levels out here a bit and is a good place to scope out your descent options across Pole Canyon Basin, like the Champagne and Northwest couloirs. At 10,900 feet, the ridge becomes steep again for a 600-foot push to the North Shoulder above Wolf Pass. From here, traverse south on the narrow summit ridge as it undulates toward the obvious summit cone. You'll have to boot pack the final few hundred steep, vertical feet to the top. Crampons and an ice ax or Whippet may be useful.

During times of stable snowpack, when the famous Champagne and Northwest couloirs are your descent goals, it's best to climb directly up the snow chutes so you can check for snow stability along the way. To get there, leave Mona Pole Road at the slide path as described above, and climb to about 8300 feet. Leave the slide path here, and head in a southwest direction into the woods, where you'll find a gully. Climb up this drainage for 0.5 mile until it exits the trees at 9100 feet into Pole Canyon Basin—a huge cathedral of rock and snow below Nebo's gigantic northwest face.

Skin directly up the basin to the bottom of your couloir of choice. The Northwest Couloir is the widest and the first you'll come to. Put your skis or splitboard on your pack and boot directly up the snow chute. The upper parts of the couloirs become very steep, so you'll want to have ice-climbing tools in case you encounter hard snow.

The Champagne Couloir puts you just north of the true summit, while the Northwest Couloir spits you out to the south, where a short 300-foot hike on loose talus gets you to the top. Either option provides a thrilling ski or snowboard descent that totals almost 3000 vertical feet to the bottom of Pole Canyon Basin.

To return, descend the wooded gully below Pole Canyon Basin. You may encounter sections of thick brush in the lower section of the gully above the road. Once you bushwhack your way through, ski down the road back to your car.

Opposite: *Getting after it on one of Bountiful Peak's northeast chutes*

NORTHERN WASATCH

MOST BACKCOUNTRY SKI TERRAIN in the Northern Wasatch is lift served through ski resort boundary gates at Snowbasin Resort and Powder Mountain. While the lifts access world-class backcountry stuff, like the Banana Couloir at Snowbasin or Powder Country on the backside of Powder Mountain, those routes are not covered here as this book is focused on backcountry skiing that doesn't require a lift ticket or snowcat ride. Yet there are some tours in the Northern Wasatch that require the use of skins and touring bindings.

The most notable backcountry skiing area is above the town of Liberty in the North Fork Park area. Cutler Ridge to Ben Lomond Peak is a classic ascent with skiable lines from moderate, powder-filled tree shots to wide, avalanche-prone bowls. The extreme terrain between Ben Lomond and Willard Peak is especially heart pounding. Other human-powered tours include the North Ogden Divide and spring skiing around Skyline Drive above Farmington and Bountiful. While the latter, accessed by Farmington Canyon, is closed in the winter and requires a snowmobile to reach, it is an unsung favorite zone for skiing and splitboarding on perfect spring corn over open bowls. Frary Peak, the highest point on Antelope Island, is also included despite the rarity of skiable snow. But when the valleys receive a massive dump of powder, touring above the Great Salt Lake is an eerie, otherworldly experience that is not to be missed.

The Northern Wasatch is narrow, without the myriad side-canyons that are found in the Central Wasatch. But what is missing in skiable terrain and unfettered access, the north makes up for with a plethora of snowfall. Ben Lomond Peak is especially snowy—perhaps the snowiest peak in the Wasatch Range, with localized snowfall at 8000 feet that is equal to Alta. If a big storm pushes in on a southwest flow, head to Ben Lomond for an epic powder day.

NOTES

Land Management. Tours in the Northern Wasatch are located in Uinta-Wasatch-Cache National Forest. Contact the Ogden and Salt Lake ranger districts for more information. Frary Peak is within Antelope Island State Park and is highly restricted. The mountain is located within an animal sanctuary, so travel is strictly limited to the summer trail route. Web addresses and phone numbers are found in Resources.

Road Conditions and Fees. Antelope Island State Park requires an entrance fee. As of this writing, it costs $9 per car to drive across the causeway. See Resources for contact information. For tours in Farmington Canyon, the road is closed to vehicles from November 1 to sometime in April or May, depending on spring road conditions. Snowmobiles are the only way to get there in the winter. Check with Uinta-Wasatch-Cache National Forest to see if the canyon is open before heading up for spring tours.

Weather. The Northern Wasatch gets pounded with snow when storms approach on a southwest track. Ben Lomond gets especially hammered, but this also means avalanche danger is always a concern. Check the Utah Avalanche Center's Ogden advisory and the National Weather Service website for current conditions. See the Resources page for web addresses and phone numbers.

Leave the road at this sign on the first switchback for a shortcut to Gold Ridge.

45 Gold Ridge

Start Point : Junction of Skyline Drive and Francis Peak Road, 7250 feet
High Point : Point 8396 on Gold Ridge, 8396 feet
Trail Distance : 5 miles
Trail Time : 3 hours
Skill Level : Beginner/Intermediate
Best Season : Spring
Map : USGS Bountiful Peak

The shortest backcountry ski tours in Farmington Canyon are found on Gold Ridge. This 2-mile-long shoulder has several skiable lines on her northeast face, but you can also ascend and descend the moderately angled ridgeline for a scenic skin up and down. Even closer to the trailhead, there are short tree shots with practically no approach on Point 7668. If you're short on time, or just want to practice your skinning skills on Francis Peak Road, the Gold Ridge area is worth checking out as soon as Farmington Canyon opens for the summer, which happens sometime in April or May.

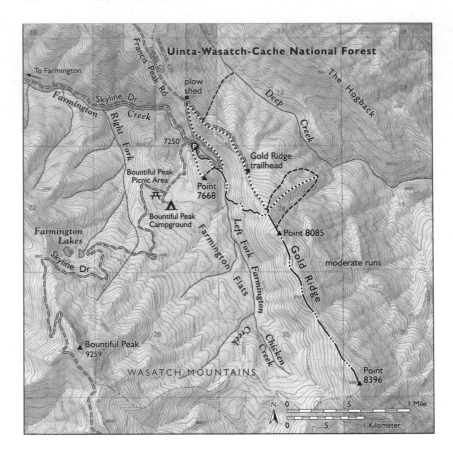

GETTING THERE

From Salt Lake City, drive north on I-15 for 15 miles to Farmington. Leave the interstate at exit 322, stay right, and continue north on 200 West. At State Street, turn right, drive east for three blocks, and curve left onto 100 East. Go north on 100 East for a mile to the mouth of Farmington Canyon. Stay right at a fork near Farmington Pond and continue up the canyon on Farmington Canyon Road, which becomes Skyline Drive, a narrow dirt road that switchbacks up into the mountains. Park at the junction of Skyline Drive and Francis Peak Road, 7.5 miles from the canyon bottom, where there is a locked gate.

THE ROUTE

Go around the gate and hike or skin up the road only 400 yards until it makes a sharp switchback to the northwest. Leave the road and continue up the canyon bottom, passing a sign that reads, "No Vehicles Permitted Beyond This Point." Follow the stream for 0.25 mile until you see an evergreen forest on the hillside to your left (southeast). Skin up this west-facing slope through the trees for around 700 vertical feet to the crest of

Gold Ridge. Head right up the ridge to the top of Point 8085. It's only a total of 1 mile from the car to this point. If the slope lacks snow, you can always follow Francis Peak Road to the official Gold Ridge trailhead for a longer alternate route.

A few good skiable runs go down the northeast side, where the best (and sometimes only) snow is found in the spring. To return, skin or boot pack up the run to the ridge crest and repeat.

If you're in the mood for a longer tour, you can continue following the ridge to Point 8396, the highest peak on Gold Ridge. Keep an eye out on your left for good ski runs as they appear along the way. You can also simply skin to the summit, then ski down the undulating shoulder for an easy return while enjoying the Northern Wasatch views.

Skiing and snowboarding with even less of an approach is found right off Francis Peak Road. From the car, follow the road for 0.8 mile as it switchbacks twice up the mountainside. When you reach a fork next to a plow shed, go right at yet another switchback and head southeast a few hundred yards on the ridge. Very moderate, low-angle tree runs on the northeast slope provide easy, short runs for around 500 vertical feet to Deep Creek. Skin back up the way you descended.

The shortest tour is on Point 7668, where skiable slopes begin practically from the car. Instead of skinning up the road, switchback west up onto a small ridge and follow it for 0.3 mile to the top. Ski or snowboard the northeast-facing tree run for a minuscule 350 vertical feet to the road's first switchback at the NO VEHICLES sign.

This whole area is a good spot to practice skinning and backcountry skills as the runs are short and it's easy to return to the car.

46 Bountiful Peak

Start Point	Junction of Skyline Drive and Francis Peak Road, 7250 feet
High Point	Bountiful Peak summit, 9259 feet
Trail Distance	5 miles
Trail Time	3 hours
Skill Level	Intermediate/Advanced
Best Season	Spring
Map	USGS Bountiful Peak

Bountiful Peak is a cool little gnar zone in Farmington Canyon that is unfortunately only accessible in the spring unless you own a snowmobile. It was possible to ski here in the winter when Skyline Drive was plowed year-round. A landslide in 2011 caused major damage to the road and closed it for years. Now that the road has been repaired, the city of Farmington has decided to cease winter maintenance, and the road is now closed from November 1 to sometime in April or May, depending on conditions. But as soon as the winter gate opens, Bountiful Peak becomes an accessible corn-skiing playground that's close to the city and sees little traffic. It is, however, a major snow-mobile area, so be prepared to share the mountain with two- and four-stroke engines.

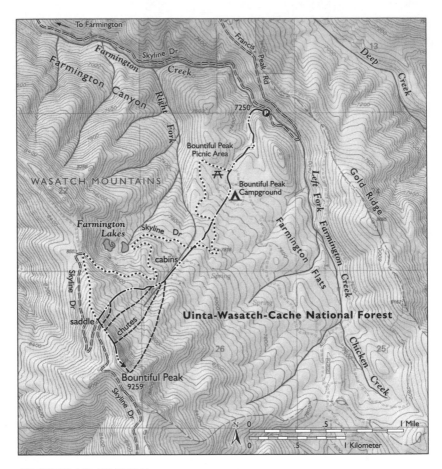

GETTING THERE

From Salt Lake City, drive north on I-15 for 15 miles to Farmington. Leave the interstate at exit 322, stay right, and continue north on 200 West. At State Street, turn right, drive east for three blocks, and curve left onto 100 East. Go north on 100 East for a mile to the mouth of Farmington Canyon. Stay right at a fork near Farmington Pond and continue up the canyon on Farmington Canyon Road, which becomes Skyline Drive, a narrow dirt road that switchbacks up into the mountains. Park at the junction of Skyline Drive and Francis Peak Road, 7.5 miles from the canyon bottom, where there is a locked gate.

THE ROUTE

Go west from the locked gate and skin up the snow-covered Skyline Drive, which will likely be packed down by snowmobile use. In 0.5 mile, you'll reach a fork at the Bountiful Creek Picnic Area. Right stays on Skyline Drive and left takes you to Bountiful Peak Campground. Both directions get you there, but when you're skinning, roads don't mean as much, so going left through the campground is more direct. Cross through the campground loop and aim southwest toward the obvious, broad peak ahead. This is Bountiful Peak.

After leaving the campground, continue skinning southwest. You'll cross Skyline Drive twice as you shortcut to the mountain. At 1.3 miles, you'll enter a neighborhood of cabins. Try to stay on the snowmobile tracks to avoid trespassing on private property.

Once beyond the cabins, jog slightly right (west) onto a small sub-ridge and a flat area. At 2 miles, you'll reach the bottom of Bountiful Peak's cliff-strewn northeast face at 8650 feet. This is a good place to scope out your lines of descent, as several chutes and slide paths drop from the peak. Head west and up an open bowl to a saddle on the summit ridge, then climb an additional 350 feet above the cliffs to the top.

You may also follow the snow-covered Skyline Drive for a more laid-back, meandering route via Farmington Lakes to the top of Bountiful Peak. Cars drive it during the summer months, so it's very low angle with a lot of switchbacks. It is 3 miles one-way to the summit ridge, where another 0.75-mile traverse puts you on the summit.

While there are no ski or snowboard options from the true summit because of cliff exposure, several lines can be found north along the ridge. These short, spicy chutes offer heart-pounding descents that can easily be lapped over and over. You can also make turns on the ascent bowl from the saddle, or find a more open, east-facing line just under the summit cliffs. An even more open area lies beneath a point south of the summit. This north-facing run has good corn in the spring for 200 feet of vertical down to the flat area below the summit cliffs, before it enters trees.

When you've had your fill, return to your vehicle by following the ascent route.

The northeast side of Bountiful Peak is a cool little gnar-zone of cliffs and chutes.

47 Mud and Rice Bowls

Start Point : Junction of Skyline Drive and Francis Peak Road, 7250 feet
High Point : Point 8735, 8735 feet
Trail Distance : 5 miles
Trail Time : 3 hours
Skill Level : Intermediate
Best Season : Spring
Map : USGS Bountiful Peak

Some of the best moderate spring skiing in Farmington Canyon can be found on Mud and Rice bowls. Each of these open faces have major corn potential and are located on the north side of Point 8735, a small high point just north of Bountiful Peak. If the late-season snowpack is deep enough, you can ski or snowboard all the way down the creek beds to Skyline Drive. Other lines like Hell Hole Creek and Miller Canyon can also be accessed from here but may hold less snow in the spring. Since Skyline Drive is now closed from November 1 until April or May, it's best to get here as soon as the road opens to make spring turns before the snow melts away.

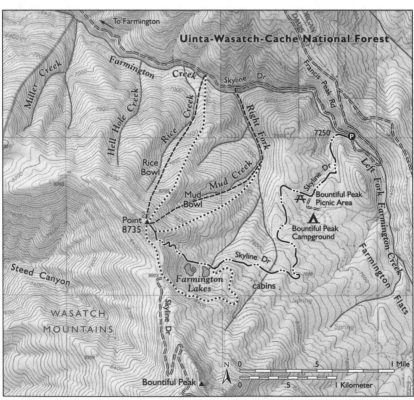

Intermediate corn skiing is what you'll find in Mud Bowl.

GETTING THERE

From Salt Lake City, drive north on I-15 for 15 miles to Farmington. Leave the interstate at exit 322, stay right, and continue north on 200 West. At State Street, turn right, drive east for three blocks, then curve left onto 100 East. Go north on 100 East for a mile to the mouth of Farmington Canyon. Stay right at a fork near Farmington Pond and continue up the canyon on Farmington Canyon Road, which becomes Skyline Drive, a narrow dirt road that switchbacks up into the mountains. Park at the junction of Skyline Drive and Francis Peak Road, 7.5 miles from the canyon bottom, where there is a locked gate.

THE ROUTE

Go west from the locked gate and skin up the snow-covered Skyline Drive. It will likely be packed down by snowmobile use. In 0.5 mile, you'll reach a fork. Go right to stay on Skyline Drive as it winds toward the Bountiful Peak ridge. At 2 miles, you'll reach Farmington Lakes, small, frozen ponds nestled beneath open bowls split by rock outcroppings. This is a good place to leave the road and shortcut toward Point 8735.

Cross or circumvent the lakes to the north side of them, and switchback up the short face for a half mile to gain the ridge. Make a careful assessment of avalanche stability before ascending this steep face. Once on the ridge, it's an easy and short traverse north to the top of Point 8735.

Alternatively, you can stay on Skyline Drive at the lakes for a longer 1-mile (but less steep) skin that ends at the same place on the ridge.

At the summit of Point 8735, as you face northeast, Mud Bowl is on the right, and Rice Bowl is on the left. Both are split by a ridge that terminates at the divide. A good option for a yo-yo tour is to make turns in Rice Bowl, skin up any of the adjoining ridges, and then enjoy Mud Bowl. For longer runs, both lines spill into creek bottoms that can be skied to Skyline Drive, but you'll need to hike more than a mile up the road to your car. Otherwise, regain the Bountiful Peak ridge and traverse south to your ascent route for a more direct descent to the trailhead.

48 Frary Peak

Start Point : Frary Peak winter trailhead, 4280 feet
High Point : Frary Peak, 6596 feet
Trail Distance : 7 miles
Trail Time : 6 hours
Skill Level : Intermediate
Best Season : Winter
Map : USGS Antelope Island

Antelope Island, a mountainous landmass in the middle of the Great Salt Lake, isn't a place one would think to go ski touring. Low elevation and a ban on off-trail travel deter many would-be skiers. But if lake-effect snow dumps powder in the valleys that measures in feet instead of inches, then it's a good opportunity to ski tour the island's highest mountain, Frary Peak. Antelope Island is a state park, and the peak is located on the protected animal-sanctuary side of the island, where encounters with bison and antelope are common. As a result, park rangers are very strict about how you

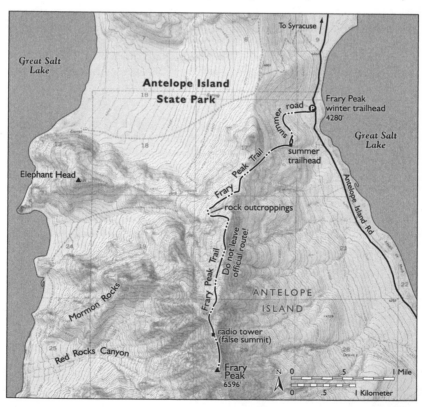

Skinning above the Great Salt Lake on Frary Peak

travel in the backcountry. You'll avoid a citation if you stay on the trail and do not ski off the marked path. And if you follow the rules, you'll be treated to an otherworldly tour high above the lake with 360-degree views that are uniquely Utah.

GETTING THERE

From Salt Lake City or Ogden, take I-15 to exit 332 (Antelope Drive) in Syracuse. Follow the Antelope Island signs and travel west on Antelope Drive to the Antelope Island State Park entrance gate. As of this writing, there is a fee of nine dollars per car to enter the park. From the gate, drive 6.5 miles across the causeway to the island. At a fork in the road, take the south (left) fork. In a half mile, take another left at another fork onto Antelope Island Road. Travel this road for 5.1 miles and turn west (right) on a paved road signed FRARY TRAILHEAD. This road is closed in winter, so park at the winter parking area on the right.

THE ROUTE

From the parking area, walk west up the closed summer road as it curves to the south. In 0.6 mile, the road ends at the official Frary Peak summer trailhead. Follow the marked trail route west as it meanders up into the foothills. Although the rules state you must stay on the trail, it can be hard to follow when it's covered in snow. Bring a trail map and try to follow the route as best you can. Intermittent carbon posts mark the route.

At 0.25 mile from the summer trailhead, you'll gain the ridge, where you are treated to sweeping views of the island and the Great Salt Lake all around you. Enjoy the scenery as the trail heads south toward Frary Peak. The official path soon curves west again and loops around rock outcroppings before going east back up onto the ridge. From here, simply follow the trail south along the ridge for 1.5 miles to a false summit

Taking a break on a rock outcropping below Frary Peak

marked by a radio tower. The true summit of Frary Peak is surrounded by cliffs and a knife-edge ridge. The route dips down onto the west face and traverses below the cliffs to a point where you can scramble to the top. While it's easy in summer, winter travel is dicey, so if you insist on bagging the peak, bring along some crampons and an ice ax.

To return, ski down the trail you came up, being careful not to deviate from the official path. Depending on snowpack, you may want to keep your climbing skins on as the rocks are very sharp on Antelope Island, and it costs far less to replace skins than skis or a splitboard.

Since Antelope Island is a state park, access and rules are ever changing. Before heading out, be sure to call the ranger station for the most up-to-date information. See Resources for contact details.

49 North Ogden Divide to Chilly Peak

Start Point : North Ogden Divide trailhead, 6200 feet
High Point : Chilly Peak summit, 9620 feet
Trail Distance : 8 miles
Trail Time : 6 hours
Skill Level : Intermediate/Advanced
Best Season : Winter
Map : USGS North Ogden

One of the most accessible backcountry touring areas in the Northern Wasatch is the North Ogden Divide. This trailhead is the start of several possible tours, the most common of which is Chilly Peak, a diminutive summit that cowers in the ever-present shadow of the much larger Ben Lomond Peak to the north. But what Chilly Peak lacks in size and fame, it makes up for with a relatively straightforward approach and tons of ski lines around her summit cone, including the challenging and spooky Rock Slab Couloirs. Other ski and snowboard descents south of the peak end at North Ogden Canyon Road above the town of Liberty, making for quick shuttle tours.

GETTING THERE
From Ogden, drive north on I-15 for 6.5 miles and get off at exit 349. Head east on State Route 134 (2700 North) for 4 miles to 1050 East. Turn left (north) and drive 0.5 mile to 3100 North. Go right (east) where the road becomes North Ogden Canyon Road. Drive into North Ogden Canyon as it winds up to the North Ogden Divide. In 3 miles, you'll see the trailhead parking lot on your right.

THE ROUTE
From the parking lot, walk north across the road to the north trailhead, located in a thick grove of scrub oak. Follow the Great Western Trail route as it switchbacks up the mountainside. The trail is usually snow covered, but the south-facing aspect and low elevation may mean you'll have to walk this first section.

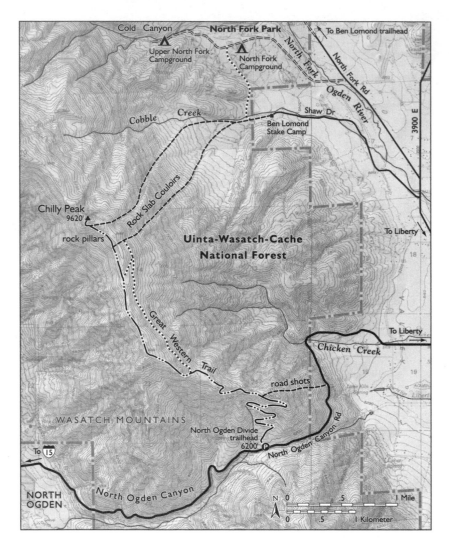

From the road, it's about 2 miles to the top of the ridge, with a few overlooks along the way that you'll want to take the time to check out to enjoy the view. Once you gain the ridge at about 7000 feet, you have the option to ski or snowboard the "road shots"—steep, 1300-foot runs that end at North Ogden Canyon Road. There needs to be a good snowpack at this lower elevation for the road shots to be feasible, and you'll either need to stash a car at the bottom to shuttle with, or hitchhike back up to the North Ogden Divide. While it's possible to skin back up the road shots, the prospect of then having to ski back down the narrow, south-facing switchbacks to the trailhead is a deterrent.

To summit Chilly Peak, keep following the Great Western Trail route for 0.5 mile as it meanders on the ridgetop. The trail soon leaves the ridge and dips down to traverse on the east face overlooking the town of Liberty far below. You can continue on this route for the next 2.2 miles to Chilly Peak. But for winter tours, the ridge is a good option, especially when there is little wind and you want to enjoy the view all along the way.

If you choose the ridge route, you'll need to leave the ridge right before Chilly Peak because of large rock pillars that stand in the way. From here, rejoin the summer trail route as it traverses the west slope, then switchback around the pillars for 200 vertical feet to the top.

There isn't much good skiing or snowboarding right from the summit, but just 200 vertical feet south of the top is the starting zone for the Rock Slab Couloirs, massive, long, narrow chutes that spill northeast through slab cliffs all the way down to Cobble Creek. It's a stout descent through extreme avalanche terrain, so only attempt this descent during times of very low avalanche danger.

Once you reach Cobble Creek, you can ski 0.5 mile to Shaw Drive near the private Ben Lomond Stake Camp, or you can put the skins back on and traverse about a mile north to the Nordic trails at North Fork Park, which is an excellent place to leave your shuttle vehicle.

Moderate, open skiing can be found all along the ridge to Chilly Peak from the North Ogden Divide.

50 Ben Lomond Peak and Cutler Ridge

Start Point : Ben Lomond trailhead at Camp Utaba, 5600 feet
High Point : Ben Lomond Peak summit, 9712 feet
Trail Distance : 9 miles
Trail Time : 7 hours
Skill Level : Intermediate/Advanced
Best Season : Winter
Maps : USGS Mantua, North Ogden

If you want to bag a winter summit in the Northern Wasatch, then Ben Lomond Peak is the one to climb. While it's not the highest summit around, it is the most prominent and therefore the bigger destination. This obelisk-shaped mountain lords over the city of Ogden, but the small town of Liberty on the peak's east side is the place where backcountry skiers begin a tour via a 3000-foot, avalanche-safe ramp called Cutler Ridge. Tons of quality untracked ski terrain can be had from this long shoulder that rises from the valley floor all the way to the Wasatch Divide, so it's among the most popular touring spots for Ogden-area locals. The ridge also provides central access for tours around Cutler Canyon and Willard Peak, where long fall lines in amazing high-alpine terrain equal unparalleled skiing and snowboarding. But avalanche danger can be notoriously high anywhere but atop Cutler, so touring on the ridge's low-angle slopes is best when the avy report is in the red.

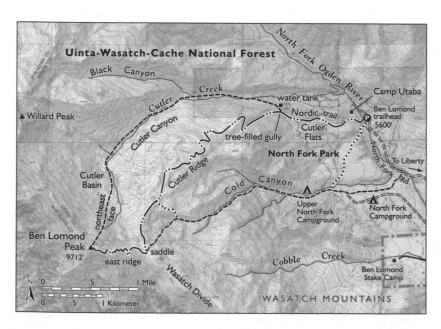

Skinning toward Ben Lomond Peak's summit cone

GETTING THERE

From Ogden, take 12th Street South (State Route 39) east to Ogden Canyon. Drive
up the canyon and turn left onto SR 158, crossing the dam at Pineview Reservoir.
Continue 4.3 miles to a four-way stop, and then go left on SR 162 toward Liberty. In
3 miles, you'll come to a three-way stop at a park. Go left on 4100 North, and take
the first right at 3300 East. In 1.5 miles, bear left at a fork onto North Fork Road, and
drive 2.8 miles to the entrance of Camp Utaba. There is a parking area on the west
side of the road.

THE ROUTE

From the parking area, walk a few steps south to the trailhead marked by a metal gate
and sign. Skin down the hill, and then head up the low-grade, groomed Nordic trails
of Cutler Flats, keeping an eye out for moose that hang out in the trees. In 1 mile,
go west into a tree-filled gully just before a water tank on the right. A skin track will
likely already be in place. The trail stays in this foliage-choked drainage for about a
half mile before climbing to the crest of Cutler Ridge.

    Routefinding is easy from here as you simply follow the wide ridgetop for 2 miles
to the bottom of Ben Lomond's northeast face. You'll be treated to wicked-awesome

views of Cutler Basin and Willard Peak to the north and the Eden Valley spreading out in all directions far below. Near the top of the ridge, contour left (south) to gain the Wasatch Divide at a saddle around 8800 feet. To summit the peak, head west on the east ridge of Ben Lomond. These upper slopes are often wind scoured or loaded, so use caution.

To descend Ben Lomond, ski down the way you ascended on the east ridge, or get gnarly on the massive northeast side where gullies split the main face that spills all the way down to the bottom of Cutler Basin. This is a big line and can only be skied safely when the snowpack is very stable. Return to your car by following Cutler Canyon back to Cutler Flats and the trailhead.

If you ski down the east ridge to 8800 feet, you can return by riding the low-angle slopes atop Cutler Ridge, or enjoy long, vertical lines of powder in the pine trees east of Cutler Ridge. After making turns for around 1000 vertical feet, climb northwest up a low-angle slope back to the top of Cutler Ridge, and proceed back down to the trailhead. You can also keep skiing into the narrow bottom of Cold Canyon, which dumps you out at the North Fork Campground. From there, skin north back to Camp Utaba, or walk the 0.85 mile up North Fork Road to the car.

Opposite: *Fast, wide, sweeping turns are possible in Deseret Peak's North Twin Couloirs.*

WEST DESERT MOUNTAINS

THE OQUIRRH MOUNTAINS, the range that creates the western border of the Salt Lake Valley and northern Utah County, is the primary region for backcountry skiing in Utah's West Desert. The Oquirrhs have vast touring potential along their 30-mile-long stretch, but unfortunately, most of it is totally locked up in private property and is terra incognita for any sort of recreational access. Mining is the law of the land. However, the southern part of the range around Ophir Canyon is one of the few exceptions. This area is ringed with 10,000-foot skiable peaks like Bald Mountain, Lowe Peak, Lewiston Peak, and the highest summit in the range, Flat Top Mountain, which tops out at 10,620 feet. Yet even these routes are surrounded by private property, so traveling with an awareness of where you are and respecting property rights by not trespassing is paramount to keeping trailheads open for future use. Also, you'll need a high-clearance 4x4 vehicle for the rocky, often snow-covered dirt roads.

The Stansbury Mountains are the other skiable range in the West Desert, though winter access is extremely limited due to road closure (or lack of any roads for that matter!). Deseret Peak, the tallest mountain in the range, is the main event. Late spring or early summer is the best season for a summit attempt, after South Willow Road opens in late May, or you and your party can strap skis to backpacks and ride bikes up the closed road to the trailhead at the Loop Campground. Deseret's North Twin Couloirs are a notch that any hard-core Salt Lake–area skier should have on their helmet.

Solitude is the main draw in the West Desert. Despite its proximity to millions of people living along the Wasatch Front, the Oquirrhs and Stansburys remain practically untouched by ski and snowboard tracks. In all the days I've spent skiing the West Desert, I've only ever seen one other touring party while skinning up Lowe Peak on a beautiful spring day. Otherwise, I've had the mountains all to myself. There is no competition for fresh tracks here!

NOTES

Land Management. Tours in the West Desert are located on a mixture of BLM and private land. Generally speaking, most of the private property is at or near the trailheads, such as with routes in upper Ophir Canyon. Serviceberry Canyon is mostly all private, but currently hikers and backcountry skiers are allowed through an access gate. Do your research and talk to landowners. Develop relationships. Leave no trace, respect the land, and help keep the backcountry open.

The Stansbury Mountains are located in the Uinta-Wasatch-Cache National Forest. Deseret Peak, however, is within the Deseret Peak Wilderness. If you're winter camping, you must camp at least 200 feet from streams and lakes. Contact the Salt Lake Ranger District for more information. Web addresses and phone numbers are found in Resources.

Road Conditions. South Willow Road is closed from November to May. In early spring, the road opens to Boy Scout Campground. From there, you can ride a bike beyond the closure gate. In winter, snowmobiles are allowed up to Loop Campground.

Ophir Canyon in the Oquirrh Mountains is open year-round, but the road is unplowed beyond the town of Ophir. Drive a high-clearance 4x4 vehicle, and start your tour where the snow becomes too deep for tires.

Weather. The West Desert Mountains get less snow than the Cottonwood Canyons of the Wasatch, though a lack of weather stations above 8000 feet means there really isn't much data. Anecdotally, wind is a big factor in the upper slopes and can have a detrimental effect on the snowpack. Also, the Utah Avalanche Center does not issue a forecast for this area. Check the Salt Lake advisory to get a ballpark idea of avalanche danger, but make your own assessment by digging pits and performing snow stability tests before skiing in avalanche terrain. The National Weather Service has current conditions. See Resources for web addresses and phone numbers.

51 Deseret Peak

Start Point : Mill Fork trailhead, 7418 feet
High Point : Deseret Peak summit, 11,031 feet
Trail Distance : 6–13 miles
Trail Time : 8–12 hours
Skill Level : Advanced
Best Season : Spring
Maps : USGS Deseret Peak West, Deseret Peak East; Alpentech
: Stansbury Touring

The Stansbury Mountains in Utah's West Desert may seem an unlikely place to go skiing and snowboarding, but classic ski and mountaineering routes exist on Deseret Peak, the highest point in the range. Three chutes, including the North Twin Couloirs and the East Couloir, allow 1300 feet of fun skiing between summit cliffs on snow that lasts well into summer. Access can be difficult as the road in South Willow Canyon closes in the winter, requiring snowmobiles or a 13-mile round-trip skin. Most parties wait for the road to open halfway to Boy Scout Campground, where bikes can be used to dispatch road miles, or for the full road opening to the Loop Campground, usually around Memorial Day weekend.

GETTING THERE

From Salt Lake City, drive west on I-80 for 23 miles to Lake Point, and leave the interstate at exit 99. Head southwest on State Route 36 toward Stansbury Park. In 3.5 miles, go right (west) on SR 138 and drive 10 miles to Grantsville. Continue through town to West Street (400 West) and turn left. Drive south as the street becomes Mormon Trail Road, following the signs to Deseret Peak Wilderness. About 4 miles from town, go right on South Willow Road and head up the canyon. In winter, the road is closed 3 miles up, just beyond some homes at the national forest boundary. If the road is open, either continue up the dirt road to the second gate at Boy Scout

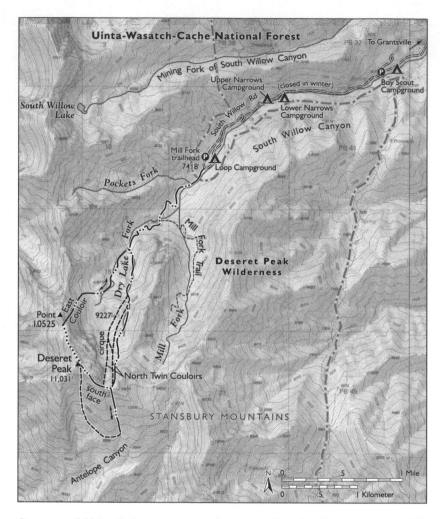

Campground (5.2 miles) or, in summer, drive to road's end at Loop Campground (7 miles) and park at the Mill Fork trailhead.

THE ROUTE

Locate the signed trail by a Forest Service outhouse, and follow it southwest into the Deseret Peak Wilderness. After hiking 0.7 mile, cross a creek at 7900 feet and reach the intersection of Mill Fork Trail and Dry Lake Fork. Mill Fork Trail goes left and is the standard summer route to the top of Deseret Peak. For a winter ascent, go right and follow the creek up into Dry Lake Fork.

Stay on the left side of the creek as you ascend (hopefully) on snow as the canyon rises steeply toward the colored cliffs of Deseret Peak. About 1 mile after leaving the trail, the terrain will flatten as it enters the Deseret Peak Cirque at 9400 feet. From

The North Twin Couloirs are must-do lines on Deseret Peak.

here, the East and North Twin couloirs are easily seen on either side of the summit cliffs. Continue up the canyon through narrow gullies and along small ridges until you're directly under the North Twin Couloirs, both gorgeous and aesthetic lines between walls of quartzite.

The easternmost Twin is generally the easiest to ascend as it's wider and not as steep as her sister to the west. Skin up the snowfield and enter the chute until it becomes too steep, then transition to boot packing. Crampons and an ice ax or Whippet may be needed, especially in the spring when morning refreezes leave ice. The couloir is 1300 feet long and can be hazardous from avalanche activity and falling rocks, so it's best to wear a helmet. At the top of the couloirs, step onto the mild south face and climb the summit ridge for 0.4 mile to the top of Deseret Peak.

There are many skiing and snowboarding options here. To ski the East Couloir, continue traversing north from the summit along the ridge for 0.4 mile to the entrance of the chute, located between the Deseret Peak summit and Point 10525. Make tight turns down the tube to your skin track in Dry Lake Fork. This couloir is also a possible boot packing ascent route, though snow doesn't stick around as long here as it does in the North Twins.

From the summit, moderate skiing and snowboarding exists on the south face, where you can lap good corn snow before ticking off the couloirs. From either the top of Deseret Peak or the North Twin Couloir entrance, make turns down the wide bowls for about 1000 vertical feet into upper Antelope Canyon (or until the snow runs out), and then skin back up to the summit ridge for your return run.

Of course the créme de la créme is a descent down the North Twin Couloirs. Carve turns from the summit partway down the south face, then either traverse or skin back up to the ridge above the couloirs' entrance. Pick your poison and ski down the gut of these fantastic hallways. When you're finished and if it's a warm spring day, be sure to sunbathe from a safe spot and watch afternoon avalanches careen down the summit cliffs.

To return, retrace your ascent route down Dry Lake Fork back to the Mill Fork Trail to the Loop Campground.

52 Flat Top Mountain

Start Point : Pole Canyon trailhead, 6600 feet
High Points : Flat Top Mountain summit, 10,620 feet;
: Lewiston Peak summit, 10,411 feet
Trail Distance : 8 miles
Trail Time : 7 hours
Skill Level : Advanced
Best Season : Spring
Map : USGS Mercur

Flat Top Mountain is the highest peak in the Oquirrh Range, and it's also one of the hardest to get to. One thing that makes this mountain special for skiers and

Staring down the south bowls on Flat Top Mountain

climbers alike is that Flat Top is one of fifty-seven mountains in the continental United States that has 5000 feet of prominence. But this overland and vertical effort is worth breaking a sweat (and possibly a vehicle axle) for, because the spectacular south face that curtains down from the summit into Pole Canyon harbors some of the most life-affirming spring corn snow you can imagine, on runs that are both long and wide. Again, the effort to get there is great, as a long and rugged 4x4 road and miles of skinning into Pole Canyon are required to pull off the adventure.

GETTING THERE

From I-15 and Main Street in Lehi, drive west through town on Main Street. At the west edge of downtown, go straight through the roundabout and continue west on State Route 73 for 14 miles to the small town of Cedar Fort. Turn right off the high-way onto Center Street and drive three blocks to 100 West. Go south four blocks to the edge of town where the road becomes dirt and turns sharply east. Instead, keep going straight on the rugged 4x4 jeep road that winds into the cedar forest. This rocky double track curves west and up into Pole Canyon. You will absolutely need a high-clearance vehicle here. A few side roads split off, but they eventually go to the same place up canyon. When in doubt, stay on the road most traveled. At around 3.5 miles on the jeep road, you'll reach a locked metal gate. Park at a pullout here.

THE ROUTE

Walk around the side of the gate and follow the road as it angles farther into Pole Canyon. In midwinter or deep snow years, you might be able to skin from here, but prepare to walk if you're gunning for spring corn.

In 1.5 miles you'll come to a split in the road. Stay right on the main road as it crosses the deep, dry creek bed where the climb becomes steeper (going left leads to private property). Almost immediately after crossing the dry creek, another road comes in on the right. Avoid this as it also heads to a private cabin. Stay on the main track another 0.25 mile until the road makes a sharp left and goes west and down into a meadow at the foot of a small ridge at 7700 feet.

At this point, you have two choices to get to the summit of Flat Top. In the winter, when the possibility of unstable snow is a concern, go around to the west side of the ridge until the road ends at a large aspen grove marred by decades of bark carvings. A huge erosion gully is found to the west. Stay on the east side of the gully and skin to the top of the ridge where it connects to a small flat at the base of Lewiston Peak's and Flat Top Mountain's huge east and south faces. You are in the middle of a major avalanche zone here at the toe of a southeast-facing sub-ridge that climbs almost to the top of Flat Top.

Ascend this sub-ridge through more aspen trees until you get above tree line at 9500 feet. From here, the ridge becomes much more obvious as it goes up and connects with the summit ridge 1000 feet above. This is a good ascent route as it minimizes your exposure to avalanche terrain. Near the top, the ridge becomes less prominent as it's gobbled up by the surrounding snow bowls. Proceed with caution as this is your most avalanche-prone spot.

Once you gain the summit ridge, it's a short 250-yard walk northeast to the 10,620-foot Flat Top. The summit has a communications tower and a mailbox that houses the summit register.

A more direct way to Flat Top from the meadow at 7700 feet is to skirt east around the sub-ridge. Skin up through an aspen grove for 0.5 mile. There is another deep erosion gully here. Stay on the west side of it. At 8300 feet, there is a crossing to the other side of the gully. Take this and head east up the side of another aspen-covered sub-ridge. Continue skinning up through the aspens for another 0.5 mile until you get above tree line. Along the way, you'll encounter yet another gully, though this one is much smaller and is easy to cross when needed.

Above the trees, you're directly under the massive south face. There is another ridge to the summit on the left, but in the spring when the snowpack is locked in from a good melt-freeze cycle, I like to go directly up the face. Switchback up for a little over a half mile to the summit ridge, and then follow it southwest a few hundred yards to the top.

After all that effort comes the reward—skiing the south- and southeast-facing bowls. At 35 degrees, these giant, wide snowfields are the perfect pitch to make huge

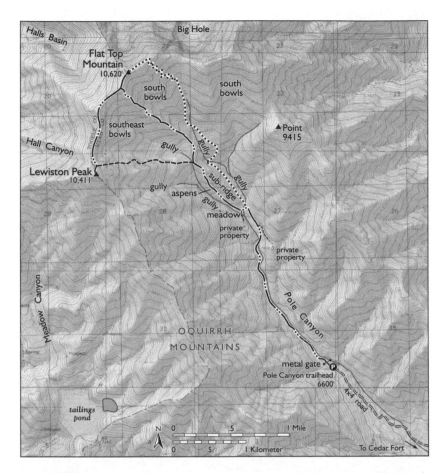

turns at high speeds. For spring corn skiing, there's nothing like it as the fall line sends you down almost 2000 vertical feet. It's like a choose-your-own-adventure book as you can ski pretty much any bowl between Lewiston Peak, Flat Top, and Point 9415.

Even more excellent skiing is found on Lewiston Peak. Although you can climb to Lewiston's summit from the bottom of Pole Canyon, the ascent is very steep and avalanche prone near the top. Instead, I prefer to link it with a tour of Flat Top for an epic day. From Flat Top, follow the undulating summit ridge south for 1 mile to Lewiston's crown. Steep, east-facing runs spill down from here. The aspect and evergreens protect the snow, so it's a good spot if you're looking for powder turns. When possible, stay skier's right to avoid small cliff bands and gullies that become serious terrain traps.

To return, follow your ascent route back down Pole Canyon to your car. Be mindful of the many erosion gullies as you finish your run off Flat Top and Lewiston. They are very deep and can cut you off, forcing you off route until you find a reasonable crossing. Be careful not to wander into private property along the way.

53 Lewiston Peak

Start Point : South Fork Ophir Canyon trailhead, 6700 feet
High Points : Lewiston Peak summit, 10,411; Flat Top Mountain summit,
: 10,620 feet
Trail Distance : 7 miles to Lewiston Peak; 9 miles to Flat Top from Ophir
: Canyon Road
Trail Time : 7–8 hours
Skill Level : Advanced
Best Season : Spring
Map : USGS Lowe Peak, Mercur

The South Fork of Ophir Canyon is a popular spot for ATV and 4x4 enthusiasts, as it is part of the Lion Hill Loop. But in the winter and early spring, the canyon is effectively shut off to wheeled vehicles and becomes a remote place for backcountry ski touring. Two main summits can be achieved from here: Lewiston Peak and the largest mountain in the Oquirrh range, Flat Top. In my opinion, this route is best used when attempting to ski or snowboard Lewiston, while Pole Canyon is a more direct option for Flat Top (Tour 52). But if you're looking to make a two-summit tour out of your day, then the South Fork of Ophir Canyon is a good option. While Lewiston can be skied all winter, spring is best as driving access becomes easier beyond the unplowed road outside the town of Ophir, especially if conditions (or your vehicle) allow you to drive all the way to the intersection with Halls Basin.

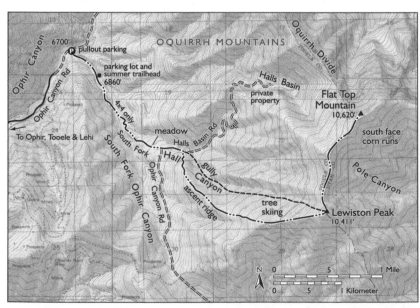

Skinning up lower Lewiston Peak from Hall Canyon

GETTING THERE

From the town of Tooele, drive south on State Route 36 for 11 miles until it intersects with SR 73. Go left (southeast), and in 4.6 miles turn left on Ophir Canyon Road. In about 3 miles, you'll reach the tiny community of Ophir, a sleepy former mining town. The road becomes dirt and is unplowed at the end of town, but if road conditions allow, drive another 0.5 mile to South Fork Ophir Canyon Road on the right. In winter, you'll need to park here and skin 0.5 mile to the trailhead.

In the spring, you can turn right here and drive 0.4 mile to the official trailhead and parking lot, where there is a wooden kiosk and map display. If you have a high-clearance 4x4 vehicle, you might be able to keep driving the remaining mile to the Halls Basin intersection. The road beyond the trailhead is narrow, rutted, extremely rocky, and treacherous if there is snow or mud.

THE ROUTE

If snow forces you to park along Ophir Canyon Road, skin southeast into South Fork Ophir Canyon by following the summer road route. In 0.4 mile, you'll come to the large summer trailhead parking lot. Continue up the road as it narrows and climbs steeply for another mile to a large meadow at 7500 feet. Here, the road splits. The right fork continues south, and the left fork heads east into Halls Basin. A sign here states that access ends in 1.6 miles because it's private property beyond that.

The meadow is at the toe of a large ridge that provides direct access to Lewiston Peak. To climb it, take the left fork for about a quarter mile, and then head up into the trees and brush on your right to gain the ridge. Follow this broad shoulder for almost 2 miles and nearly 3000 vertical feet to the summit. Along the way you'll skin through steep aspen groves, skirt rock outcroppings, traverse across open meadows, and finally switchback up through the evergreens to the undulating summit ridge to the 10,411-foot top.

For a shorter tour, descend back to the car by skiing or snowboarding down the northwest-facing evergreen forest that falls into Hall Canyon. The run starts out as fun tree skiing that holds good, protected snow, but it soon constricts into a massive and deep gully. The gully is navigable in places, but you'll have to make your way around giant logjams and fallen trees. To avoid this, it's best to stay in the evergreens south of the gully for as long as possible. Either way, you'll come to an aspen grove that leads back to the intersection of Halls Basin Road and South Fork Ophir Canyon Road.

For a longer tour, you can summit Flat Top Mountain from Lewiston. Simply traverse the ridgeline north as it first descends to a small saddle and then gradually climbs for exactly 1 mile to Flat Top's wide summit. You'll know you're there based on the communications tower and large mailbox that holds a summit register.

From here, the best skiing in the spring is down the immense south-facing bowls, which are a classic corn run. However, I prefer to ski here only if I parked in Pole Canyon (Tour 52), otherwise you'll have a long skin back up and over to Lewiston to return to your vehicle in Ophir Canyon. The west face is a long, tempting run, but it goes into private property, so don't do it. The safest bet is to instead ski down the ascent ridge back to the saddle below Lewiston, and then ski the wooded, west-facing run into Hall Canyon.

54 Serviceberry Canyon

Start Point	Serviceberry Canyon trailhead, 6800 feet
High Point	Bald Mountain East summit, 10,006 feet
Trail Distance	6 miles
Trail Time	4 hours
Skill Level	Intermediate/Advanced
Best Season	Winter
Maps	USGS Lowe Peak, Stockton

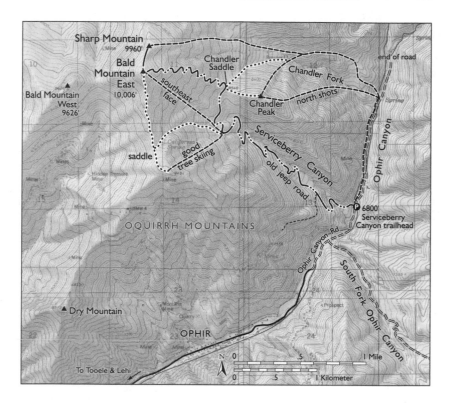

Serviceberry Canyon is a one-two punch of wide-open bowls and cold, north-facing evergreen tree runs with an uppercut of easy access thrown in. In fact, Bald Mountain East and her twin peak, Sharp Mountain, are the quickest summits to access in the southern Oquirrhs and are therefore the best to ski during the short, dark days of winter. A low-angle 4x4 road gets you to the goods easily, but you can also find steep ridges to climb if you're hankering for more adventure.

GETTING THERE

From the town of Tooele, drive south on State Route 36 for 11 miles until it intersects with SR 73. Go left (southeast), and in 4.6 miles turn left on Ophir Canyon Road. In about 3 miles, you'll reach the tiny community of Ophir, a sleepy former mining town. The road is unplowed at the end of town, but if the snow is shallow, you can usually drive to the mouth of Serviceberry Canyon at an obvious parking area by an old, abandoned tractor.

THE ROUTE

Enter Serviceberry Canyon through the green gate with a posted NO MOTORIZED VEHI-CLES sign. Much of the area is private property, so stay on the switchbacking jeep road as you skin up. In 0.5 mile, you'll reach another road that goes to the south. Avoid

View of Bald Mountain East from the south saddle in Serviceberry Canyon

this road and keep going up the canyon. The route soon enters spruce and fir territory, and the switchbacks become more common. It is possible to shortcut between some of the curves at the canyon bottom to save mileage.

At around 8050 feet the view opens up and Bald Mountain is revealed in all her snowy glory. At mile 2, the road heads north to Chandler Saddle. This is Grand Central Station for your touring destination. You have the option here to head east up the ridge to the top of Chandler Peak (8776 feet), where quality, north-facing shots into Chandler Fork will take you back down to Ophir Canyon Road, or you can skin back up to the saddle to continue touring in Serviceberry Canyon.

For the prize tour, skip the shots into Chandler Fork and instead summit Bald Mountain East, a twin peak just south of Sharp Mountain. From the Chandler Saddle, climb the east ridge to the top and descend the impressive southeast face for 1500 feet to the canyon bottom. You can also summit from a saddle to the southwest of Chandler Saddle, which is easier but adds mileage. From Bald Mountain East, you can traverse the summit ridge north to Sharp Mountain, where an east-facing run takes you into Chandler Fork. Return via the Chandler Saddle.

From the saddle south of Bald Mountain, very good tree skiing on northeast-facing slopes is a safe bet for soft, protected snow for about 800 vertical feet. But prepare to bushwhack at the bottom as the terrain narrows into gullies that lead back to the jeep road you skinned up.

55 Picnic Canyon

Start Point : Ophir Canyon trailhead, 7100 feet
High Point : Point 9925, 9925 feet
Trail Distance : 6 miles
Trail Time : 5 hours
Skill Level : Intermediate
Best Season : Winter
Map : USGS Lowe Peak

Powder-filled mountainsides, tree skiing, tremendous views, and relatively easy access—Picnic Canyon has everything you could want in a backcountry tour. Plus, there's a sweet public cabin below the best ski terrain where you can have lunch, escape nasty weather, or even stay the night. The prize line is a 1200-foot northwest face called Cabin Run, where you'll want to farm powder all day. As is always the case with the Oquirrh Mountains, private property is everywhere, so obey all NO TRESPASSING signs.

GETTING THERE

From the town of Tooele, drive south on State Route 36 for 11 miles until it intersects with SR 73. Go left (southeast), and in 4.6 miles turn left on Ophir Canyon Road. In about 3 miles, you'll reach the tiny community of Ophir, a sleepy former mining town. The road becomes dirt and is unplowed at the end of town, but if the snow is

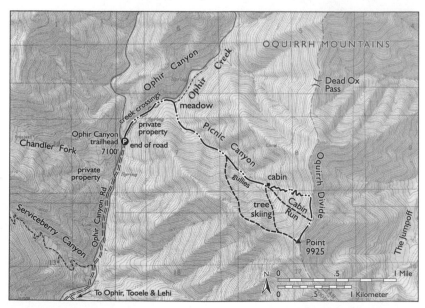

Getting to Picnic Canyon requires several crossings of Ophir Creek.

shallow, drive the remaining 1.5 miles to road's end, where you can park at a small turnaround. Otherwise, go as far as the snow level allows, and walk the remaining distance to the trailhead.

THE ROUTE

At the end of Ophir Canyon Road, find the trailhead by immediately crossing the creek. The start is marked by a NO MOTORIZED VEHICLES sign. At this point, the trail crosses through private property, so stay on the designated trail. Begin by hiking with your skis strapped to your pack because you'll maddeningly cross the creek several times as the trail meanders up Ophir Canyon. Even in winter, the creek can be exposed in places because of a warm spring up canyon. After about a half mile, you'll come to the intersection with Picnic Canyon on the southeast side of Ophir Canyon. This junction at 7400 feet is unmarked, but you'll know you're there when you enter a large meadow. There is also a plaque commemorating a horseback rider named Ronald Johnson.

Go right and start skinning southeast up the bottom of Picnic Canyon while finding the easiest way through scrub brush and aspen forests. About 1 mile up canyon at 8200 feet, the terrain narrows into three V-shaped gullies. Go up the leftmost gully for 0.25 mile and 400 vertical feet until you can find a way out on the right into old-growth aspen forest. Within the trees is a historic log cabin that is open to the public; it's a great place to eat lunch or even stay the night.

Behind the cabin, the landscape steepens up to the Oquirrh Divide and Point 9925. The open, northwest-facing Cabin Run goes from the divide all the way to the cabin. To ski or snowboard it, skin up through the trees north of the run. The trees provide a modicum of protection from avalanches and are a safer option than switchbacking straight up the face.

After about 1000 feet of climbing, you'll reach the divide, where an easy traverse south along the ridge puts you above Cabin Run. The highest place at the head of the canyon is Point 9925, just south of Cabin Run above north-facing trees. From this high point, you can access Picnic Canyon's south ridge. Ski or snowboard down the ridge, and choose one of many excellent tree shots back down to the bottom of Picnic Canyon.

To return, follow your ascent route down to get back to Ophir Canyon and the trailhead.

56 Lowe Peak

Start Point	Ophir Canyon trailhead, 7100 feet
High Points	Rocky Peak summit, 10,273; Lowe Peak summit, 10,589 feet
Trail Distance	6–9 miles
Trail Time	5–7 hours
Skill Level	Advanced
Best Season	Spring
Map	USGS Lowe Peak

A corn-skiing mecca. That is what Lowe Peak and neighboring Rocky Peak become when spring hits the Oquirrh Mountains and warm, sunny days are followed by below-freezing nights. When that consistent corn cycle engages, grab your skis or splitboard and head to Ophir Canyon, pronto! A hike-in-your-ski-boots approach over dozens of creek crossings keeps things interesting, but the trouble is worth it as both mountains sport massive southeast-, south-, and southwest-facing headwalls and bowls that catch the morning sun, which softens the snow into al dente corn so you can carve crescent curves for thousands of vertical feet. If conditions are prime, you can easily link both peaks together for an epic late-season day. As is always the case with touring in the Oquirrh Mountains, private property is everywhere, so obey all NO TRESPASSING signs.

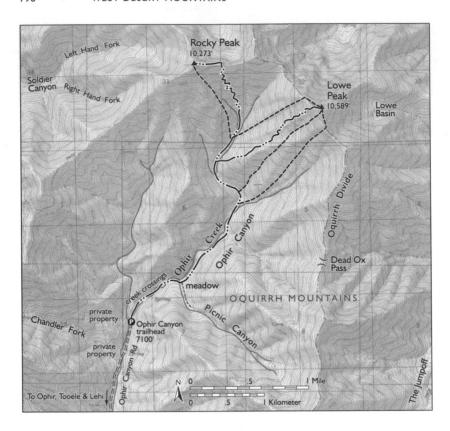

GETTING THERE

From the town of Tooele, drive south on State Route 36 for 11 miles until it intersects with SR 73. Go left (southeast), and in 4.6 miles turn left on Ophir Canyon Road. In about 3 miles, you'll reach the tiny community of Ophir, a sleepy former mining town. The road becomes dirt and is unplowed at the end of town, but if the snow is shallow, drive the remaining 1.5 miles to road's end, where you can park at a small turnaround. Otherwise, go as far as the snow level allows, and walk the remaining distance to the trailhead.

THE ROUTE

At the end of Ophir Canyon Road, find the trailhead by immediately crossing the creek. The start is marked by a NO MOTORIZED VEHICLES sign. At this point, the trail crosses through private property, so stay on the designated trail. Begin by hiking with your skis strapped to your pack because you'll maddeningly cross the creek several times as the trail meanders up Ophir Canyon for about a half mile to the intersection with Picnic Canyon on the southeast side of Ophir Canyon. This junction at 7400 feet is unmarked, but you'll know you're there when you enter a large meadow. There is also a plaque commemorating a horseback rider named Ronald Johnson.

There are no more creek crossings at this point, so you can start skinning. Continue northeast up Ophir Canyon by generally following the summer trail. If you lose it, simply stay above the creek bed. You'll skin through an old-growth aspen forest for 1.75 miles from the Picnic Canyon intersection all the way to the foot of the massive Rocky Peak–Lowe Peak Cirque at 8500 feet.

To climb Rocky Peak, which is the best bet for a morning tour as its face is more easterly and gets the sunlight first, skin up one of two sub-ridges that fall east of the summit for around 1200 feet to the main ridge. Both shoulders get steeper the higher you go, so you may need to boot pack and use crampons if the snow is still firm. Once you reach the divide, head west and climb and traverse the remaining 0.3 mile and 300 vertical feet to the top. You may have to negotiate rock outcroppings on the way, so be prepared for a bit of mountaineering fun (there's a reason they call it Rocky Peak).

To descend, ski down between the boulders and small cliff bands that guard the summit until you can open up the throttle and make fast, sweeping turns on the broad southeast face for 1500 vertical feet to the canyon floor.

To ski or snowboard Lowe Peak, begin at 8600 feet and climb the distinct ridge that goes directly to a point just below the top. The ridge begins in aspen trees where a mellow half-mile ascent gets you above tree line at about 9400 feet. At this point, the ridge gets steeper and may even be wind scoured to the point that you'll have to put skis and boards on packs to hike on rocks and low-lying bushes. Even so, the ascent is

Spring skiing doesn't get much better than on one of Lowe Peak's southwest-facing runs.

a simple climb to the divide, where you'll find a communications shack and tower at 10,500 feet. Go right and follow the ridge a few dozen yards to the 10,589-foot summit, the second-highest in the Oquirrh Mountains.

Three distinct runs fall from the summit, separated by sub-ridges. All are open bowls on a south aspect that offers more than 2000 vertical feet of skiing, and each will have you salivating when the corn snow glistens under a bluebird sky. Pick your poison, enjoy the ride all the way down to Ophir Creek, and cruise through the aspen trees back to Picnic Canyon, where you can follow your footsteps back to the trailhead.

Opposite: *Boosting air off a cornice near the summit of Castle Peak, Uinta Mountains*

UINTA MOUNTAINS

THE TALLEST PEAKS IN UTAH are found in the Uinta Mountains. Also noted as the highest range in the contiguous United States running east to west, this range, just south of the Wyoming border, is a summer playground for hikers and backpackers. But the main roadway through these mountains, the Mirror Lake Highway, closes for the winter, leaving the Uintas empty save for snowmobilers that motor in from Kamas or Evanston. As a result, backcountry skiing here requires a machine to access ski terrain in the winter months. Fortunately, the highway opens early enough in the spring (usually around Memorial Day weekend) that skiers can shred corn snow right off the highway until it completely melts.

Since spring is the only time for skiers and snowboarders who don't own snowmobiles to experience much of the Uintas, the Mirror Lake Highway routes around Bald Mountain Pass and Hayden Pass described in this chapter reflect late-season conditions. The Wolf Mountain Pass routes are good to visit in the fall before State Route 35 closes for the winter. Smith and Morehouse and the Ridge, Boundary Creek, and Castle Peak yurts are all best in the winter, especially in March when the snowpack is deep and tends to settle down.

The yurts are a great way to explore the Uinta Mountains. Castle Peak Yurt is operated by White Pine Touring in Park City, where short but good ski runs are found on Castle Peak and Duke Mountain. The Ridge and Boundary Creek yurts, located on the north slope, can be reserved through the Bear River Outdoor Recreational Alliance, or BRORA, in Evanston, Wyoming. See Resources for details.

NOTES

Land Management. These routes are located in the Uinta-Wasatch-Cache National Forest. Land east of the Hayden Peak ridgeline is within the High Uintas Wilderness. Follow all wilderness regulations and practice Leave No Trace principles. If you're winter camping, you must camp at least 200 feet from streams and lakes. Contact the Heber-Kamas and Evanston–Mountain View ranger districts for more information. Web addresses and phone numbers are found in Resources.

Road Conditions and Fees. The Mirror Lake Highway closes when snow starts flying, usually in November. It reopens around Memorial Day weekend, depending on conditions. There is a recreation fee of $6 per day, or $45 for an annual pass. State Route 35 over Wolf Creek Pass closes when the state decides to stop plowing. Some years, I've skied there as late as December. Check with UDOT for current road closures in the area.

Weather. Avalanches are a big concern in the Uintas. These mountains have a continental snowpack similar to conditions found in Colorado, where the air is cold, weak layers in the snow are common, and constant high winds load slopes to their breaking points. Before heading out, check the Utah Avalanche Center's Uintas advisory and the National Weather Service website for current conditions. See the Resources page for web addresses and phone numbers.

57 Smith and Morehouse

Start Point : Forest Road 33 winter closure, 7400 feet
High Point : Point 10002, 10,002 feet
Trail Distance : 6 miles
Trail Time : 4 hours
Skill Level : Advanced
Best Season : Winter
Maps : USGS Slader Basin, Hidden Lake

Smith and Morehouse Reservoir is a beautiful place nestled into the western edge of the Uintas, where ice fishermen, snowmobilers, and Nordic skiers can be found recreating. You might even get lucky and run into a sled dog tour on Forest Road 33

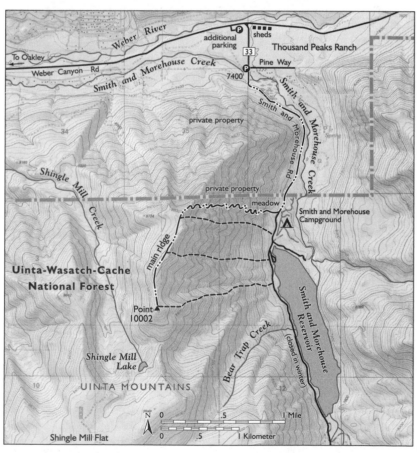

Skinning up above Smith and Morehouse Reservoir

on your way to the mountains north of the lake. These steep, forested slopes are the closest skiing from the trailhead and rise up to a broad ridge, terminating at Point 10002. Shoulders, gullies, and numerous terrain traps guard some challenging tree skiing, but avalanches are a huge concern here, so be confident of slope stability before setting off on the skin track. Also, everything north of national forest land is private property, so take care not to trespass.

GETTING THERE

From Oakley, drive east on Weber Canyon Road for 12 miles until you reach the Park City Powder Cats and Heli-Ski snowcat skiing operation at Thousand Peaks Ranch. West of the snowcat sheds is a large, plowed parking lot where snowmobilers unload their sleds. You can park here, or turn right onto Smith and Morehouse Road (FR 33)

and drive toward Smith and Morehouse Canyon for 0.25 mile to the gated entrance
of Pine Way, a small neighborhood of cabins. There is a tiny row of parking spaces
along a fence next to the gate. If parking can't be found here, go back to the large lot
by Weber Canyon Road.

THE ROUTE

Skate-ski, skin, or snowmobile across the bridge over Smith and Morehouse Creek and
follow the snowpacked road south into Smith and Morehouse Canyon for just under 2
miles. There, you will pass the signed Uinta-Wasatch-Cache National Forest boundary near the Smith and Morehouse Campground entrance. Soon after the sign, look
for a small meadow to the west. Leave the road here and skin toward the mountains.

Numerous sub-ridges that look like good ascent routes line up to the west, but
all are steep and brushy. Pick your switchbacking poison to gain the top. I've found
the easier way is perhaps a generally lower-angle shoulder to the north that skirts
the edge of private property. Switchback up for the long, steep, 2300-vertical-foot
slog to the ridge. All the while, be mindful of the private property just to the north.
Also, these low-elevation, south- and east-facing slopes can be sun crusted or even
have little snow coverage, which sometimes makes the ascent a challenge.

Once you gain the main ridge, follow it southwest for 1 mile to the indistinct
top of Point 10002. Along the way, you can choose to ski any of the choice-looking,
steep glades and slide paths that spill back down to Smith and Morehouse Road, or
make turns from the point all the way down to the shore of Smith and Morehouse
Reservoir. Choose your descent route carefully, because avalanches are common in
the Uintas' generally weak snowpack. Also, the trees can be thick in places and hide
small cliffs and boulders.

When finished, skate-ski north on the road to return to your vehicle.

58 Wolf Creek Pass

Start Point : Wolf Creek Pass summit, 9485 feet
High Point : Point 9750, 9750 feet
Trail Distance : 2 miles
Trail Time : 2 hours
Skill Level : Beginner
Best Season : Fall
Map : USGS Wolf Creek Summit

Snowmobile mecca. That's what Wolf Creek Pass becomes when the snow flies and
the summit campground closes. But along with the immense plateaus and ridges that
snowmobilers love to ride, there is plenty of obvious ski terrain that rises directly from
the road. These 400-vertical-foot descents are short, but they make for good yo-yo
tours on a powder day. The pass closes in winter but is open early- and late-season

as long as you can still drive up the road. A 4x4 vehicle or chains are highly recommended. Once the pass officially closes, you'll need a snowmobile to get there.

GETTING THERE

From Kamas, drive 2 miles south on State Route 32 to the town of Francis. Go left (east) at a four-way intersection on SR 35. Continue into the mountains for 20 miles to the summit of Wolf Creek Pass. There are several pullouts along the road, or park on the shoulder near the campground.

THE ROUTE

Wolf Creek Pass has several options for low-angle touring on all aspects from the closed campground. The most obvious run is a prominent ridge just to the northwest. Follow snowmobile tracks on the summer road past camp outhouses and picnic tables. Bear right toward a low-angle shoulder that splits the northeast and southeast faces of the ridge. Snowmobilers enjoy high marking on the open faces, but small cliffs farther north keep them at bay. After skinning 0.5 mile, you'll gain the ridge and then head north above the rock bands below Point 9750, where you can ski down a short 35- to 40-degree 400-foot east face.

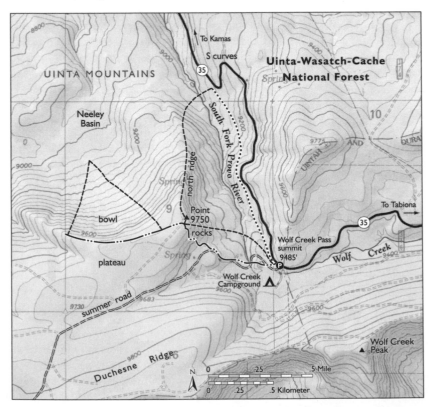

On the way to Point 9750 at Wolf Creek Pass

For a longer tour, continue from Point 9750 west across the large plateau on the north end of Duchesne Ridge another 0.5 mile along the rim of a wide, north-facing bowl that spills into Neeley Basin. The slopes are often wind loaded here, but good, protected snow can be found if you make turns near or in the trees on either side of the bowl. To return, skin back up to the plateau rim and traverse back to Point 9750.

Another option with a bit more vertical is to go north from the top of Point 9750 toward a triangle-shaped prominence, then ski the low-angle, 600-foot north ridge down to the S curves of the road and the banks of the South Fork Provo River, which should be buried under the snow. If the river is buried, cross it to reach the highway. A 1-mile skin or hitchhike south along the road returns you to the pass and your car.

59 Wolf Creek Peak

Start Point	Wolf Creek Pass summit, 9485 feet
High Point	Wolf Creek Peak summit, 9949 feet
Trail Distance	1.5 miles by shortcut; 3 miles by road
Trail Time	1–2 hours
Skill Level	Beginner
Best Season	Fall
Map	USGS Wolf Creek Summit

Wolf Creek Peak is an evergreen-covered high point that rises above Wolf Creek Pass on State Route 35. It may not look like much, but what it lacks in stature, it makes up for in excellent Uinta Mountain views and low-angle tree skiing that's easy and quick to get to. Mellow terrain and snow-covered summer roads make Wolf Creek Peak an ideal place for backcountry beginners to learn skinning technique or for anyone seeking a quick morning lap in the glades.

GETTING THERE

From Kamas, drive 2 miles south on State Route 32 to the town of Francis. Go left (east) at a four-way intersection on SR 35. Continue into the mountains for 20 miles to the summit of Wolf Creek Pass. There are several pullouts along the road, or park on the shoulder near the campground.

THE ROUTE

From Wolf Creek Pass summit, skin south through the flats and campground toward a saddle west of Wolf Creek Peak. Enter the pine trees and head uphill by following a summer road that's popular with snowmobilers.

Experienced ski-touring parties with skins can shortcut the road for a tour that's half the distance. Just before the major switchback 0.3 mile from the highway, leave the road and keep going south straight up the mountainside. You'll skin through an evergreen forest that can be thick at times. Climb 0.2 mile and 200 vertical feet to the summit ridge, then go east, following the ridge an additional 0.4 mile to the summit.

For a longer but very easy, almost flat approach, just keep following the road. In 0.3 mile from the highway, the road makes a sharp left and heads east as it angles to the top of the summit ridge. After 0.8 mile, the road switchbacks again just below the ridge and goes west for an additional 0.5 mile to the summit. This road route is a very good option for anyone learning how to skin, or for cross-country skiers.

The true summit is located on a gray, rocky knob, so it's not necessary to top out for the ski tour. If you insist, leave the road and go south for a couple dozen yards to get the panoramic view from Wolf Creek Peak's 9949-foot summit.

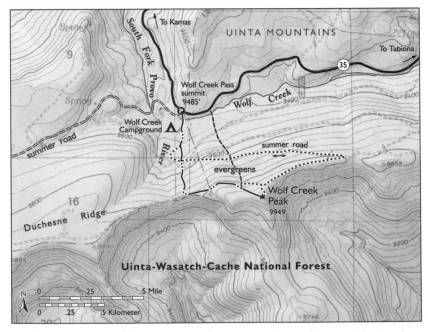

The north side of Wolf Creek Peak harbors excellent tree skiing.

To descend, skate down the summer road route for the easiest option, or drop into the evergreen-gladed north face. The trees are spaced out enough in some areas to allow for turns in protected powder all the way back to the highway and your vehicle.

60 Phelps Brook Slide Path

Start Point	Phelps Brook trailhead, 8700 feet
High Point	Top of Phelps Brook Slide Path, 9350 feet
Trail Distance	1.5 miles
Trail Time	1 hour
Skill Level	Intermediate
Best Season	Fall
Map	USGS Wolf Creek

The Phelps Brook Slide Path is a hidden surprise just east of Wolf Creek Pass. Located right across the highway from the north and south forks of Phelps Brook in Uinta-Wasatch-Cache National Forest, this old avalanche path is now filled in with young aspens but is littered with downed trees and boulders. It's also one of the longer ski descents in the area and a nice alternative to the short runs at Wolf Creek Peak (Tour 59). If snow coverage is good and Wolf Creek Pass is still open, you can ski this open, 650-foot shot or make low-angle turns in the aspens in a quick hour or two, and then link it with the runs at Wolf Creek Peak for a full day of touring.

GETTING THERE

From Kamas, drive 2 miles south on State Route 32 to the town of Francis. Go left (east) at a four-way intersection on SR 35. Continue into the mountains for 20 miles to the summit of Wolf Creek Pass. Drive down the other side for another 3.5 miles to the Phelps Brook trailhead and park at a large, signed pullout on the north side of the highway.

THE ROUTE

From the parking pullout, walk south across the road and go down a few yards to Wolf Creek, which will likely be buried under snow. Cross the creek and locate a small opening in the thick trees. Enter here. You will be able to see the lower slide path above, along with a large cliff and boulder field to the west.

In 200 yards, cross a summer ATV road and then skin up and over a low-angle slope while angling south toward an aspen-covered ridge. Switchback up through thick vegetation for 0.5 mile to attain the ridgetop, where you'll be treated to southern views of Tims Hole. Go right (west) and up along the ridge another 0.25 mile to the top of the obvious avalanche path at around 9350 feet.

To descend, ski down the open, low-angle slide path, keeping skier's right all the way back to Wolf Creek. If you ski left, you'll end up in a steep gully that terminates

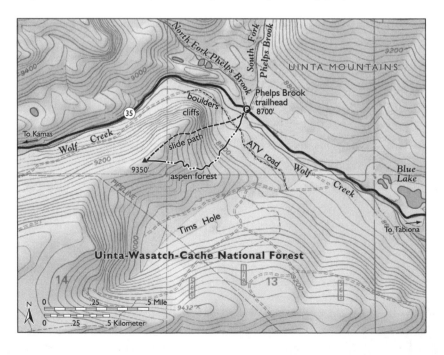

The start of the Phelps Brook Slide Path tour is easy to find.

with cliffs and that nasty boulder field below. Also, be careful if you arrive during a dry fall with low snow because the place is lousy with fallen logs; keep those tips up or risk a season-ending knee injury.

61 Castle Peak Yurt

Start Points : Upper Setting Road, 7400 feet; Castle Peak Yurt, 9600 feet
High Points : Castle Peak summit, 10,234 feet;
: Duke summit, 10,605 feet
Trail Distance : 10 miles roundtrip to yurt; 5 miles roundtrip from yurt
: to Duke
Trail Time : 5 hours one-way to yurt; 4 hours for tours to Duke
: from yurt
Skill Level : Intermediate
Best Season : Spring
Maps : USGS Hoyt Peak, Erickson Basin

The Castle Peak Yurt, operated by White Pine Touring in Park City; is my favorite winter shelter in all of Utah. On the surface it looks just like any other Utah yurt, but with one exception: it has a wood-fired sauna. While the ability to ease your tired muscles in a sauna is reason enough to book a trip to the yurt, the mountains that surround the place aren't half bad either. Two peaks with skiable terrain lie a short day tour north of the yurt—Castle Peak and a mountain known only as Duke. Both rise above 10,000 feet and offer short but steep lines on northwest- and southeast-facing aspects. Spring is the best time to visit, as the Uinta Mountains have a fussy snowpack and anything above tree line is highly avalanche prone here. But if you happen to plan a trip to Castle Peak during high avalanche danger, you can always play it safe and hang out in the sauna.

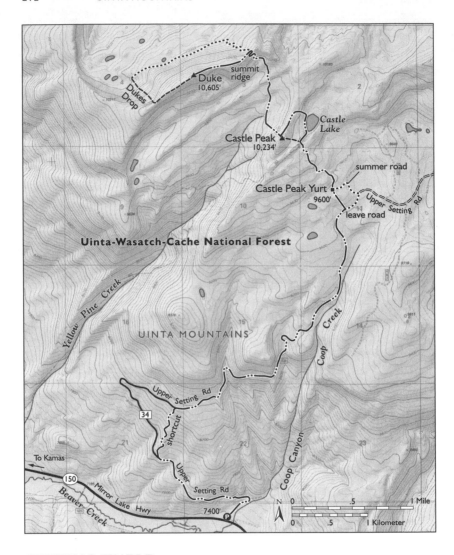

GETTING THERE

From the town of Kamas, drive east on the Mirror Lake Highway (State Route 150). You'll pass through the town of Samak and in 6 miles reach a turnoff with a Forest Service fee booth where you'll pay a recreation fee. After the booth, continue on the highway for 2.3 miles and park on the north side of the highway at the winter gate for Upper Setting Road.

THE ROUTE

Skin up the wide, flat road as it goes northeast. It almost immediately switchbacks and heads west, contouring along the mountainside. Continue on the road for 1.5

miles, at which point you can leave the road at an obvious ridge. This is a shortcut that bypasses a large switchback located 0.5 mile farther up the road. Follow the ridge northeast for 0.5 mile through widely spaced scrub oak to where you rejoin the road.

Go east on the road as it heads toward Coop Canyon. From the top of the shortcut, stay on the road for another 3.25 miles as it slowly curves north and ascends into the alpine. At about 9400 feet keep an eye out for a brightly colored ribbon tied to a tree on your left, which indicates where to leave the road. If it hasn't snowed in a while, there may already be a skin track in place. Take this path northwest as it ascends less than a quarter mile through the evergreens to the yurt, which is nestled on top of a small hill at 9600 feet.

If you can't figure out where to leave the road, keep following it another 0.25 mile to where it makes a big turn east. Leave the road here and head west on a smaller Forest Service road that leads 0.4 mile directly to the yurt, but in a more roundabout way. This is the summer route to the yurt and will likely be packed down by snowmobile tracks. Either way, it's a good idea to bring along a GPS receiver just in case.

From the yurt, you have access to both Castle Peak and Duke. Skin northwest through well-spaced evergreens over terraced terrain that is like a staircase leading up to Castle Peak. Much of the mountain is protected by small cliff bands, so to reach the summit you must first go to Castle Lake, which rests at the base of the peak to the east. It is 0.75 mile from the yurt to the lake. From the lake, contour halfway around the west

The Castle Peak Yurt can be hard to find when buried in snow up to its white roof.

shoreline, and ascend west for 200 vertical feet to the top of a ridge. Follow the ridge southwest for 0.25 mile and another 160 vertical feet to Castle Peak's broad summit.

On a clear day, the view from Castle Peak is spectacular. The south slopes of the Uinta Mountains surround you, and Duke squats to the northwest. But most impressive is the view of Mount Timpanogos and Provo's Cascade Mountain far to the southwest. From here, you can ski back to the yurt on the short but fun east face or make turns on the northwest aspect down to the head of Yellow Pine Creek. This north side is avalanche prone, however, so only attempt it during times of stable snow.

To ski Duke, it's best to get yourself a two-for-one by first skiing the northwest face of Castle Peak. Then from the bottom of Yellow Pine Creek, traverse north over more undulating ridges for 0.75 mile to the east side of Duke. Again, cliffs protect the mountain, but if you stay east, there is a way up to 10,500 feet at a saddle on Duke's summit ridge.

Go west on the low-angle ridge for 0.5 mile to the indistinct, 10,605-foot summit. The headliner descent is Dukes Drop, a massive avalanche path on the northwest face just west of the summit that is also very avalanche prone. Like most ski runs in the area, it's pretty short (800 vertical) for all the effort it takes to get there. To return, skin northeast below Duke and up to rejoin your ascent route at the saddle, then retrace your steps back to the Castle Peak Yurt via Castle Lake.

62 Mount Watson

Start Point : Crystal Lake trailhead, 10,030 feet
High Point : Mount Watson summit, 11,521 feet
Trail Distance : 5 miles
Trail Time : 4 hours
Skill Level : Intermediate
Best Season : Spring
Map : USGS Mirror Lake

Mount Watson is a beautiful peak, and all eyes turn to her impressive east face when driving west from Bald Mountain Pass on the Mirror Lake Highway. Despite her intimidating presence, the mountain is easy to reach in spring and offers descent routes from advanced steeps to intermediate shoulders. Unless you own a snowmobile, you'll have to wait until Memorial Day weekend to ski her, when the road opens and allows access to the Trial Lake area. Otherwise, the approach route will be too long for a day tour. Also, because the best skiing and snowboarding is east facing, an early start is recommended so you can make turns before the spring snow gets too wet and dangerous.

GETTING THERE

From the town of Kamas, drive east on the Mirror Lake Highway (State Route 150). You'll pass through the town of Samak and in 6 miles reach a turnoff with a Forest Service fee booth where you'll pay a recreation fee. After the booth, continue on the

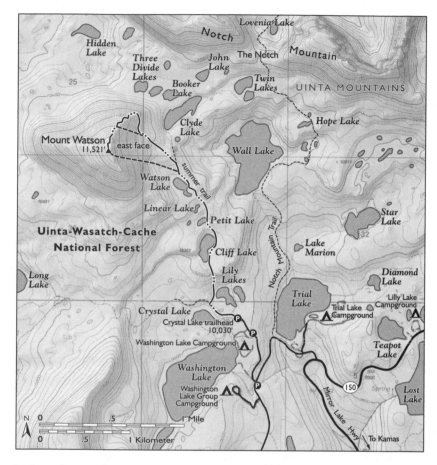

highway for 19 miles. Turn left at the signed road for Trial Lake and Notch Mountain, and follow signs for 1.25 miles to the Crystal Lake parking area located just past the Washington Lake Campground. Drive as far as the snow will allow and find parking at turnouts along the road.

THE ROUTE

From where you parked, follow the snow-covered road north to the Crystal Lake parking area. There are a few trailheads here, but you want to locate the trail on the northwest corner of the large lot. There will be a trail post for Long and Island lakes. Follow this summer path about a quarter mile to a small metal sign pointing the way to Cliff Lake on the right. Leave the main trail and head north. Although the trail will be snow covered, generally follow the summer route toward Cliff and Watson lakes. A GPS receiver and topo map are helpful here.

After the fork in the trail, the path skirts a row of cliffs as it switchbacks up to Cliff Lake, which you'll reach nearly half a mile from the trailhead. Cross the frozen water, or circumnavigate on the east side if it's melted out, and continue north. You'll soon

Snowboarding down Mount Watson's north ridge

pass Petit Lake, followed by Linear Lake and then Watson Lake at 10,400 feet. It's a little over 1 mile from the trailhead to this point.

Watson Lake is where you'll get your first look at the mountain's east face, so it's a good spot to plan your descent. Cross or go around the lake and keep going north under the peak's eastern flank. Stay well away from the avalanche run-out zone as you aim for the mountain's northeast shoulder. This is a safe and easy ascent route that spans about 1 mile from the lake to the shoulder. Depending on snow conditions, you may have to boot pack or even use crampons. Follow the ridge as it curves up and south 700 vertical feet and almost a half mile to the top of Mount Watson.

Descent routes are varied but limited in the spring. The east face has the steepest lines but can be dangerous if you summit later than noon on a warm day. Perhaps the safest place to make turns is the north-facing ascent route, followed by a descent of a large bowl on the northernmost side of the east face.

To return, retrace your skin track back to the car. Unfortunately, you'll have to skin back out as the elevation loss is minimal. In late season, expect to hike some portions of the route and be prepared for creek crossings.

63　Bald Mountain

Start Points : Bald Mountain trailhead, 10,693 feet; Mirror Lake pullout, 10,235 feet
High Point : Bald Mountain summit, 11,943 feet
Trail Distance : 3 miles
Trail Time : 2 hours
Skill Level : Intermediate/Advanced
Best Season : Spring
Map : USGS Mirror Lake

Bald Mountain is the most accessible of the major Uinta Mountain peaks. She sits just off Mirror Lake Highway on Bald Mountain Pass and can be skied after the road is plowed, around Memorial Day weekend. The route up is pretty straightforward as you can either follow the summer trail from the pass for south-facing shots, or boot straight up the east side of the mountain from Mirror Lake. But don't let the ease of access fool you, because the runs on Bald Mountain are steep and rocky, so it's best to make spring turns after a big snow year, or bring your rock boards so you won't worry about the inevitable core shot.

GETTING THERE

From the town of Kamas, drive east on Mirror Lake Highway (State Route 150). You'll pass through the town of Samak and in 6 miles reach a turnoff on the right at a Forest Service fee booth where you'll pay a recreation fee. After the booth, continue on the highway for 23 miles to the Bald Mountain trailhead, just before the top of Bald Mountain Pass. There are also several other pullouts where you can park along the top of the pass. The summer parking area usually is not plowed.

For the start at Mirror Lake, continue on SR 150 for an additional 2 miles as it descends on the north side of the divide. Park at the semi-plowed turnoff for Mirror Lake, where a few cars can usually fit, or find space along the road shoulder.

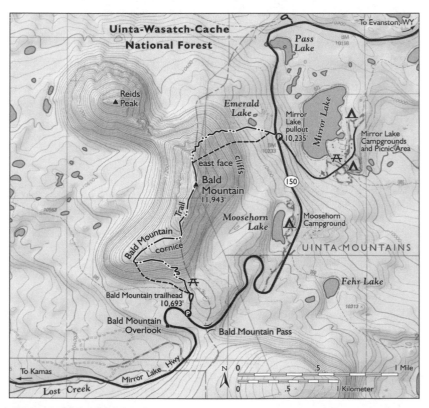

Springtime on Bald Mountain means sometimes you have to scramble to get the goods.

THE ROUTE

At Bald Mountain Pass, locate the summer trailhead at the end of the (probably snow-covered) parking lot on the north side of the highway. The mountain's south face has many cliff bands, so it's best to follow the summer trail route as best you can. For 0.5 mile, the trail makes several short, sharp switchbacks before traversing west to the end of a corniced cliff. If the cornice is too big to get around, ski down from here. Otherwise, once you get up onto the broad summit ridge, it's an easy, low-angle half-mile skin to the top of Bald Mountain. If snow conditions don't allow for skinning, you can boot pack your way up as well.

Low angle is the key word for descending the summit ridge, but then it gets steep and cliffed-out when you get back to the south face. Carefully make your way back down to the highway. In most years, the spring skiing here is about linking together remaining snow patches, and on this southern exposure, it's pretty much a guarantee.

Much better spring skiing is found on the east side. From the Mirror Lake pullout, skin up the meadow toward Emerald Lake. You'll reach the lake in just under a quarter mile. From here, the terrain becomes too steep for skins, especially if you're making the ascent on a spring morning when the snow is hard. Crampons and an ice ax or Whippet might come in handy.

From Emerald Lake, skirt around the south shore and begin booting up the steep east face. It's about 1600 vertical feet in 0.5 mile to the summit ridge, where a short skin south puts you on the true summit. Most years, the spring snowpack doesn't cover the rocky top of the mountain above 11,400 feet, so if you're intent on climbing to the top, prepare to scramble up boulders and loose scree in your ski boots. Otherwise, ski down the east face from the top of the snow line back to Emerald Lake and your vehicle. As you ski, traverse skier's left of the face as skier's right has large cliffs at the bottom. Also, get an early start for this run as the eastern exposure soaks in the morning sun, and the snow turns sloppy by noon.

64 Murdock Mountain

Start Point : Bald Mountain Pass, 10,715 feet
High Point : Murdock Mountain summit, 11,212 feet
Trail Distance : 1.5 miles
Trail Time : 1 hour
Skill Level : Beginner/Intermediate
Best Season : Spring
Map : USGS Mirror Lake

Murdock Mountain is a flat-topped, fairly uninspiring mound that loses even more prominence when compared to Bald Mountain, its neighbor across the road. But

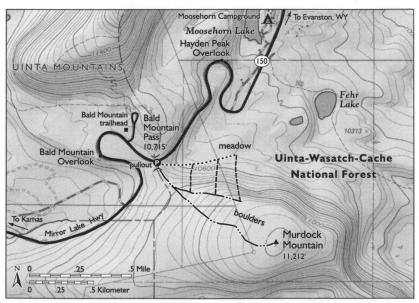

Snowboarding down Murdock Mountain with Bald Mountain in the distance

what Murdock lacks in dramatic beauty, it makes up for in super easy access and very fun skiing and snowboarding. The mountain's west side allows quick skinning from the car to the top and is low angle enough for novice ski tourers to practice skinning technique, while more advanced skiers and riders will enjoy making laps on the north face's steep chutes. However, access is limited to snowmobilers until Memorial Day weekend when the Mirror Lake Highway opens, so the boulder-filled top may be exposed and require scrambling to reach any skiing on the north side.

GETTING THERE

From the town of Kamas, drive east on Mirror Lake Highway (State Route 150). You'll pass through the town of Samak and in 6 miles reach a turnoff on the right at a Forest Service fee booth where you'll pay a recreation fee. After the booth, continue on the highway for 23 miles to the top of Bald Mountain Pass. There are several pullouts along the top of the pass, but the closest one for Murdock is on the south side of the road, just 1000 feet beyond the Bald Mountain trailhead parking area.

THE ROUTE

Navigation on Murdock Mountain is super easy. Just head southeast from the car up the mountain's west flank. You'll first pass over a snowy, open flat that gives way to sparsely wooded, rolling terrain that ascends toward the top. After 0.25 mile and only 160 feet of vertical, you'll hit the boulder fields. It's likely you'll have to remove your skis or splitboard and hike the remaining 330 feet to the summit. This is only necessary if you insist on bagging the peak. Otherwise, make easygoing turns through the trees back down for a beginner-friendly tour.

Intermediate to advanced skiers should stay left upon reaching the boulders, and follow the north edge of the mountain, where expansive views of the Uinta Mountains' north slope provide a picture-perfect backdrop for the climb. A series of steep chutes and short tree shots fall off the north side for 500 vertical feet of skiing. Good corn lasts well into spring here, but exercise caution because this is serious avalanche terrain. The north face, with its short vertical and easy return, allows you to make several laps in short order.

To get back to the start from the bottom of the north face, traverse west across the flats, and then skin up to the highway and your car.

65 Reids Peak

Start Point : Mirror Lake pullout, 10,235 feet
High Point : Reids Peak summit, 11,708 feet
Trail Distance : 3.5 miles
Trail Time : 3 hours
Skill Level : Advanced
Best Season : Spring
Map : USGS Mirror Lake

Reids Peak is practically Bald Mountain's twin, as the two proudly stand side by side above the Mirror Lake Highway. But even though Reids shares the same easy access from the road, it's a bit steeper, rockier, and more intimidating. If you have a

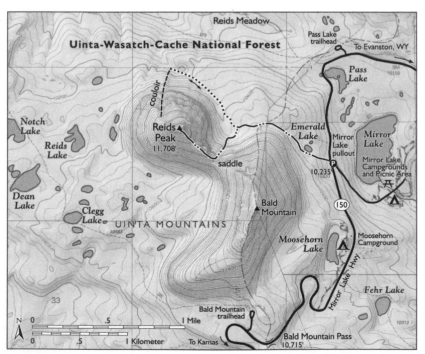

Note the large chute on the right in this view of the north side of Reids Peak from Kamas Lake.

snowmobile and can get to Mirror Lake in the winter, there are a couple of skiable shots off the summit. But spring is not kind to Reids Peak as her boulder-strewn crown melts off quickly, and skiing from the top is nearly impossible. However, when the road is finally plowed, there are usually a few snow-filled lines that stubbornly remain, just waiting for your skis or snowboard. These lines are the ones described here.

GETTING THERE

From the town of Kamas, drive east on the Mirror Lake Highway (State Route 150). You'll pass through the town of Samak and in 6 miles reach a turnoff on the right at a Forest Service fee booth where you'll pay a recreation fee. After the booth, continue on the highway for 23 miles to the top of Bald Mountain Pass. To reach Mirror Lake, continue on SR 150 for an additional 2 miles as it descends on the north side of the divide. Park at the semi-plowed turnoff for Mirror Lake, where a few cars can usually fit, or find space along the road shoulder.

THE ROUTE

From the Mirror Lake pullout, skin northwest up and across a meadow toward Emerald Lake, which is nestled at the foot of Bald Mountain. You will reach the lake in just under a quarter mile. From here, follow the tree line in a northerly direction beneath Bald Mountain's east face for another 0.25 mile, and then curve around the north ridge. From here, the saddle between Bald Mountain and Reids Peak is right in front of you.

Switchback directly up the wide, northeast-facing snowfield for 500 vertical feet to attain the saddle at 11,050 feet. If the snow isn't soft enough for skinning, you may need to hike up with crampons and an ice ax or a Whippet. For a short tour, make turns back down your ascent route. This is a fun line for multiple laps.

To reach the summit from the saddle, climb up the ridge to the top. If you're making a spring ascent, you'll probably be climbing exposed rocks in your ski boots, and the skiing from the summit may be sketchy. I only suggest doing this if you have snowmobile access during the winter months, or if you're intent on bagging the peak in the spring.

One excellent spring line is a couloir found on the north side of Reids Peak. Instead of switchbacking up to the saddle between Bald and Reids, keep skinning north along the tree line and wrap around the base of Reids Peak's east-facing slopes for 0.7 mile to the far north side of the mountain. There you will find the wide and obvious couloir. Boot pack directly up as far as you can go until you run out of snow. In the spring, you can climb to an elevation of about 11,190 feet and get around 1000 feet of vertical. The couloir does not go to the summit but rather terminates at large cliffs. Ski or snowboard back down the steep chute, and be aware of a rocky choke at 11,000 feet.

To return, simply follow your skin track south beneath the two mountains back to the pullout at Mirror Lake.

66 Mount Marsell

Start Point	Pass Lake trailhead, 10,160 feet
High Point	Mount Marsell summit, 11,340 feet
Trail Distance	5 miles
Trail Time	4 hours
Skill Level	Advanced
Best Season	Spring
Map	USGS Mirror Lake

Mount Marsell just can't get any love. Despite the fact that, at over 11,000 feet, it proudly stands alongside some of the larger peaks in the area. But skiers and even

Skiing down from Lofty Lake to Kamas Lake with Bald Mountain and Reids Peak beyond

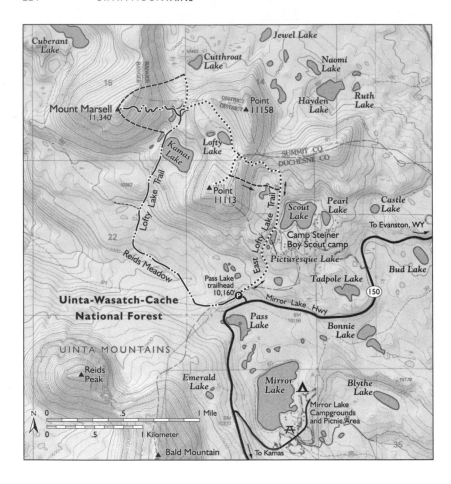

summer hikers eschew Marsell for sexier-looking mountains along the Mirror Lake Highway. What Marsell's humped summit lacks in picturesque quality, it makes up for with steep skiing on her east face and an approach route via Kamas Lake that's more scenic than any other in the Uinta Mountains. In addition, two lesser summits to the south that surround Lofty Lake (Point 11158 and Point 11113) have good skiing and snowboarding above Camp Steiner Boy Scout camp and Scout Lake. But get here as soon as the highway opens around Memorial Day weekend because Marsell's rocky slopes melt out fast.

GETTING THERE

From the town of Kamas, drive east on the Mirror Lake Highway (State Route 150). You'll pass through the town of Samak and in 6 miles reach a turnoff on the right at a Forest Service fee booth where you'll pay a recreation fee. After the turnoff, continue on the highway for 23 miles to the top of Bald Mountain Pass. Drive over the pass and continue another 3 miles to the Pass Lake trailhead turnoff on the north side of the highway. Turn left here and drive a few dozen yards on a dirt road to the parking area. If the dirt road is still snowed in, find a pullout along the highway shoulder.

THE ROUTE

From the parking area, locate the start of the Lofty Lake Trail on the west end of the dirt lot. Follow the summer trail route as it goes west through the evergreen forest. After 0.3 mile, the trail splits. Go right (north). The trail gradually begins to descend and in just over a half mile from the parking area enters Reids Meadow. In late spring and summer, the meadow is a wet, boggy place, so the trail circumnavigates around the east side. Be sure to slow down and take in the unobstructed view of Bald Mountain and Reids Peak from here.

Beyond Reids Meadow, the trail begins to climb north toward Mount Marsell and Kamas Lake. The terrain is steep in places, and if you're here when there's little snow at lower elevations, the trail is very rocky (most uncomfortable hiking in ski boots). In 1.25 miles from the trailhead, you'll come to another intersection. Left goes to Cuberant Lake on the opposite side of Mount Marsell, while right goes to Kamas Lake. Take the right fork, and climb an additional 0.5 mile to reach Kamas Lake, nestled between Marsell and Point 11113. Go around the west side of the lake and climb an additional 0.25 mile to a wide pass. From here you have two choices: climb and ski Mount Marsell, or explore Point 11113.

For Marsell, head west and switchback up the east side, which usually has enough snow to warrant keeping skis and skins on. From the pass, it's about a half mile and 700 vertical feet to the mountain's very wide, low-angle summit. The true summit is on the far west end of the top near stunted evergreens, but unless you're raring to officially bag the peak, it's not necessary to go there. Skiing lies on the northeast through southeast aspects. You can go back along your ascent route for moderate corn skiing, or ski northeast down the mellow summit ramp until you're above the steep and rocky east face. Narrow chutes hold enough snow to ski here, but late spring brings treacherous conditions. If you determine that the chutes are skiable, pick your way down to the low-angle slopes just above Cutthroat Lake, and return by skinning south 0.25 mile back to the pass.

For another option, you can skin to Point 11113. To get there, go right (east) from the pass and skin up the moderately steep slopes that level off en route to Lofty Lake. The ascent is 0.5 mile to the lake, but you'll want to continue another 0.5 mile until you're nearly to the summit. A few good, 500-vertical-foot lines exist on the east face above Scout Lake and the Camp Steiner Boy Scout camp. Avoid skiing too far into the camp property, even though it's closed until July. To return to the trailhead, follow the East Lofty Lake summer trail above the west shore of Scout Lake as it goes past Picturesque Lake and then south for 0.75 mile to the parking area.

Alternatively, if you just want to ski on Point 11113, find the East Lofty Lake trailhead on the east side of the parking lot, and travel along the east path 0.75 mile to Scout Lake. From the lake, angle northwest and climb another 0.5 mile by switch-backing or boot packing up to the saddle between Point 11113 and Point 11158. From here, go south on the ridge to the ski shots described above.

67 Hayden Peak

Start Point : Highline trailhead at Hayden Pass, 10,360 feet
High Point : Point 11820, 11,820 feet
Trail Distance : 3 miles
Trail Time : 2 hours
Skill Level : Advanced/Expert
Best Season : Spring
Map : USGS Hayden Peak

Hayden Peak literally stands out among the summits that rise along the Mirror Lake Highway. As you drive over Bald Mountain Pass from Kamas, Hayden is the most intimidating, jagged, and prominent mountain in the sawtooth skyline. But fear not, because the skiing and snowboarding is not found off the impossible summit cliffs, but rather on a few couloirs to the southwest and moderate runs off Point 11820. Access

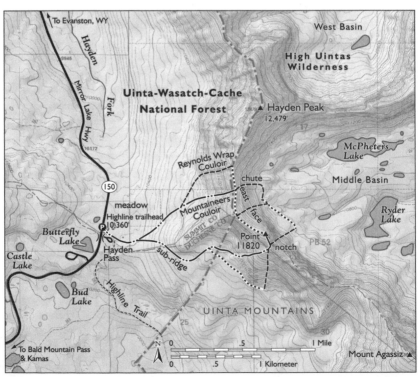

Spring skiing off Point 11820 just south of the Hayden Peak summit

is fast and relatively easy from the Highline Trail at Hayden Pass, which means you can spend an entire spring day picking off lines that are ripe for the taking.

GETTING THERE

From the town of Kamas, drive east on the Mirror Lake Highway (State Route 150). You'll pass through the town of Samak and in 6 miles reach a turnoff on the right at a Forest Service fee booth where you'll pay a recreation fee. After the booth, continue on the highway for 23 miles to the top of Bald Mountain Pass. Drive over the pass and continue another 5.2 miles to the Highline trailhead, just after crossing Hayden Pass. The trailhead parking is snowbound, but once the highway is plowed, a few parking spots are carved into the snowbanks on the side of the road. If the parking area is full, park at the turnout next to Butterfly Lake, less than a quarter mile south.

THE ROUTE

If you just want to ski the couloirs, skin east from the Highline Trail turnoff across a vast meadow directly toward Hayden Peak. Along the way, you'll pass Forest Service outhouses and parking infrastructure for the Highline trailhead. In 0.25 mile, on the far side of the meadow, head northeast into the evergreen trees. In 0.75 mile from the trailhead, you'll reach the bottom of the twin couloirs—Mountaineers Couloir is to the south (also known as the Southwest Couloir), and Reynolds Wrap Couloir is to the north. Climb up the wider and shorter Mountaineers Couloir (ice ax and crampons recommended) for around 1400 feet to the top of the ridge overlooking Middle Basin.

From here, you can descend Mountaineers Couloir, or climb along the ridge north for 0.16 mile to the entrance to Reynolds Wrap Couloir. The former is really steep at the top with a rollover that can be spooky. The latter often has an exposed rock ledge about halfway down, which makes it a pretty extreme descent in the spring.

To ski or snowboard terrain that's a bit less stout, head to the summit of Point 11820. To get there, cross the meadow from your car as described above, but just before you reach the far side, turn southeast into the evergreens and contour up along the bottom of Hayden's lower cliffs and a small, cliff-strewn sub-ridge that lies on the Summit County and Duchesne County line.

When you reach the other side of the cliff ridge in Duchesne County, you'll get a view of a narrow, west-facing snowfield. Make your way east along undulating terrain to the bottom of the snowfield. It's about 1 mile from the trailhead to this point. Switchback up with your skis and skins if the snow is soft from the afternoon sun. If you're on a morning tour, this west-facing slope will likely be hard, so crampons and ice axes may be needed when you boot pack up. The ascent is around 870 vertical feet to ridgetop cliffs that resemble a gun sight. The east-facing couloir found in this notch is a beautiful descent into Middle Basin.

To continue to the top, skin north from the notch an additional 120 vertical feet to the summit of Point 11820. From here you'll have impressive views of Hayden Peak to the north, Mount Agassiz to the south, Middle Basin to the east, and Bald Mountain and Reids Peak to the west.

Descent options are plenty from here. Traverse the ridge north for 0.25 mile and descend a wide east face to the bottom of Middle Basin. Return by skinning up the same route (this is also a good return route if you skied the couloir in the notch). Another descent option into Middle Basin is from the top of Mountaineers Couloir. Keep going north on the ridge for an additional 0.25 mile to where the couloir meets the ridgetop, and ski down the obvious, east-facing chute.

To return to the trailhead, you can ski down your west-facing ascent route from Point 11820, or ski a wider, more southerly facing slope on skier's left, and then skin northwest back to your skin track and follow it to the car. Many skiers will descend these lines, then skin back up to the ridge and ski Mountaineers Couloir, which spits you out much closer to the trailhead.

68　Ridge Yurt

Start Points : Bear River Snowpark, 8375 feet; Ridge Yurt, 9320 feet
High Point : Point 10356, 10,356 feet
Trail Distance : 10 miles roundtrip to yurt; 4 miles roundtrip from yurt to Point 10356
Trail Time : 4 hours one-way to yurt; 2 hours for tours from yurt
Skill Level : Beginner
Best Season : Winter
Maps : USGS Deadman Mountain, Christmas Meadows

The Ridge Yurt is one of five yurts operated and maintained in a cooperative venture between the US Forest Service and the Bear River Outdoor Recreational Alliance,

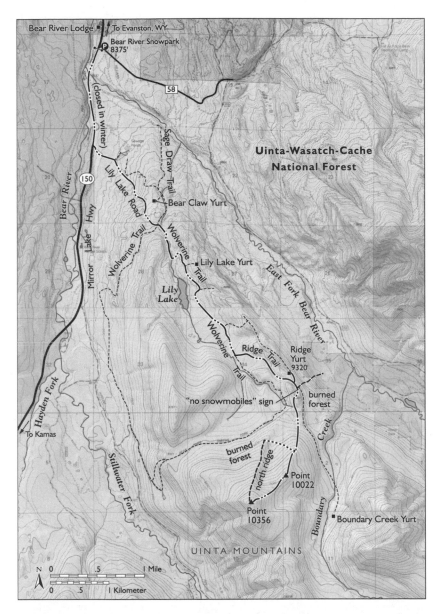

or BRORA. These yurts on the north slope of the Uinta Mountains are for use by backcountry and Nordic skiers, snowshoers, and even snowmobilers. The Ridge Yurt is the fourth in the system and located where snowmobile access ends, 4.5 miles from the highway winter closure. It is also one of two yurts in the BRORA system that has any skiable terrain around it, including an unnamed mountain (Point 10356) and a zone below the yurt that are both covered in burned-out trees from a long-ago forest

"Mountain Livin'" at the Ridge Yurt

fire. Skiing or snowboarding through the burn is a unique, eerie experience that is best described as making turns through a forest of black toothpicks. The Ridge Yurt is also a good stopover for touring parties on their way to the Boundary Creek Yurt.

GETTING THERE

From Evanston, Wyoming, drive south toward the Uinta Mountains on Mirror Lake Highway (State Route 150) for 30 miles to the Bear River Snowpark, located just east of the road-closure gate. This is also the location of the Bear River Lodge, where you can stay the night or stock up on supplies from the general store.

THE ROUTE

From the trailhead at the Bear River Snowpark, go around the ROAD CLOSED gate at the highway and skin south on the groomed snow for 1 mile. At the signed intersection, go left (southeast) on Lily Lake Road. Continue flat-tracking on the road as it gradually climbs through rolling terrain. You'll pass several intersections for other destinations such as the Bear Claw and Lily Lake yurts. Although this maze of Nordic and snowmobile trails can be confusing, it's best to simply follow the signs to Lily Lake.

Around 1.3 miles from the highway, you'll come to a crossroads for Lily Lake Road, Sage Draw Trail, and Wolverine Trail. Keep skinning south on Wolverine Trail. In 1 mile you'll pass Lily Lake to the west. From the lake, it's about 1 mile to another intersection with a sign showing the way to the Ridge Yurt. Go east (left) on the Ridge Trail as it climbs up 0.75 mile to the top of the ridge. From the ridgetop, go north for a few hundred yards to the yurt, which is nestled in a stand of evergreen trees.

The Ridge Yurt is home base for mellow, low-angle ski terrain in burned-out forests. The most accessible runs are short, northeast-facing hits that spill from the ridge 500 vertical feet to the East Fork Bear River valley. The low elevation means snow coverage can be sketchy, and you'll have to watch out for hundreds of fallen logs. Keep those tips up! To return, switchback up the way you descended.

For a longer tour, the summit of Point 10356 is a good destination. From the yurt, skin south on the ridge for 0.25 mile. You'll pass a sign indicating that snowmobiles are not allowed beyond this point. From here, go west up the hillside for 100 feet to the top of a broad ridge. Head south along this higher ridge for 0.8 mile as it slowly climbs up through the burned forest to Point 10022.

For a shorter tour, you can stop where the ridge flattens at Point 10022 and ski back to the yurt from here. To reach the mountaintop, keep following the ridge as it curves southwest for another 0.75 mile to the summit of Point 10356.

The best descent from the summit is on the north ridge. It's all low-angle skiing through charred ghost trees to the flats. At the bottom, skin east 0.25 mile on a traverse back to the primary ascent ridge, and then ski your original climbing route back to the yurt.

69 Boundary Creek Yurt

Start Points	Bear River Snowpark, 8375 feet;
	Boundary Creek Yurt, 9500 feet
High Point	Point 10959, 10,959 feet
Trail Distance	13 miles roundtrip to yurt;
	2.5 miles roundtrip from yurt to Point 10959
Trail Time	6 hours one-way to yurt; 1.5 hours for tours from yurt
Skill Level	Intermediate/Advanced
Best Season	Winter
Maps	USGS Deadman Mountain, Christmas Meadows

The Boundary Creek Yurt is, by far, the best yurt for backcountry skiing out of all five yurts operated and maintained in a cooperative venture between the US Forest Service and the Bear River Outdoor Recreational Alliance, or BRORA. These yurts on the north slope of the Uinta Mountains are for use by backcountry and Nordic skiers, snowshoers, and snowmobilers. The Boundary Creek Yurt is the last in the system, located 6.5 miles from the Mirror Lake Highway winter closure. The best skiable terrain in Boundary Creek is right behind the yurt on the slopes of Point 10959 and Point 10485. Open aspects, burned forests, and glades of evergreens dot the north- and west-facing runs, which hold soft snow long after a storm and spill back down to the yurt deck. Talk about ski-in, ski-out!

GETTING THERE
From Evanston, Wyoming, drive south toward the Uinta Mountains on Mirror Lake Highway (State Route 150) for 30 miles to the Bear River Snowpark, located just east of the road-closure gate. This is also the location of the Bear River Lodge, where you can stay the night or stock up on supplies from the general store.

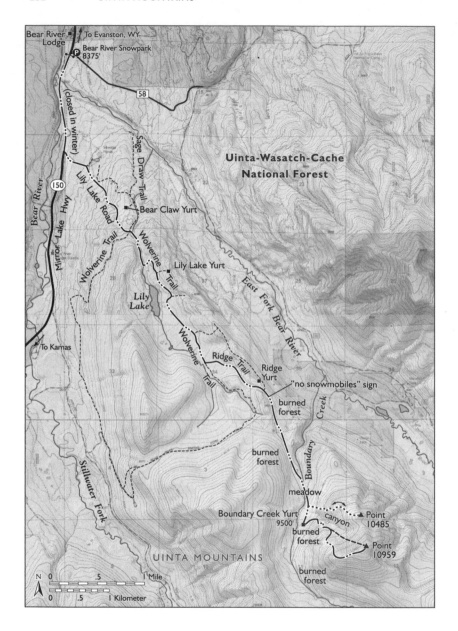

THE ROUTE

From the trailhead at the Bear River Snowpark, go around the ROAD CLOSED gate at the highway and skin south on the groomed snow for 1 mile. At the signed intersection, go left (southeast) on Lily Lake Road. Continue flat-tracking on the road as it gradually climbs through rolling terrain. You'll pass several intersections for other destinations such as the Bear Claw and Lily Lake yurts. Although this maze of Nordic and snowmo-bile trails can be confusing, it's best to simply follow the signs to Lily Lake.

Around 1.3 miles from the highway, you'll come to a crossroads for Lily Lake Road, Sage Draw Trail, and Wolverine Trail. Keep skinning south on Wolverine Trail. In 1 mile you'll pass Lily Lake to the west. From the lake, it's about 1 mile to another intersection with a sign showing the way to the Ridge Yurt. Go east (left) on the Ridge Trail as it climbs up 0.75 mile to the top of the ridge. From the ridgetop, go south (north goes to the Ridge Yurt, Tour 68). You will immediately pass signs marking this as the boundary where no snowmobiles are allowed. If it snowed recently, you may have to break trail from this point.

Luckily, blue diamonds are nailed to trees to mark the route. Follow the diamonds as the path winds through burned forests for 1.5 miles to the Boundary Creek Yurt, nestled in the trees below Point 10959.

Threading turns through burnt evergreens above the Boundary Creek Yurt is a totally different skiing experience. (Mike DeBernardo)

From the yurt, start skinning up the northwest face into the trees. For the most low-angle and avalanche-safe route, make your way east and follow the rim of the canyon that separates Point 10959 and Point 10485 to the north.

About a half mile and 700 vertical feet from the yurt, the forest will thin out on a wide bench. This is a great place to ski down through the burned trees for short laps to the yurt, especially if avalanche danger is high since the terrain gets much steeper above this point. To continue to the summit, go south across the bench for 0.25 mile and switchback up the steep slope for around 200 feet to the ridge. Follow the ridge northeast for 0.5 mile to the top of Point 10959.

To return, ski or snowboard down a nearly 1500-foot run through the steep treed slopes and open glades back to the yurt. Be aware of the small canyon between the two mountains though, as it is a serious terrain trap when avalanches are a consideration. Besides, it's best to make tracks on the lines above the yurt anyway because you'll be skiing right back to the deck, which is a beautiful way to end a tour!

To ski Point 10485, leave the yurt and retrace your approach route north across a huge meadow. You'll see the small canyon to your right (east). Just beyond the meadow, less than a quarter mile from the yurt, you'll be at the toe of Point 10485. Leave your skin track and break trail up through the aspen trees. In about 500 vertical feet, the trees fade into open terrain on the mountain's west face.

After 0.5 mile of switchbacking, you'll reach a small outcrop where the terrain flattens before the final climb to the summit. The exposed upper mountain is often wind scoured, so this may be a good spot to descend. Otherwise, continue up the ridge another 0.25 mile and 200 vertical feet to the top.

The skiing and snowboarding is a bit trickier here as far as snow is concerned. The more south- and west-facing slopes may be wind and sun crusted, but evergreens lower down can hide soft powder. There's also an excellent aspen grove with perfectly spaced trees for skiing. To return from the bottom, you'll have to skin to traverse back to the yurt.

Opposite: *Escaping the cliffs below Point 7488 in Wood Camp Hollow*

BEAR RIVER AND
WELLSVILLE MOUNTAINS

SOME OF THE BEST BACKCOUNTRY SKIING in the state is found among the mountain ranges that surround the city of Logan. The Bear River Mountains are a large range that runs from Soda Springs, in southeastern Idaho, south all the way to the Ogden Valley. The backcountry skiing potential is huge here, but it's mostly limited to peaks found along US Highway 89 through Logan Canyon, which connects Logan to Garden City and Bear Lake. Plowed pullouts along the highway near trailheads give access to side canyons like Wood Camp Hollow, Bunchgrass Creek, and Hells Kitchen Canyon.

Routes are a bit longer than those found in the Central Wasatch but short enough for day tours. Also, the Bear Rivers are perhaps the best place to visit for early-season turns, as higher-elevation areas like Tony Grove and the Garden City Bowls consist of low-angle, grassy slopes that sometimes see enough coverage by October and November. Come winter, the Bear Rivers are excellent for yurt trips. Yurts operated by Powder Ridge Ski Touring and Utah State University are cozy backcountry shelters where you can explore farther into the range and find untracked powder. Though not covered in this book, there is also lift-served backcountry skiing at Beaver Mountain Ski Area off the Harrys Dream chairlift. Check in with ski patrol for current access policies.

Outside Logan Canyon, tours from Dry Canyon to Logan Peak and Providence Canyon to Millville Peak are long and challenging. The latter, however, is always filled with the buzzing of snowmobiles.

The Wellsville Mountains west of Logan are steep, hard to access, and devoid of people, especially in winter. The range is also notorious for massive avalanches. But if you time it right and are willing to put in the effort, you can say you skied the steepest range in North America.

NOTES

Land Management. These routes are located in the Uinta-Wasatch-Cache National Forest. In general, areas west of the Bear River Divide are within the Mount Naomi Wilderness. The Wellsvilles are within the Wellsville Mountain Wilderness. Follow all wilderness regulations and practice Leave No Trace principles. If you're winter camping, you must camp at least 200 feet from streams and lakes. Contact the Logan Ranger District for more information. Web addresses and phone numbers are found in Resources.

Road Conditions. US Highway 89 through Logan Canyon is open year-round. There are plowed pullouts and ample parking at trailheads. Tony Grove Road is unplowed but remains open. Drive at your own risk. Check with UDOT for current road conditions. The Utah Avalanche Center's Logan advisory also has updated Tony Grove road conditions in the fall. Contact information is found in Resources.

Weather. The Bear Rivers are perhaps the coldest region in Utah. In fact, on February 1, 1985, Peter Sinks near Bear Lake Summit saw the second-lowest temperature ever recorded in the contiguous United States at -69° F. Before heading out, check the Utah Avalanche Center's Logan advisory and the National Weather Service website for current conditions. See the Resources page for web addresses and phone numbers.

Skinning up to Box Elder Peak from just below the summit ridge with Mitton Peak behind

70 Wellsville Mountains

Start Point : Rattlesnake Canyon trailhead, 5400 feet
High Point : Box Elder Peak summit, 9372 feet
Trail Distance : 7 miles
Trail Time : 5 hours
Skill Level : Advanced
Best Season : Winter
Maps : USGS Honeyville, Wellsville, Mount Pisgah, Brigham City

Ski or snowboard the Wellsville Mountains and you supposedly make turns on the steepest mountain range in North America. The Wellsvilles earn this distinction based on the fact that they are narrow (only 5 miles wide) but rise from the Cache Valley floor for 4500 feet to a top elevation of 9372 feet on Box Elder Peak. There are no foothills, which gives the Wellsvilles an intimidating presence, as if the mountains are a giant wall. Of course this means the peaks are a breeding ground for avalanches, but you can find great skiing with tons of vertical assuming the snowpack

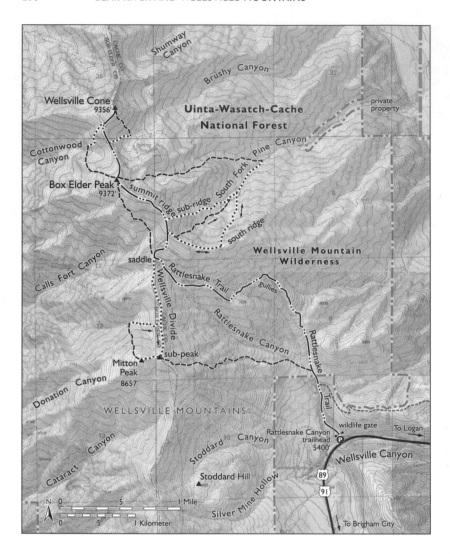

is very stable. While there are four official access points, Rattlesnake Canyon is the most efficient trailhead for skiable terrain on the highest peaks in the south end of the range, so it is the only approach described here.

GETTING THERE

To reach Rattlesnake Canyon from Logan, drive southwest on US Highway 89/91 for 13 miles to Sardine Canyon. Just after entering the canyon as it goes up toward Sardine Pass, park at the first pullout on the right. There is a large chain-link fence with a gate. A sign on the gate says, "Prevent wildlife on road. Close gate." This is the Rattlesnake Canyon trailhead.

If you're approaching from Brigham City, drive 14 miles northeast up US 89/91 over Sardine Pass. Because there is a concrete barrier dividing the highway, you'll have to drive an additional 4 miles to the turnoff for the town of Wellsville. Make a U-turn and drive back up the canyon to the pullout on the right.

THE ROUTE

Go through the chain-link gate, making sure to close it behind you, and follow the Rattlesnake Trail north into the canyon. The trailhead is on private property until the wilderness boundary, but the owners graciously allow public access. Also, the low elevation of this trailhead means you might have to hike to reach snow line, especially during spring tours.

The trail begins as double track as it crosses a meadow and then enters a forest. In just over a half mile, the double track makes a sharp switchback to the right, while the Rattlesnake Trail continues as single track to the left. Go left and follow the trail as it enters the Wellsville Mountain Wilderness, which is marked by a sign and map.

Beyond the wilderness boundary, the trail rises steeply through the trees toward the upper peaks and parallels a deep gully. After 1.7 miles from the trailhead, at 7300 feet, the path turns left (west) and crosses a series of gullies. These drainages are magnets for avalanches from above, so cross quickly one skier at a time.

Beyond the gullies, the trail enters a large meadow, with a prominent ridge to the west. Skin to the top of this ridge, and continue following the summer trail route northwest along the ridgetop. This ridge peters out and the trail descends a west-facing slope to a large, wide gully, which is the top of the Rattlesnake Canyon drainage. Quickly follow this gully up to the top of a saddle on the Wellsville Divide at around 8500 feet. It is 3 miles from the trailhead to this point.

From the saddle, there are a couple of options. For a shorter tour, traverse the divide south for one mile to Mitton Peak, where you can ski short but sweet north-facing runs that are dotted with evergreens. This is one of the best places in the Wellsvilles to find powder turns. After your run, it's an easy skin back up to the divide, so you can do laps if you choose.

To get back to the trailhead from Mitton Peak, take a huge, east-facing run back into Rattlesnake Canyon. From a small sub-peak east of Mitton, ski or snowboard down the wide bowl until it constricts above small cliff bands. To avoid the cliffs and gullies below them, traverse skier's right (south) until you reach the next bowl over and ski down that. Repeat as necessary all the way down to the bottom of Rattlesnake Canyon for a long, 3000-vertical-foot-plus run. Afterward, expect to bushwhack until you regain the trail.

For a longer tour, ski or board Box Elder Peak or Wellsville Cone. From the saddle at the divide, go north and, still following the summer route, switchback 500 vertical feet up the large, west-facing slope to Box Elder Peak's summit ridge at around 9000 feet. When you gain the ridge, traverse northwest for a view-laden half mile to the 9372-foot summit of Box Elder Peak, the highest mountain in the Wellsville Range.

Descent options abound. Good south-facing runs that return to your ascent route in Rattlesnake allow wide turns if the snow is good. This is especially true if you're looking for spring corn. From the summit, traverse back to the summit ridge south of the peak and descend from there, staying skier's left rather than going too far into Calls Fort Canyon.

For steep skiing, short, east-facing couloirs guarded by large cornices and cliffs spill into Pine Canyon. Choose a viable entrance and ski down into the bowls and rollovers and then finally the canyon proper as it constricts into a narrow valley. At around 6500 feet, stop at the intersection of Pine Canyon and South Fork. Private property owners recently closed the entrance to the bottom of Pine Canyon to the public. To avoid trespassing, return to the summit ridge by skinning west up South Fork for a mile, where a small sub-ridge among the steep bowls and cliffs provides the best access back to the divide. The large bowl south of this sub-ridge also has good skiing, as does Pine Canyon's south ridge, where northeast-facing tree shots can be lapped or used as another ascent route to gain the summit ridge. This south ridge is another viable ascent route back to the divide. Only enter this area if you are 100 percent sure of snowpack stability. Massive avalanches are common in upper Pine Canyon.

A north-facing descent into Cottonwood Canyon is another good place to make turns and often holds cold, soft snow. This is also the most fun way to reach the Wellsville Cone. Ski the open bowl 700 vertical feet into an evergreen forest, and then skin north on the south-facing slope back to the summit ridge. Follow the ridge northeast for 0.25 mile to the Wellsville Cone's 9356-foot summit. The less-fun way is to follow the summit ridge from Box Elder Peak for 0.6 mile to the top of the Wellsville Cone.

From the Wellsville Cone, there are tons of good ski and snowboard descents, but most create problems for returning back to the divide and Rattlesnake Canyon. The best bet is to ski or snowboard the southeast face into Brushy Canyon as far as you'd like, then skin or boot back up to the saddle between the Wellsville Cone and Box Elder Peak. To return, follow the divide south back to your ascent route and descend Rattlesnake Canyon to the trailhead.

71 Millville Peak

Start Point : Providence Canyon, 5500–6500 feet
High Point : Millville Peak summit, 9282 feet
Trail Distance : 6–9 miles
Trail Time : 4–7 hours
Skill Level : Intermediate/Advanced
Best Season : Winter/Spring
Maps : USGS Logan, Logan Peak

Millville Peak is a gem of a mountain located at the head of Providence Canyon. The entire area is swarming with snowmobiles, but that shouldn't deter you from

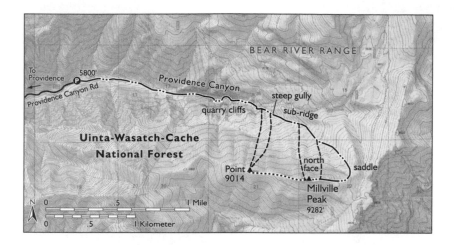

experiencing the spectacular ski lines off Millville's north side. In fact, if you make friends with the snowmobilers, you might get lucky enough to hitch a ride. Winter access can be long and difficult when the unmaintained canyon road is snowed in, but short spring tours are possible if you can drive all the way to the old quarry.

GETTING THERE

In the town of Providence just south of Logan, at the corner of Center Street and 100 East, drive south on 100 East for 0.8 mile until it curves left (east) and becomes Canyon Road. Continue east for 1.3 miles to the mouth of Providence Canyon. The road becomes dirt, its name changes to Providence Canyon Road, and plowing ends at a large pullout where snowmobilers unload their sleds. In early or late season you can drive about 3 miles farther to the old quarry. There are other pullouts along the way as well. Your approach time will be dependent upon how far up the canyon you can drive.

THE ROUTE

After parking as far as you can up Providence Canyon, skin up the wide, 4x4 Providence Canyon Road toward an old quarry. Massive cliffs mark the area and dominate both sides of the canyon. Beyond the quarry, the road becomes steep and narrow as it switchbacks into the upper drainage. Just after the largest switchback at 7300 feet and 0.3 mile beyond the quarry, you'll reach a fork where snowmobile tracks go right or left around a small sub-ridge. Left stays on the summer road and continues up the bottom of Providence Canyon. Instead, angle right and up a steep gully for 400 vertical feet where it ends at an open bench.

At this point, you can see the north face of Millville Peak rising to the south. Continue skinning along the path of least resistance southeast another mile toward a saddle at 8750 feet, and then follow the summit ridge for 0.5 mile and 530 vertical feet as it curves west to the top of Millville Peak.

Consistent powder skiing is found on the north face of Millville Peak.

The best skiing and riding is on the north side of the mountain, where both glades and open shots fall 1000 vertical feet to the canyon floor. It's an ideal place to make laps, especially if you have the use of a snowmobile.

Alternatively, you can continue west from the summit along the ridge toward Point 9014, where several other tempting slide paths and gullies line up in a row. But be careful not to traverse too far west or you'll end up above the quarry cliffs.

To return, follow your ascent route from the bottom of Millville's north face back down Providence Canyon to the car.

72 Logan Peak

Start Point	Dry Canyon trailhead, 5125 feet
High Point	Logan Peak summit, 9710 feet
Trail Distance	9 miles
Trail Time	6 hours
Skill Level	Intermediate/Advanced
Best Season	Winter
Maps	USGS Logan, Logan Peak

Getting to Logan Peak (also called Mount Logan) can be quite a haul for a day tour, especially if you're breaking trail. But the reward for earning those turns is some of the best skiing you'll find in Logan's backyard, easily accessed by a trailhead on the edge of town. The summit elevation is 9710 feet, making it the tallest mountain south of

Logan Canyon in the Bear River Range—reason enough to make the climb. A nearly 5-mile approach through Dry Canyon entertains with a low-grade skin through beautiful scenery, and quality skiing on the mountain's north and west aspects are the prize lines and should not be overlooked.

GETTING THERE

At the intersection of Main and Center streets in downtown Logan, go east on Center Street. In 1.1 miles, the street becomes Mountain Road as it winds up into the foothills through a nice neighborhood. Follow the street another 1.2 miles to its end at a large cul-de-sac at the mouth of Dry Canyon with a sign that reads, "Devere and Velda Harris Nature Park and Preserve." If it isn't too snowy or muddy, you can park a few yards farther up in a dirt parking area.

THE ROUTE

Head up into Dry Canyon, where you will immediately pass a closed metal gate that states that motorized vehicles are not allowed. If it hasn't snowed in a while, a path well worn by skiers and snowshoers will wind up the canyon bottom as it follows the summer trail route through maple and juniper trees. Small rock formations form the lower canyon walls. The trail crosses several drainages that spill down from the south ridge between Temple Baldy and Little Baldy. The foliage is quite thick lower down but opens up about 3 miles into the ascent.

From here, the canyon narrows into a gully, so it's best to switchback climber's left (still following the summer route) onto a flat bench. The trees become aspen and evergreen here, and straight ahead you can see Logan Peak with its communications tower on top, which is partially obscured by trees.

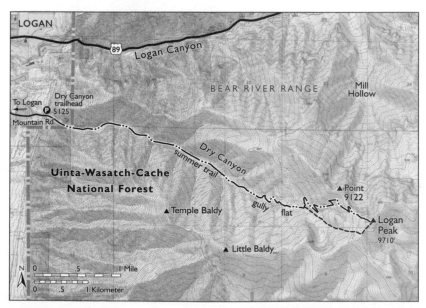

View of Logan Peak's north side from the saddle below Point 9122

Continue up, staying north of the gully for another 0.7 mile, and then turn north and actively head up the mountainside. The summer trail makes several switchbacks here, but you can skin up any way you like as you aim for the saddle between Logan Peak and Point 9122. It's about 1000 feet from the canyon bottom to the ridgetop. Once you gain the divide, go east along the ridge. It is 0.5 mile and 600 vertical feet of switchbacking up the steepening ridge to the Logan Peak summit and her massive communications tower. The total trip from trailhead to summit is a hair under 5 miles, one-way.

To descend, ski the perfectly spaced pine glades or open meadows on Logan Peak's west side back down into Dry Canyon. If you traverse southwest from the top, you'll find open, west-facing meadows and gladed, north-facing trees, both of which offer extremely fun skiing and snowboarding when the snow is soft and deep. On your exit run, be careful not to get caught in that gully you avoided on the way up as it is a serious terrain trap. To return, follow your ascent route on the bottom of Dry Canyon, but be careful skiing down in the lower section as it is narrow, choked with vegetation, and usually full of uphill traffic.

73 Wood Camp Hollow

Start Point : Wood Camp trailhead, 5400 feet
High Point : Point 9065, 9065 feet
Trail Distance : 7 miles
Trail Time : 5 hours
Skill Level : Advanced
Best Season : Winter/Spring
Map : USGS Mount Elmer

Summer is an extremely busy time in Wood Camp Hollow, because it's home to the Old Jardine juniper, the oldest-known Rocky Mountain juniper tree. Estimates put the tree at 3200 years old, so it attracts curious hikers like a magnet. But in the colder

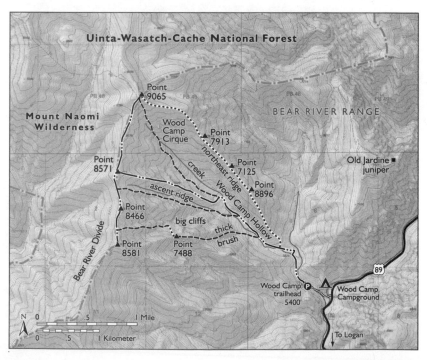

months, Wood Camp's bowls and steep ridges are empty, save for backcountry skiers in search of winter powder and spring corn. The skiable area is massive and can be accessed by a steep ridge climb to the Bear River Divide. It's slow going though, as limestone rock bands block the way and must be climbed over or circumnavigated. The effort pays off as soon as you make big turns on open, south-facing headwalls below point 9065 or slalom through north-facing trees south of Point 8571.

GETTING THERE

From the intersection of Main Street and 400 North in Logan, drive east on US Highway 89 for 2.5 miles to Logan Canyon. From the mouth of the canyon, travel 10 miles to the signed Wood Camp Campground. Turn left onto a dirt road and drive a few hundred yards up to the trailhead.

THE ROUTE

Skin along the Wood Camp summer trail for 0.5 mile to the mouth of Wood Camp Hollow, a large canyon that opens up to the west. Leave the trail here and follow the creek toward Wood Camp Cirque. It's a brushy hike, but navigation is straightforward. In 1 mile from the canyon mouth, you'll reach the toe of a large ridge that splits Wood Camp Hollow in half.

Switchback up the steep bottom of the ridge to its wide shoulder and continue up. This is a somewhat safe ascent option as far as avalanche danger is concerned, but you will have to routefind your way over small rock crags. The ridge is just over 1 mile long and will put you on the Bear River Divide at Point 8571.

From the top, your descent options are enormous. Go north to Point 9065 for south- and east-facing bowl skiing that is particularly good during the spring corn cycle. The runs are wide, long, and open and dump you right back to your ascent track at the bottom of Wood Camp Hollow.

You may also traverse south from Point 8571 in search of powder stashes tucked away in north-facing trees on small sub-ridges that return to the Wood Camp trailhead via narrow side-canyons. But be very careful skiing down the face between Point 8466 and Point 8581, especially if the snowpack is unstable. Massive cliffs guard the gully exit, so after your run, you'll either have to skin back up to the divide at Point 8466 or traverse south above the cliffs to gain another large shoulder below Point 7488, where you can ski or snowboard directly to the trailhead through a hateful bushwhack. As a result, this line is best avoided altogether if you're adverse to adventure.

Alternatively, if you just want to access the south-facing slopes of Wood Camp Cirque, you can skin up Wood Camp Hollow's northeast ridge. From the trailhead, follow the summer trail and split off into Wood Camp Hollow as for the primary route, but after 0.25 mile into Wood Camp Hollow, cut right (north) across the creek toward the toe of the obvious, brushy northeast ridge. Switchback up to the ridge proper and follow the ridge for just over 2 miles to Point 9065. It's an efficient way up, but the lower elevations and south aspects around this ridge can be subject to bad or thin snow.

Opposite: *Exit run on the north ridge of Point 7488*

74 Tony Grove

Start Point : Tony Grove Lake, 8050 feet
High Point : Point 8942, 8942 feet
Trail Distance : 2 miles
Trail Time : 1 hour
Skill Level : Beginner/Intermediate
Best Season : Fall
Map : USGS Naomi Peak

Tony Grove Lake is often called the crown jewel of the Bear River Range. But the mountains that surround the water are of more interest to skiers and snowboarders, as everything from mellow runs to steep chutes to cliff bands can be found above the frozen shore. Tony Grove is also a popular haven for snowmobilers, so you'll likely be sharing the mountains with machinery. Fall is the best time of year to tour, when access is short and easy from the lake or campground. But as soon as the 7-mile access road is snowbound and becomes impassable to vehicles, snowmobiles are required to reach the lake. While longer tours in the Bear River Range are possible from the lake, this route sticks to the lower bowls that can be lapped for a short day.

GETTING THERE

From the intersection of Main Street and 400 North in Logan, drive east on US Highway 89 for 2.5 miles to Logan Canyon. From the mouth of the canyon, travel

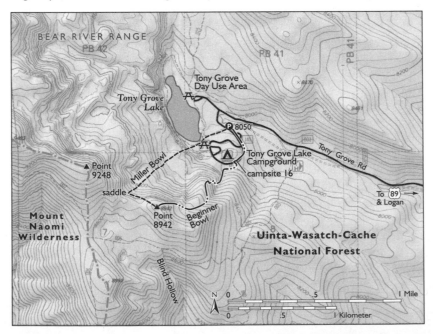

A snowboarder hikes up Beginner Bowl at Tony Grove.

19 miles to Tony Grove Road. Following the signs, turn left on a paved road and drive 7 miles up past the Tony Grove Lake Campground to the lakeside parking at the Tony Grove Day Use Area. Either park here or at the closed campground. When Tony Grove Road is buried in snow, you'll have to skin or snowmobile 7 miles from the highway.

THE ROUTE

From the campground entrance, go south toward the mountains by skinning around the campground loop to campsite 16. There's probably a skin track in place that starts here, but if there isn't, it's still a good spot to start breaking trail. Head into the evergreens and start switchbacking up.

In 0.5 mile from the campground entrance, you'll exit the trees where an open meadow splits the thick forest. This is a good, mellow run called Beginner Bowl (also known as Early Bowl). Stay right (west) near the trees to avoid being in the middle of avalanche terrain and continue up for another quarter mile.

At 8700 feet you'll reach a flat area below a short but steep slope. Avoid this avalanche start zone by going right, where there will likely be a low-angle snowmobile track that contours northwest to the top of the ridge at Point 8942. It's only 1 mile from the campground entrance to the top.

From here, you can traverse back above the steep slope and ski the northeast-facing, 30-degree Beginner Bowl you just skinned up.

Another popular run is Miller Bowl, a northeast-facing, steeper, and more challenging shot below a cliff band above the lake. From the saddle between Point 8942 and Point 9248, carefully ski north, and look for a traverse skier's right under the cliffs. There are also a few expert-only chutes with hidden entry between the rocks that start in the trees on the ridge.

75 Upper Cottonwood Canyon

Start Point : Tony Grove Day Use Area, 8050 feet
High Point : Point 9493, 9493 feet
Trail Distance : 9 miles
Trail Time : 10 hours
Skill Level : Intermediate/Advanced
Best Season : Fall/Winter
Maps : USGS Naomi Peak, Mount Elmer

Upper Cottonwood Canyon is another excellent touring area that can be easily accessed from Tony Grove Lake in the fall when the road is still passable. The canyon is huge and features a series of large peaks along the Bear River Divide for an amazing ski traverse and quality skiing on north and east faces. The whole area is part of the Mount Naomi Wilderness, which means Cottonwood Canyon is free of snowmobiles so you can enjoy your tour without any user conflicts once you go south and west of Tony Grove and Blind Hollow. You can ski and snowboard short laps at the head of the canyon or spend all day traversing to high points along the Bear River Divide.

The Utah State University Yurt is also a good start point in the winter, with easier access to the south end of the canyon and Mount Elmer, but you need to have a current student or faculty member in your party to rent it. Since it's not open to the general public, directions to and from the yurt are not covered here.

GETTING THERE

From the intersection of Main Street and 400 North in Logan, drive east on US Highway 89 for 2.5 miles to Logan Canyon. From the mouth of the canyon, travel 19 miles to Tony Grove Road. Following the signs, turn left on the paved road and drive 7 miles up past the Tony Grove Lake Campground to the lakeside parking at the Tony Grove Day Use Area. When Tony Grove Road is buried under deep snow, you'll have to ski or snowmobile the 7 miles from the highway.

THE ROUTE

From the parking area, skin south around the east side of Tony Grove Lake on what is normally the summertime Tony Grove Nature Trail. Contour around the south

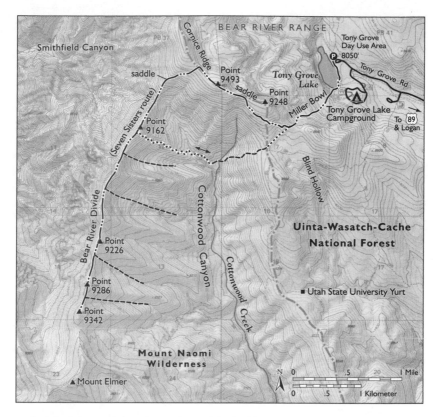

end of the lake, and then leave the trail by heading west into the pine trees where a summer picnic area is located. Switchback southwest up a steep hill for about 200 vertical feet until you reach an open flat beneath the popular Miller Bowl. Continue angling right and skin into some more trees on a small ridge that curves around the cliffs above the bowl. You will gain the ridge between Tony Grove and Blind Hollow at around 8875 feet after 0.75 mile of skinning.

From the ridge, go right (northwest) toward Point 9248, staying below the actual peak as you contour around its western flank. Overall it's a mellow grade for 400 vertical feet until you gain a saddle between Point 9248 and Point 9493. This is the start of Cornice Ridge.

Follow the ridge on a likely snowmobile track, and then ski southwest down to a saddle at the head of Cottonwood Canyon. You may be tempted to just use the Smithfield Canyon Trail summer route, but staying on the ridgeline is safer from avalanches. However, you can save some vertical and mileage if you choose the summer route.

From the saddle on the Bear River Divide, travel south along the ridge crest toward Mount Elmer, following the Seven Sisters route (so named by locals because of the many high points along the way). You'll be witness to incredible views of the Bear River Mountains from this long perch. Several distinct peaks line up before you with the largest, Mount Elmer, 3 miles south of the saddle.

Skinning the "Seven Sisters Route" above Cottonwood Canyon

An alternate way to access the divide is to ski down from the Tony Grove area. At the flats above Miller Bowl, continue left (west), and then ski down the tree-covered, west-facing slopes into the bottom of Cottonwood Canyon. Due to the aspect, the snow can be shallow here, and the slopes are rocky. Erosion gullies and creek beds in Cottonwood Canyon are steep and deep, so you'll have to navigate wisely. Pick your way to the base of the nearest ridge and skin up it for around 1100 vertical feet to Point 9162.

Each peak from Point 9162 to Point 9342 has good open bowls and tree skiing into Cottonwood Canyon on the north and east faces, as well as steeper runs on the ridges that spill like fingers down to the bottom of the canyon. It's best to just lap the upper faces for 500- to 1000-vertical-foot shots as the lower canyon funnels into terrain traps and is littered with small cliffs that guard steep, maze-like erosion gullies.

To return, skin west up the closest ridge that regains the divide, and traverse back the way you came to the head of Cottonwood Canyon and down to Tony Grove Lake. Or you can retrace the alternate descent route into the canyon back to the top of Miller Bowl for a final run back to the car.

76 Cornice Ridge

Start Point	Tony Grove Day Use Area, 8050 feet
High Point	Point 9676 on Cornice Ridge, 9676 feet
Trail Distance	4 miles
Trail Time	3 hours
Skill Level	Intermediate/Advanced
Best Season	Fall
Map	USGS Naomi Peak

Cornice Ridge is a fleeting place for backcountry skiers. In winter, access to the Tony Grove parking area requires a snowmobile, and the ridge grows an impassable, giant cornice (hence the name). But this playground for snowmobilers is prime for autumn backcountry skiing and snowboarding when the snow is too shallow for heavy machinery, the cornice is still an infant, and Tony Grove Road hasn't snowed in yet. If you time it right, you can make laps below Cornice Ridge on open, north- and east-facing bowls that consistently have the deepest early-season snow in the Bear River Range.

GETTING THERE

From the intersection of Main Street and 400 North in Logan, drive east on US Highway 89 for 2.5 miles to Logan Canyon. From the mouth of the canyon, travel 19 miles to Tony Grove Road. Following the signs, turn left on the paved road and drive 7 miles up past the Tony Grove Lake Campground to the lakeside parking at the Tony Grove Day Use Area. When Tony Grove Road is buried under deep snow, you'll have to ski or snowmobile the 7 miles from the highway.

THE ROUTE

From the parking area, skin south around the east side of Tony Grove Lake on what is normally the summertime Tony Grove Nature Trail. Contour around the south end of the lake, and then leave the trail by heading west into the pine trees where

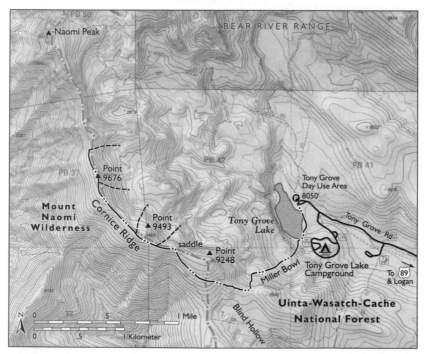

Cornice Ridge in autumn is a safe bet for untracked powder skiing.

a summer picnic area is located. Switchback southwest up a steep hill for about 200 vertical feet until you reach an open flat beneath the popular Miller Bowl. Continue angling right and skin into some more trees on a small ridge that curves around the cliffs above the bowl. You will gain the ridge between Tony Grove and Blind Hollow at around 8875 feet after 0.75 mile of skinning.

From the ridge, go right (northwest) toward Point 9248, staying below the actual peak as you contour around its western flank. Overall it's a mellow grade for 400 vertical feet until you gain a saddle between Point 9248 and Point 9493. This is the start of Cornice Ridge. Continue northwest along the top of the ridge. You will likely be following a snowmobile track all the way to the highest part of the ridge, Point 9676.

There are many options for skiing and snowboarding from Cornice Ridge on 500- to 600-vertical-foot open runs along the northeast and east aspects, the safest being from a saddle just north of Point 9676, where a lower-angle bowl beckons. Of course, as the name suggests, there will likely be a massive cornice all along the ridge, but it may be passable in early season. Also, the skiable runs are in avalanche terrain, so make a thorough snow stability assessment before dropping in.

To return, skin back up to Cornice Ridge and follow your ascent route back to Miller Bowl, where you can make some easy turns for a bonus home run down to Tony Grove Lake.

77 Bunchgrass Creek

Start Points	Bunchgrass Creek trailhead, 6300 feet; Bunchgrass Yurt, 8415 feet
High Point	White Pine Knob summit, 9134 feet
Trail Distance	8 miles roundtrip to yurt; 1 mile roundtrip from yurt to White Pine Knob
Trail Time	5 hours one-way to yurt; 1 hour for tours from yurt
Skill Level	Beginner/Intermediate
Best Season	Winter
Maps	USGS Tony Grove Creek, Naomi Peak

There's nothing more memorable in backcountry-ski life than staying a night or two at a yurt. The Bunchgrass Yurt, owned by Powder Ridge Ski Touring in Logan, is one such tidy shelter nestled beneath acres of righteous ski and snowboard terrain. The summits of White Pine Knob and Chicken Hill are a mere half-mile skin from the front door, and each has runs on several aspects so you can generally find good snow, even weeks after a storm.

GETTING THERE

From the intersection of Main Street and 400 North in Logan, drive east on US Highway 89 for 2.5 miles to Logan Canyon. From the mouth of the canyon, continue

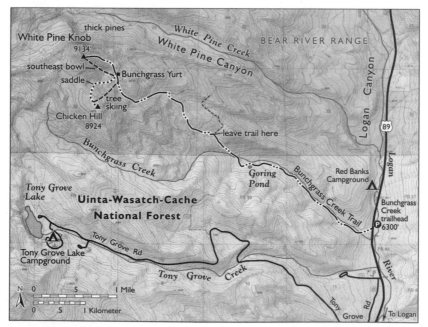

Tucked inside an aspen forest, the Bunchgrass Creek Yurt is an idyllic base camp for powder tours.

19.6 miles to the Bunchgrass Creek trailhead. There is a large, plowed pullout on the east side of the highway between Tony Grove Road and the Red Banks Campground.

THE ROUTE

From the parking lot, cross the highway and skin west through a sagebrush meadow until you connect with Bunchgrass Creek and the trail. Follow the trail as it parallels the creek up the canyon in a northwest direction. In 1.8 miles, you'll reach Goring Pond. The trail crosses the creek at 7400 feet before going up a steep hill. Soon you'll see the top of White Pine Knob in the distance to the northwest.

Just over a half mile from Goring Pond, leave the main trail by heading toward White Pine Knob. At this point, the route can be difficult to find. There's usually a skin track in place to the yurt from previous occupants, but if you're breaking trail, White Pine Knob is your guide (assuming it's a clear day). It's a good idea to have a map, compass, and GPS, with coordinates to the shelter, which are provided by Powder Ridge Ski Touring.

Once you leave the main trail route, skin in a northwesterly direction as the terrain becomes more wooded. It's just over 2.1 miles from the creek to the Bunchgrass Yurt, located at 8415 feet in a stand of aspen near the base of White Pine Knob's southeast face. If the snowpack is deep or if there is fresh powder, it may be difficult to find the white-roofed yurt against all the snow. Again, GPS coordinates are helpful.

Once you reach the yurt, a smorgasbord of skiing surrounds you. It's only 0.5 mile and 720 vertical feet to the summit of White Pine Knob, which can be climbed by its east ridge. Steep runs on the southeast bowl are the main course, but if avalanches are a concern, ski or snowboard down the ridge you ascended. There's also steep, north-facing tree skiing that falls into White Pine Canyon.

Chicken Hill is just south of White Pine Knob and features short tree runs on north and east aspects, where powder stashes can be found long after a storm. From the yurt, go west through the trees to a saddle at 8720 feet between White Pine Knob and Chicken Hill, and then go south on the ridge to the top of Chicken Hill and take your pick from several gladed runs you can ride back down to the yurt.

After your yurt adventure is over and every shred of snow has been tracked out, follow your ascent route down Bunchgrass Creek to return to the highway and your vehicle.

78 Hells Kitchen Canyon and Steam Mill Yurt

Start Points	Franklin Basin winter trailhead, 6670 feet; Steam Mill Yurt, 8100 feet
High Point	Steam Mill Peak summit, 9282 feet
Trail Distance	7 miles roundtrip to yurt and Steam Mill Peak; 4 miles roundtrip from yurt to Steam Mill Peak
Trail Time	4 hours one-way to yurt; 3 hours for tours from yurt
Skill Level	Beginner/Intermediate
Best Season	Winter
Map	USGS Tony Grove Creek

Hells Kitchen Canyon is a favorite backcountry skiing area for Logan locals. A long but mellow approach from a large parking area leads to remote, snowmobile-free ski runs in the upper canyon and on the area's highest point, Steam Mill Peak. For those of us who don't reside in Logan, the Steam Mill Yurt is conveniently located in a spot where you can spend days tracking every open face on every aspect. Hells Kitchen Canyon is an ideal spot for every ability, from beginner to expert, as terrain options range from low-angle aspen trees to moderate bowls on broad mountain shoulders and even gnarly, cliff-strewn chutes below the canyon's highest points.

GETTING THERE

From the intersection of Main Street and 400 North in Logan, drive east on US Highway 89 for 2.5 miles to Logan Canyon. From the mouth of the canyon, continue 22 miles to the Franklin Basin Road turnoff on the left, where there is a plowed winter trailhead with Forest Service outhouses. This is a very popular spot for snowmobilers, many of whom travel all the way to Idaho on Franklin Basin Road, so parking spots can be difficult to find on weekends.

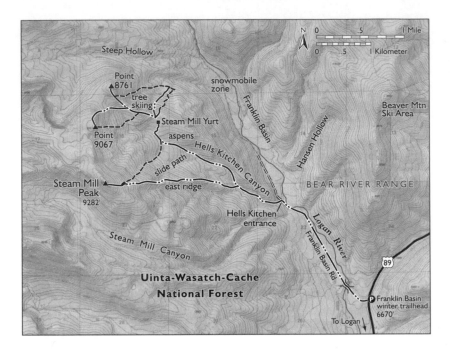

THE ROUTE

Follow Franklin Basin Road as it heads northwest into the mountains. You'll soon cross a bridge over the Logan River. The road is flat and will probably be packed down by snowmobiles, so skinning the 1.5 miles to Hells Kitchen Canyon will be a piece of cake. If the snowmobilers are nice enough, you may even get a ride or tow to the turnoff.

Hells Kitchen Canyon begins at 6890 feet at the toe of an obvious ridge where the entrance is blocked off with bamboo poles and orange fencing in an attempt to keep snowmobiles out. Get off the road here and head northwest up the canyon. You'll soon be enveloped in aspen trees as you ascend a narrow gully.

If your only destination is a day tour of Steam Mill Peak, leave the gully 0.6 mile from the road at about 7300 feet and ascend west up a wooded ridge. This is the east ridge of Steam Mill Peak. It is 1.5 miles from the gully to the summit. Along the way, the ridge alternates between flat meadows and woods of fir trees and aspens. At 8400 feet, you'll cross a major slide path. Scope out this area and dig a pit to check snow stability, because here is some of the best skiing on the mountain. From the avalanche path, you'll cross undulating, open terrain to the bottom of the summit at 8950 feet. From here, switchback up the steep east face for 300 vertical feet to the top. Small cliff bands and boulders guard the wind-scoured upper peak, so you may have to take off your skis to reach the true summit.

Ski and snowboard options abound on Steam Mill Peak. Descend the east ridge to the bottom of Hells Kitchen Canyon, or link moderate, open slopes between the trees on the mountain's northeast face. Rejoining your skin track is easy from the canyon bottom so you can yo-yo laps all day.

If you're going to the Steam Mill Yurt, stay on the canyon bottom after leaving Franklin Basin Road. In 1.8 miles from the canyon mouth, you'll reach a meadow at about 8030 feet, below Steam Mill Peak to your left. To your right is a large aspen grove. Head north up into the aspens, where you will find the Steam Mill Yurt about 0.2 mile and 700 vertical feet above the canyon floor, just below the ridge that divides Hells Kitchen Canyon and Franklin Basin.

The yurt, operated by Powder Ridge Ski Touring, sleeps up to eight people and is well appointed. If you stay at the yurt, it's a good base camp for ski tours in all directions. For tours on Steam Mill Peak, ski down the mellow aspen slopes to the base of the mountain and ascend the east-facing slopes to gain the east ridge for an ascent to the summit. You can also find good, north- and east-facing tree skiing behind the yurt into Franklin Basin. Skin from the yurt north to the ridge and ski down the other side, or traverse northwest to Point 8761. Descent options are possible all along here. The trees start out thick but widen just below the ridgetop. Return to the yurt by switchbacking up your descent route. Be warned, though, because Franklin Basin is snowmobile heaven, and it may be tracked out.

The best terrain near the yurt lies below Point 9067. Skin from the yurt northwest on the ridge for 0.5 mile. Just before reaching Point 8761, leave the ridge and cut west directly toward Point 9067. You'll have to switchback up a very steep evergreen slope to the top of the ridge between Hells Kitchen Canyon and Steep Hollow. At the top at 8950 feet, the terrain flattens out. Turn south and stop above a large, east-facing bowl just below the summit of Point 9067, which is guarded by rock bands.

The east face of Point 9067 is one of the premier lines in Hells Kitchen Canyon.

This east-facing cirque is a sweet pitch and fall line where you can make multiple short but fun laps. When you've had your fill, return to the yurt by skinning southeast for 0.5 mile through the aspen trees.

79 Garden City Bowls

Start Point : UDOT plow garage at Swan Flat Road, 7600 feet
High Point : Point 8802 on the Garden City Canyon west ridge, 8802 feet
Trail Distance : 5 miles
Trail Time : 3 hours
Skill Level : Beginner/Intermediate
Best Season : Winter
Map : USGS Garden City

The east-facing runs of Garden City Canyon, known as the Garden City Bowls, are a bona fide powder paradise. Wide-open meadows at a low-angle pitch, coupled with a bird's-eye view of Bear Lake in the distance, make this a must-do tour for any season. While winter is the best time to visit, the grassy slopes of the Garden City Bowls have few rocks, which makes the area perfect for scoring some early-season turns. All of this can be had with a relatively short and safe approach.

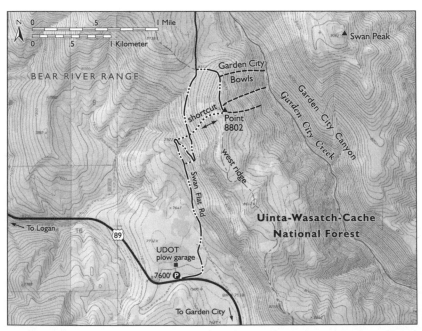

Icicles glitter in the morning sun on the ascent to the Garden City Bowls.

GETTING THERE

From the intersection of Main Street and 400 North in Logan, drive east on US Highway 89 for 2.5 miles to Logan Canyon. From the mouth of the canyon, travel 27 miles to the UDOT plow garage near Bear Lake Summit. The route starts at a plowed parking area just up canyon from the start of Swan Flat Road.

THE ROUTE

From the plowed pullout between the highway and plow garage, skin northeast across the flats for 0.4 mile until you reach Swan Flat Road, a summer route that goes all the way to the Utah-Idaho border. Go left on the road, heading north for 0.8 mile until you reach the first switchback. If the snow is deep enough, shortcut east to the second switchback and head up the brush-covered, southwest-facing slope beneath a cliff band with a small arch feature. Otherwise, stay on the road for another mile until you cross the ridge, and then leave the road and head southeast up into the evergreens to gain the west ridge of Garden City Canyon, which marks the border between Rich and Cache counties.

At the top, drop into the powder-filled Garden City Bowls beneath your skis. There are three main ski shots that drop 1000 feet to the canyon bottom and Garden City Creek at an easy slope angle of 25 to 30 degrees. Near the bottom of the canyon, however, the slopes get steeper and funnel into triangular gullies. You can easily avoid these by just lapping the upper slopes.

To return, skin back up to the saddle above the bowls to find Swan Flat Road, where you can skate-ski back to the car. If snow coverage allows, traverse south on the ridge to Point 8802 and descend the shortcut ascent route back to the road.

80 Swan Peak

Start Point : UDOT plow garage at Swan Flat Road, 7600 feet
High Point : Swan Peak, 9082 feet
Trail Distance : 6–9 miles
Trail Time : 6 hours
Skill Level : Intermediate
Best Season : Winter
Map : USGS Garden City

Swan Peak is a summit in the Bear Lake Mountains that can be climbed as a long Nordic tour, or linked up with the open bowls of Garden City Canyon (Tour 79).

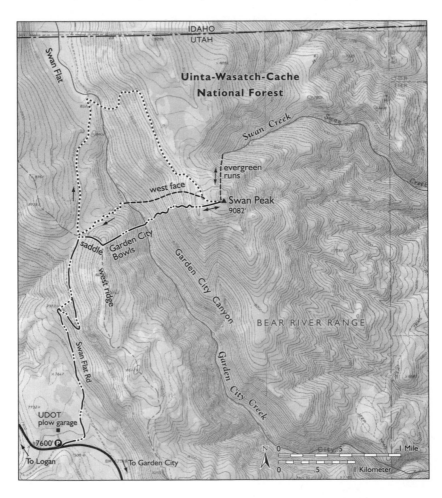

A cathedral of evergreens on the way to Swan Peak via Swan Flat

The longest ski descents are 1000-foot shots on the sun-exposed west and south faces, which require fresh snow to be any fun. The peak's evergreen-sheltered, northeast aspect that funnels into Swan Creek has better snow, but it will make for a long day in the skin track. Whatever poison you pick, the views of the Bear River Mountains, Franklin Basin, and Bear Lake shimmering far below are outstanding and are worth the tour.

GETTING THERE

From the intersection of Main Street and 400 North in Logan, drive east on US Highway 89 for 2.5 miles to Logan Canyon. From the mouth of the canyon, travel 27 miles to the UDOT plow garage near Bear Lake Summit. The route starts at a plowed parking area just up canyon from the start of Swan Flat Road.

THE ROUTE

From the plowed pullout between the highway and plow garage, skin northeast across the flats for 0.4 mile until you reach Swan Flat Road, a summer route that goes all the way to the Utah-Idaho border. Go left on the road, heading north for 0.8 mile until you reach the first switchback. If the snow is deep enough, shortcut east to the second switchback. Continue up the road for 0.5 mile until you reach a point where the road crosses the Garden City Canyon ridge at a saddle on the Cache County–Rich County line.

From here, you have two options. For a shorter tour that maximizes downhill vertical, double back by curving south another 0.25 mile on the pine-covered west ridge to the Garden City Bowls (Tour 79). Ski these excellent, east-facing shots for about 1000 vertical feet all the way to the bottom of Garden City Canyon. Cross the creek and switchback up the brushy west face of Swan Peak to the top for just under a mile of climbing. The summit is located at the end of a large flat, so unless you're super motivated to officially bag the peak, it's best to just ski down as soon as the ground levels.

If the snowpack is low or avalanche conditions are a dangerous concern, you can reach the summit by continuing up the road from the saddle for another 1.3 miles to Swan Flat, which is just a half mile from the Utah-Idaho border. Topo maps show a summer trail that goes from here to the top of Swan Peak, and this is a good route to emulate. From the Swan Flat meadow, an obvious shoulder rises to the east and becomes a ridge. Make a few switchbacks up to this ridge, and then traverse it southeast for 1 mile to the Swan Peak summit.

On a clear day, you should be able to see Bear Lake far below to the east. From here, you can make a few turns among the evergreens on the north side above Swan Creek. But the return route requires you to ski or snowboard the west face. Again, it may be low snow and brushy, so keep those tips up. When you reach the bottom of Garden City Canyon, skin west back up to the saddle at the county line and return to the car via Swan Flat Road.

Opposite: *Making turns from the summit of Shelly Baldy Peak*

TUSHAR MOUNTAINS

SOLITUDE AND EASY ACCESS. That's what you get when you backcountry ski
or snowboard the Tushar Mountains. Located east of Beaver, the Tushars are the
third-highest range in the state after the Uinta and La Sal mountains. With peaks
that rise above 12,000 feet and a geographic location that favors southwest storm
tracks, the range can get tons of snow that transforms these wind-scoured peaks into
a skier's Shangri-la.

State Route 153 provides the easy-access part, as the highway connects the town
of Beaver to Eagle Point Resort, 19 miles up Beaver Canyon. From the ski area, quick
tours to Mount Holly and Lake Peak are easy through the backcountry gates managed
in conjunction with the US Forest Service. Although ski terrain outside the resort
boundary is some of the best in Utah, you can easily tour to these peaks without
having to purchase a lift ticket. The trailhead at Puffer Lake is the gateway to the
aforementioned mountains, plus City Creek Peak, the playground of touring parties
staying at the Puffer Lake Yurt.

Solitude comes in the north end of the range, where Delano Peak, the Great White
Whale, and Shelly Baldy Peak reside. While a longer tour from Eagle Point will get

Scoping out lines on Shelly Baldy Peak

you there, staying at the Snorkeling Elk Yurt is the perfect base camp to tick off the mountain summits one by one. Tushar Mountain Tours operates the yurts and provides guiding services. See Resources for details.

Even farther north are the impressive Mount Baldy and Mount Belknap massifs. These mountains are remote and pretty much require overnight camping for a successful mission. As a result, neither peak is included in this book. However, if the Tushars get a good winter with a deep snowpack, it is possible to find summer snow that you can drive to after the dirt roads reopen. It's a great place to explore all year!

NOTES

Land Management. The Tushar Mountains are located in Fishlake National Forest. Contact the Beaver Ranger District for more information. Web address and phone number are found in Resources. There are parcels of private property around Eagle Point and Puffer Lake. Obey all NO TRESPASSING signs.

Road Conditions. State Route 153 is the only road into the Tushar Mountains that is open all year. Plowing ends at Puffer Lake, and parking can be found at pullouts there and at Big John Flat Road. Otherwise, park at Eagle Point. Check with UDOT for current road conditions. Contact information is found in Resources.

Weather. The Tushar Mountains are very windy, which can scour the upper peaks to bare rock and leave behind bad avalanche danger. Unfortunately, due to the lack of backcountry use and population centers, the Utah Avalanche Center does not provide an avalanche advisory. You are on your own to assess the snowpack and make informed decisions before skiing into avalanche terrain. Check with Eagle Point Resort and the National Weather Service for current conditions. See the Resources page for web addresses and phone numbers.

81 Shelly Baldy Peak

Start Points : Big John Flat Road, 8640 feet; Snorkeling Elk Yurt,
: 10,400 feet
High Point : Shelly Baldy Peak summit, 11,321 feet
Trail Distance : 9 miles roundtrip to yurt; 4.5 miles roundtrip from yurt to
: Shelly Baldy Peak
Trail Time : 4 hours one-way to yurt; 5 hours for tours from yurt
Skill Level : Advanced
Best Season : Winter
Map : USGS Shelly Baldy Peak

Shelly Baldy Peak is the most visible mountain on the horizon when you're staying at the Snorkeling Elk Yurt. Therefore, many a backcountry skier's eye is drawn to her delicious-looking snowfields. Although the mountain isn't as easy to access as Delano Peak or Mount Holly because of several ridges and gullies that must be traversed on

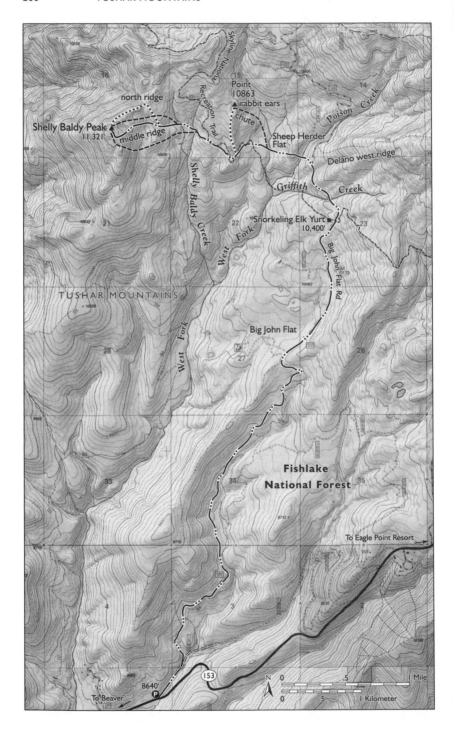

the approach, the effort to get there is well worth it. Plus, you can find good skiing and snowboarding options all along the way.

GETTING THERE

From Main Street in Beaver, drive east on 200 North as this street becomes State Route 153. Follow the road for 16 miles to the start of Big John Flat Road and park in a plowed pullout on the north side of the highway.

THE ROUTE

Skin north up the road for 4.6 miles as it gradually climbs toward Big John Flat and reach the Snorkeling Elk Yurt. The yurt is next to a Forest Service outhouse near the junction of the road and the Skyline National Recreation Trail.

From the yurt, continue up the road until it crosses Griffith Creek and contours around the foot of Delano Peak's west ridge. Around a half mile from the yurt, leave the road and head west, aiming for Shelly Baldy Peak, which is visible to the west.

There is no easy way to get to the mountain other than going up and down at least three drainages and ridges. That means you'll spend a lot of time transitioning from skin to ski mode, and the whole roundtrip affair can take all day. On the plus side, you'll get some turns in as you descend toward each small valley. This route generally follows the Skyline National Recreation Trail, which is a good point of reference.

Immediately after leaving the road, you'll descend down to and cross over Poison Creek. On the other side of the first drainage, you'll skin across the south end of Sheep Herder Flat. This large meadow has commanding views of Shelly Baldy. On the other side of the flat, 1 mile from the yurt, you'll cross West Fork and reach the bottom of a small ridge with rust-colored rocks that guard the top. At the ridge's highest point, twin rocks stick out like rabbit ears. This is the summit of Point 10863. Between these stone outcroppings is a snow-filled chute that is fun skiing for a short tour, or a last hurrah on the return trip. To continue to Shelly Baldy, switchback up to the top of the ridge, south of the rocks, and skin west down the other side.

In 1.75 miles from the yurt (6.4 miles from the trailhead) you'll reach the drainage of Shelly Baldy Creek, which cuts below the foot of the mountain. There are a couple of options to climb the summit from here: the rocky middle ridge or the windy north ridge. The middle ridge is more direct, but because of the usual exposed rocks, you'll probably have to boot pack to just below the summit. It isn't difficult though, and this route is a pretty efficient 0.5 mile and 750 vertical feet to the top.

The alternate choice is the north ridge. From the base, head northwest and climb to the obvious saddle above a wide bowl, and then follow the ridge west to the top. This route is highly exposed and windy, but it offers breathtaking views of Mount Baldy and Mount Belknap to the north.

To return, ski either the east-facing main bowl between the ridges, or make careful turns down three distinct snowfields on the southeast face. The latter option is a bit of a rocky minefield, so tread lightly. At the bottom, retrace your ascent route back to the yurt or trailhead.

82 Delano Peak

Start Points : Big John Flat Road, 8640 feet; Snorkeling Elk Yurt,
: 10,400 feet
High Point : Delano Peak summit, 12,169 feet
Trail Distance : 9 miles roundtrip to yurt; 4 miles roundtrip from yurt to
: Delano Peak
Trail Time : 4 hours one-way to yurt; 3 hours for tours from yurt
Skill Level : Intermediate/Advanced
Best Season : Winter
Map : USGS Shelly Baldy Peak, Delano Peak

Delano Peak is the highest mountain in the Tushar Range, yet it's one of the easiest to get to and ski down as long as you're staying at the Snorkeling Elk Yurt. In two hours you can reach the summit from the yurt, otherwise you're looking at a full day in the skin track if starting at State Route 153. You can also reach it from the Eagle Point Resort. Powder tours and spring corn are par for the course on Delano Peak, depending on the season, and you can ride it on either low-angle bowls on her west face, steep chutes to the south, or moderate runs into Poison Creek on a northwest aspect, all of which allow an easy return to the yurt.

GETTING THERE
From Main Street in Beaver, drive east on 200 North as this street becomes SR 153. Follow the road for 16 miles to the start of Big John Flat Road and park in a plowed pullout on the north side of the highway.

THE ROUTE
From the highway pullout, skin north up the closed Big John Flat Road for 4.6 miles as it gradually climbs toward Big John Flat and reach the Snorkeling Elk Yurt at 10,400 feet. The yurt is next to a Forest Service outhouse near the junction of the road and the Skyline National Recreation Trail.

From the yurt, continue up the road 0.3 mile to where you cross Griffith Creek at a wide drainage. Head east up the drainage beneath Delano's west ridge, which also has good skiing from the top in north-facing pine trees. This ridge can be a good ascent route but is rarely covered with enough snow to skin the entire way thanks to the Tushars' ripping winds.

Below the west ridge, traverse along the north side of Griffith Creek for about 1 mile until you're at 11,200 feet under the broad, low-angle southwest face of Delano Peak. Ascend the face by switchbacking northeast for just over a half mile and 1000 vertical feet all the way to the small, peaked summit marked by a mailbox on a pole.

If the Tushar Mountains have gotten recent, heavy snow and the ridges aren't too scoured, then the west ridge is a safer and more efficient ascent route. From the yurt,

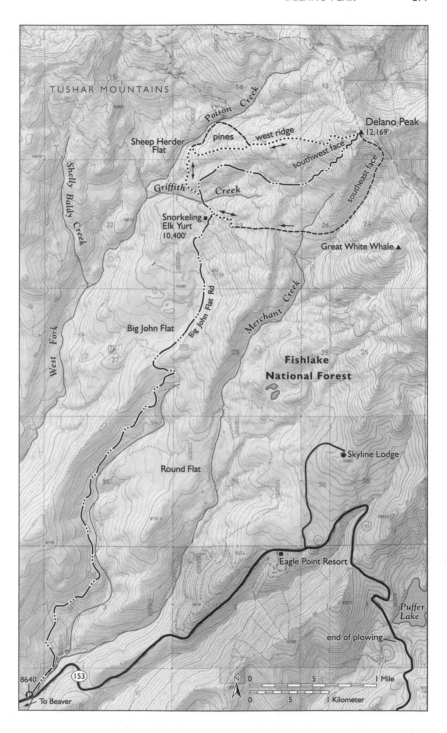

TUSHAR MOUNTAINS

Poison Creek

15   14   13

Delano Peak
▲ 12,169'

pines   west ridge   southwest face

Sheep Herder
Flat

Shelly Baldy Creek

Griffith   Creek

Snorkeling
Elk Yurt
10,400'

22

southeast face

23   24

Great White Whale ▲

West Fork

Big John Flat

Big John Flat Rd

Merchant Creek

27   26   25

Fishlake
National Forest

Skyline Lodge

Round Flat

34   35   36

Eagle Point Resort

Puffer
Lake

end of plowing

8640'
153

P
To Beaver

N   0   .5   1 Mile

0   .5   1 Kilometer

View of Delano Peak from the Great White Whale

go north on the road for 0.5 mile to the toe of the west ridge, just north of Griffith Creek. Make steep switchbacks to the ridgetop and then follow the wide ridge for 1.5 miles and upward of 1700 vertical feet to the top.

There are several wide-open descents from Delano's 12,169-foot summit on the south, west, and northwest aspects. Following your ascent route on the southwest face is a long and mellow cruise to the bottom of Griffith Creek. The west ridge is feasible if the snow is deep, and it offers easy turns if avalanche conditions are spooky. Off the lower elevations of the west ridge, good tree skiing is found on short, north-facing slopes that fall into Poison Creek. For a thrill, ski the southeast face. The upper elevations are littered with cliffs, but a few chutes offer passage to the bowl below. You can also stay skier's left off the summit where a narrow ramp circumvents the cliffs. At the bottom, traverse skier's right out of the Merchant Creek drainage back around to the Griffith Creek side.

At the bottom of upper Griffith Creek, you'll need to climb a short, 100-vertical-foot, pine-covered ridge west of the mountain to ski mellow, well-spaced trees to get back down to the yurt.

83 The Great White Whale

Start Points : Big John Flat Road, 8640 feet; Snorkeling Elk Yurt,
: 10,400 feet; Skyline Lodge at Eagle Point Resort,
: 10,500 feet
High Point : The Great White Whale summit, 11,526 feet
Trail Distance : 9 miles roundtrip to yurt from SR 153; 4 miles roundtrip to
: Great White Whale from Skyline Lodge; 3.5 miles roundtrip
: from yurt to Great White Whale
Trail Time : 4 hours one-way to yurt; 3 hours for tours from yurt;
: 4 hours for tours from Skyline Lodge
Skill Level : Intermediate/Advanced
Best Season : Winter
Map : USGS Shelly Baldy Peak, Delano Peak

The Great White Whale is a short mountain squatting between Mount Holly and Delano Peak. On official maps, it's labeled as Point 11526, but locals have dubbed it the Great White Whale, perhaps due to its broad, rounded shape. Getting there is a short tour from the Snorkeling Elk Yurt, but the approach is much longer from the trailhead at State Route 153 or Eagle Point Resort. Winter and spring are the best times to ski or snowboard here as the mountain is often covered in either powder or corn, respectively, but the Tushars' high winds can wipe the snow away, leaving rocky ground behind. As for descents to ski or snowboard, you can choose from the moderate west ridge or steeper shots on the north face.

GETTING THERE

From Main Street in Beaver, drive east on 200 North as this street becomes SR 153. Follow the road for 16 miles to the start of Big John Flat Road and park in a plowed pullout on the north side of the highway. For the Eagle Point Resort start, keep driving up the highway another 2.8 miles through the lower resort, and turn left on the road that leads to the upper lodge and ski runs. Park in the lot by the Skyline Lodge.

THE ROUTE

From the highway pullout, skin north up the closed Big John Flat Road for 4.6 miles as it gradually climbs toward Big John Flat and reach the Snorkeling Elk Yurt at 10,400 feet. The yurt is next to a Forest Service outhouse near the junction of the road and the Skyline National Recreation Trail. From here, leave the road and go southeast up and into the trees behind the yurt, generally along the route of the summer Skyline Trail. After 0.6 mile at around 10,800 feet, you'll top out on the ridge. Ski or slide on your skins down the very short east aspect to the bottom of the Merchant Creek drainage. Straight ahead you can see the wide west ridge of the Great White Whale between Delano Peak to the north and Mount Holly to the south.

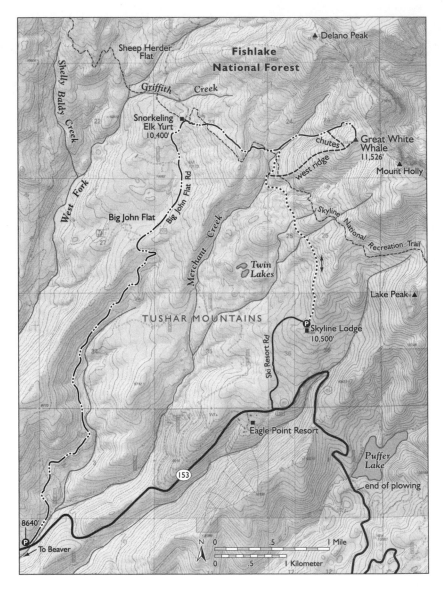

Skin up the drainage between the Great White Whale and Delano Peak for another 0.5 mile and go right where it forks at around 10,800 feet, which is pretty much where the tree line ends. Continue up toward an obvious saddle on the ridgeline, but then climb a low-angle ramp to your right at about 11,300 feet that shortcuts directly south to the large, flat summit of the Great White Whale.

From Skyline Lodge at Eagle Point Resort, begin at the upper lot and skin north into the woods. The route follows a series of small drainages that spill from Mount Holly,

Turning on the humpback of the Great White Whale

which looms on the northeast horizon. It's tedious travel as you go up and down several times for 1.5 miles before reaching Merchant Creek, then head north for another 0.25 mile to join the ascent route to the Great White Whale as described above.

The actual top is very indistinct, but there are a few good options for skiing or snowboarding down. Descend the west ridge (which can be rocky in low-snow years) or trust your edges on the steep chutes on the north face. Back at the bottom of Merchant Creek, you'll need to climb a short, 100-vertical-foot, pine-covered ridge west of the mountain to ski mellow, well-spaced trees to get back down to the yurt or follow your ascent route to return to Eagle Point.

84 Mount Holly

Start Points	Skyline Lodge, 10,500 feet; Puffer Lake, 9672 feet
High Point	Mount Holly summit, 11,985 feet
Trail Distance	3 miles from Skyline Lodge; 7 miles from Puffer Lake
Trail Time	2 hours from Skyline Lodge; 6 hours from Puffer Lake
Skill Level	Beginner/Intermediate
Best Season	Winter
Map	USGS Delano Peak

Mount Holly is a behemoth chunk of mountain that towers over Eagle Point Resort. It's easily the most prominent peak in the area, and her broad shoulders lure the eyes

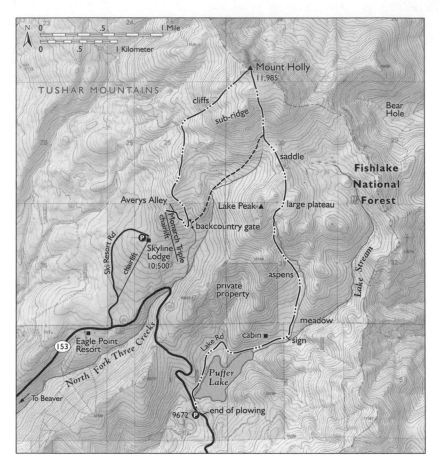

of backcountry skiers like a magnet. Luckily, the resort has backcountry gates that provide easy access to Holly's low-angle snow bowls. Plus, if you're looking for a long tour that avoids the use of ski lifts, an approach from Puffer Lake fits the bill.

GETTING THERE

From Main Street in Beaver, drive east on 200 North as this street becomes State Route 153. Follow the road for 18.8 miles to Eagle Point Resort. Just past the lower section of resort, turn left on the road that leads to the upper lodge and ski runs. Park in the lot by the Skyline Lodge, purchase a ticket, and ride the Monarch Triple chairlift. At the top, you'll find a backcountry gate.

To avoid the resort, park at Puffer Lake. Continue on the highway for another 2.5 miles as it goes through the resort and dips down to the end of plowing at Puffer Lake.

THE ROUTE

For a tour unassisted by chairlifts, follow the Lake Peak route from Puffer Lake. Skin north on the closed-for-the-winter Lake Road along the northwest shore of the lake.

In about 0.75 mile, you'll reach a fork in the road at the far end of the lake. Ignore the left path, which goes up a drainage into private property, and instead go right to the end of the lake's northeast arm. About 1 mile from the trailhead, you'll come to an old green cabin and soon after to a rotting NO TRESPASSING sign in a large meadow. While the vicinity around the lake is technically private property, the public is currently allowed access. From the old sign, turn north into an unnamed drainage toward Lake Peak. The meadow soon becomes a huge aspen grove. Continue following the drainage bottom through the forest along a small creek.

Around 1.25 miles from the old sign, you'll reach a large plateau east of Lake Peak. Continue north and switchback up Mount Holly's south side for an additional 1.25 miles to the top. Although it may seem low-angle here, this face can avalanche, so be aware. To return, you can ski the impressive southeast face for a long corn tour. Stay east of the saddle between Mount Holly and Lake Peak and descend into the Lake Stream drainage where you can follow the road back to Puffer Lake, or ski the fall line as it curves southwest into Three Creeks to Eagle Point Resort.

If you want to use the backcountry gate at Eagle Point, ride up the Monarch Triple chairlift and ski or snowboard down Teddys Twist to Averys Alley. Exit the backcountry gate found here.

From the access gate, skin up a small ridge toward Mount Holly for 0.75 mile. At the toe of a broad sub-ridge that leads to the summit, go northwest (left) and contour around the bottom of the ridge, and then head up a relatively low-angle snow ramp

View of Mount Holly's south side from the summit of City Creek Peak

to the right of a series of small cliffs. Skin up this ramp for an additional mile to the wind-blown summit.

The top of Mount Holly is a vast, flat meadow, which makes it difficult to find the highest point. This also means that it's not necessary to go that far unless you're set on bagging the peak, though it may be worth it just to stare down the gargantuan northeast cliffs. Otherwise, start skiing or snowboarding down the west face from wherever you choose on your ascent route. Another good, mellow run that gets you back to the resort boundary is on the south face. It ends in a valley between Holly and Lake peaks, where you can make your way down the North Fork Three Creeks drainage back to the resort.

85 Lake Peak

Start Points : Puffer Lake, 9672 feet; Skyline Lodge, 10,500 feet
High Point : Lake Peak summit, 11,310 feet
Trail Distance : 5 miles from Puffer Lake; 2.5 miles from Skyline Lodge
Trail Time : 4 hours from Puffer Lake; 2 hours from Skyline Lodge
Skill Level : Intermediate
Best Season : Winter
Map : USGS Delano Peak

Lake Peak, while not a small mountain, is tiny compared to her big sister, Mount Holly, which towers over everything to the north. But what Lake Peak loses in relative stature, she more than makes up for with excellent, accessible skiing from either Puffer Lake or the backcountry gates at Eagle Point Resort. Moderate ski shots fall from the peak on all aspects, but timing is critical as the Tushars' notoriously high winds can scour the upper peak, leaving bare talus behind. No matter what the conditions, you'll probably have to downclimb to the snow if you insist on bagging the summit before descending.

GETTING THERE

From Main Street in Beaver, drive east on 200 North as this street becomes State Route 153. Follow the road for 18.8 miles up Beaver Canyon to Eagle Point Resort. Continue on the highway for another 2.5 miles as it goes through the resort and dips down to the end of plowing at Puffer Lake.

THE ROUTE

From the end of the plowed road at Puffer Lake, travel north on the closed-for-the-winter Lake Road along the northwest shore of the lake. In about 0.75 mile, you'll reach a fork in the road at the far end of the lake. Ignore the left path, which goes up a drainage into private property, and instead continue right to the end of the lake's northeast arm. About 1 mile from the trailhead, you'll come to an old green cabin and soon after to a rotting NO TRESPASSING sign in a large meadow. While the vicinity around the lake is technically private property, the public is currently allowed access.

From the old sign, skin north into an unnamed drainage toward Lake Peak. The meadow soon becomes a huge aspen grove. Continue following the drainage bottom through the forest along a small creek. The trees become a bit thick in spots but eventually thin out as you gain elevation. Around 1 mile after leaving the road, you'll exit the trees at 10,500 feet below a series of large, red cliffs. Keep going up the gut of the valley for 0.25 mile until it flattens on an enormous plateau that stretches out east of Lake Peak. At 11,100 feet, go west up the remaining 200 vertical feet on the mountain's broad east face to the summit.

For another option, you can get to Lake Peak from the backcountry gates at Eagle Point Resort. Ride up the Monarch Triple chairlift and ski or snowboard down Teddys Twist to Averys Alley. Exit the backcountry gate found here. A short 1-mile skin up the North Fork Three Creeks drainage will get you to the summit. Simply follow the drainage north from the resort boundary, and then contour around to Lake Peak's north ridge and follow it to the top.

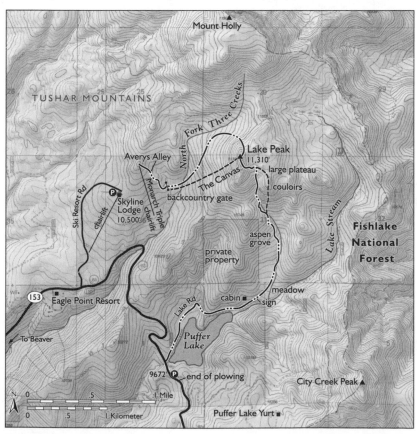

The couloirs south of Lake Peak add some spice to the tour.

For a return to Puffer Lake, ski or snowboard back the way you came on the east face and then south through the well-spaced aspen trees to the water's edge. For an adrenaline fix, check out the couloirs on a point southeast of Lake Peak. Ski east off the summit and traverse across the plateau to the obvious sub-peak. These chutes are narrow and south-facing, so conditions have to be prime before you can make turns here. The chutes spit you out at the aspen grove. To return to Eagle Point, ski the west face, known by locals as the Canvas.

86 City Creek Peak

Start Points : Puffer Lake, 9672 feet; Puffer Lake Yurt, 10,000 feet
High Point : City Creek Peak summit, 11,161 feet
Trail Distance : 3–5.5 miles roundtrip to yurt; 2 miles roundtrip from yurt to City Creek Peak
Trail Time : 1–2 hours one-way to yurt; 2 hours for tours from yurt
Skill Level : Intermediate
Best Season : Winter
Map : USGS Delano Peak

City Creek Peak is one of the most accessible mountains in the Tushars, even more so from the Puffer Lake Yurt, located below the mountain's slopes. The yurt, which is run by Tushar Mountain Tours, is ideally situated in an open meadow above low-angle glades that spill down to Puffer Lake, and is only a ten-minute skin from the access ridge for an ascent of City Creek Peak. Of course you don't have to use the yurt to ski good terrain that isn't far from the trailhead, but booking the yurt will maximize your turn-to-time ratio. As for the peak, you'll find everything from slide paths to the east to mellow bowls and glades to the west that you can lap from the yurt.

GETTING THERE

From Main Street in Beaver, drive east on 200 North as this street becomes State Route 153. Follow the highway for 18.8 miles up to Eagle Point Resort. Continue on the highway for another 2.5 miles as it goes through the resort and dips down to the end of plowing at Puffer Lake.

THE ROUTE

To get to the Puffer Lake Yurt, skin up the closed summer road for 2 miles on snowmobile tracks. Turn left onto the signed Cullen Creek Road. In 0.5 mile, veer right off the road and locate the yurt 0.25 mile farther in an open meadow. There will likely be snowmobile tracks all the way to the yurt, which sits at an elevation of 10,000 feet.

Alternatively, you can shortcut a large switchback to get there in less time. About 0.5 mile from the trailhead, go east and up into the spruce trees. The evergreens are thick, but it's less than a quarter mile of skinning before you rejoin the road. Continue up the road 0.25 mile, then head east, leaving the road when it makes a sharp curve south. In 0.2 mile, you intersect with Cullen Creek Road. Go north for 0.4 mile to

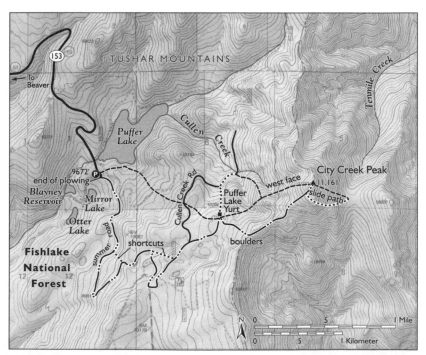

Atop the City Creek Peak summit

the yurt, veering right off the road as described above. Until you're familiar with the area, it might be best just to stay on the road.

There is plenty of good skiing right below the yurt, mostly of the low-angle, gladed variety. From the yurt, ski northwest through the woods back down to Puffer Lake, and then head back up the way you came.

To ski City Creek Peak from the yurt, skin east for 0.25 mile to the top of a steep face marked by large boulder fields. Just north of these boulder fields, you can switchback up through the trees to gain the mountain's south ridge at 10,630 feet. Follow the ridge northeast for just under 0.75 mile as it becomes a wide face near the 11,161-foot summit. High winds tend to scour the exposed peak, so you may have to take your skis off for the remaining few hundred vertical feet to the top.

Ski descents are found on every aspect of City Creek Peak, including the east-facing avalanche path. Ski down for 700 vertical feet to the bottom of a narrow gully that becomes Tenmile Creek, and re-ascend the peak by skinning up left of the slide path on an indistinct shoulder punctuated by scattered trees. This slide path ends in a bad terrain trap, so only ski or snowboard it when the snowpack is stable.

To return to the yurt, it's best to either descend the south face the way you came (if the aspect isn't wind scoured) or go big on the wide, 1000-vertical-foot, gladed swath of the peak's money shot—the west face. This is a fun run that starts with wide-open turns and ends in playful sub-ridges that spit you out very close to the yurt on Cullen Creek Road where it crosses the creek. From here, skin west on the road for 0.5 mile, and then turn south and leave the road by heading up the hillside through the trees for 0.3 mile to the yurt.

Opposite: *Skiing one of many slide paths that spill down Mount Ellen's North Summit*

HENRY MOUNTAINS

THE HENRY MOUNTAINS ARE THE MOST REMOTE and hard to reach mountain range that you will find in this book. Need proof? The Henrys were the very last mountain range to be added to the map of the continental United States in 1872. Previous to that, they were known as the "Unknown Mountains." The tiny burg of Hanksville, population 215, is the only town within 50 miles. The only access is on dirt roads, which are impassable in winter. Some years they remain blocked by snowdrifts until July. When the snow does melt, or if it rains, the roads become a muddy morass, slick as snot. Timing is everything if you want to ski or snowboard the Henrys. The key is to arrive in spring when the roads are snow free and dry, but there is still enough snow in the upper elevations for backcountry skiing. Keep checking the weather, contact the BLM office in Hanksville, and plan way ahead so you can pull the trigger when the stars align.

If you make it to the Henry Mountains with skis in tow, you'll be treated to some of the most adventurous ski touring in Utah. From below, it is surreal to drive through desolate desert to ski. From a distance, the peaks appear to float above the vastness— white caps in a sea of brown and red. At elevation, you may have to hike on dirt until you reach snow line. After skinning to the top, you will carve turns in spring corn above stunning geologic views of the San Rafael Swell, Capitol Reef and Canyonlands national parks, and the Waterpocket Fold—"ripping the peak" on an island in the sky. It's an alien, unforgettable experience.

Skiable peaks in the Henry Mountains are northwest of State Route 276, where trucks towing boats are en route to Bullfrog Marina and Lake Powell. Mount Hillers, Mount Pennell, and Mount Ellen all see enough snowfall for skiing, but Ellen is the largest, highest, and easiest to get to; therefore she's the only mountain featured here. Ellen is divided into two summits—north and south. Bull Creek Pass splits the mountain in half. Each side requires different approach routes, as the pass is snowbound into the summer. While spring allows access by car, winter touring is possible if you drive in as far as you can, and then backpack the rest of the way and camp.

NOTES

Land Management. The Henry Mountains are located entirely on BLM land. The Henry Mountains Field Station, your best bet for information on current conditions and road accessibility, is located in Hanksville. Contact information is found in Resources.

Road Conditions. As stated above, the road can be impassable during weather events. Snow and rain create mud that is impossible to drive on. Before making the trip, be sure the roads are dry, and always have a full tank of gas. This area is extremely remote and if you get into trouble, help is far away.

Weather. The Henry Mountains are a desert range, so they get less snow than other peaks in Utah. The window of skiing and snowboarding opportunity is short. Also, the Utah Avalanche Center does not provide an avalanche advisory here. You are on your own to assess the snowpack and make informed decisions before skiing into avalanche terrain. Check the National Weather Service for current conditions. See the Resources page for web addresses and phone numbers.

The Henry Mountains are an "Island in the Sky" in the southern Utah desert.

87 Mount Ellen North Summit Ridge

Start Point : Dandelion Flat, 8000 feet
High Point : Mount Ellen North Summit, 11,522 feet
Trail Distance : 7 miles
Trail Time : 6 hours
Skill Level : Advanced
Best Season : Spring
Map : USGS Mount Ellen

The North Summit Ridge of Mount Ellen has some of the most accessible ski touring in the Henry Mountains, but that doesn't mean it's easy to get to. Roads are inaccessible when wet or snow covered; rocky, steep terrain abounds; and many miles must be traveled before you ever start skiing or snowboarding. The highest point in the Henry Mountains is located here on the North Summit Ridge yet is unnamed on topographic maps. Meanwhile, a smaller yet more prominent point to the north is graced with the moniker Mount Ellen Peak. It seems unfair, but if you want to make turns off the highest point in the Henrys, then Mount Ellen's North Summit at an elevation of 11,522 feet is your goal. The skiing and snowboarding is better here anyway, as long slide paths spill down from the ridge all the way to Log Flat for up to 2500 vertical feet. These avalanche paths hold snow through late spring, so you can ski thin ribbons of corn until summer.

GETTING THERE

In Hanksville, go to the intersection of State Route 24 and 100 East. Drive south on 100 East. The road quickly exits town and becomes Sawmill Basin Road. Stay on the well-maintained dirt road, following signs for Lonesome Beaver Campground. It can be confusing because some signs call Sawmill Basin Road "Lonesome Beaver Road." Just continue on the main route as it climbs up toward the Henry Mountains. You'll pass Bull Mountain rising to the east as you switchback into the canyon. The road can get rough here with snowdrifts and creek crossings, so four-wheel-drive may be needed.

In about 21 miles, you'll reach a large parking and picnic area at Dandelion Flat, just below the Lonesome Beaver Campground. If you are able to reach it, this is the best place to leave your car for day tours. If snow still covers the road, you'll have to park as far as your vehicle can make it and hike the remainder of the road.

THE ROUTE

From Dandelion Flat, go up the road about a quarter mile while keeping an eye out for East Pass Road, an old, unmarked jeep trail on your right that's been abandoned and overgrown and is difficult to spot. If you reach the campground, you've gone too far. When you've located the jeep road, follow it west as it crosses Bull Creek and then switchbacks up into a ponderosa forest.

In 0.5 mile from the start of the road, you'll reach Log Flat at 8600 feet. A wildfire consumed many of the trees here, making travel difficult as you have to navigate over

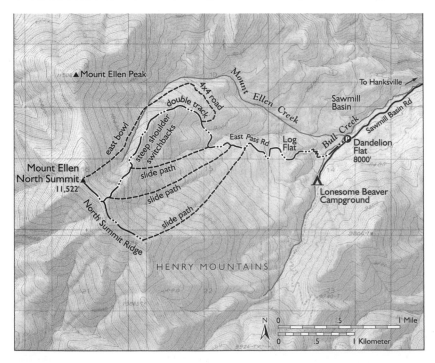

Spring tours may require hiking on bare ground on Mount Ellen's North Summit.

fallen, charred logs. At this point, you can see all the skiable terrain above you as it spills from the north ridge. During safe avalanche conditions, you can climb directly up these slide paths and open bowls to gain the ridge. For a safer route, continue past the slide paths to a ridge about 1.75 miles from the start. If it isn't snow covered, a faint double track leaves the 4x4 road here and goes left up the mountainside at 9230 feet (the main road goes down into the Mount Ellen Creek drainage).

Go left on the double track, climb 0.25 mile, and get off the double track at around 9575 feet. From here, a steep shoulder covered in piñon pines provides an efficient route directly to the North Summit Ridge. Go south and switchback up the shoulder where the view soon opens up and you can see the vast Mount Ellen massif. The route steepens as you gain elevation, so you may need to boot pack the remainder of the climb. Once you gain the North Summit Ridge at around 11,450 feet, it's a short quarter-mile walk northwest along the divide to Mount Ellen's North Summit, the highest peak in the Henry Mountains.

To descend, an east-facing bowl can be skied just north of the summit into the Mount Ellen Creek drainage down to East Pass Road, where you can follow the 4x4 road southeast to rejoin your ascent route. But the best ski terrain is along the south end of the summit ridge, so once you bag the high point, traverse back south and take your pick among the several long, northeast-facing slide paths. In good snow years, or if you get there early enough, you can ski and board almost 3000 vertical feet all the way down to Log Flat and East Pass Road. To return to your car, simply follow the jeep trail back to Dandelion Flat.

88 Mount Ellen South Summit Ridge

Start Point : McMillan Spring Campground, 8389 feet
High Point : Mount Ellen South Summit, 11,419 feet
Trail Distance : 9 miles
Trail Time : 7 hours
Skill Level : Advanced
Best Season : Spring
Map : USGS Mount Ellen

Skiing high above the red rocks of Capitol Reef is a surreal experience only found in the Henry Mountains.

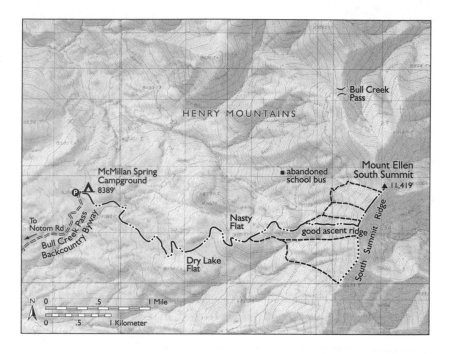

Mount Ellen's South Summit is really a long ridge with three small peaks that extends south of Bull Creek Pass. In the snowy months it can only be approached from the west, which requires long and remote driving on desert dirt roads. If you time it right and are able to park near the McMillan Spring Campground, you'll find efficient access to ski- and snowboard-friendly lines that stack up all along the west face. The terrain here is more open and exposed than the east-facing canyon and tree shots of the North Summit and (depending on how far you're able to drive) can be a playground for short day tours. The trip alone is worth making for turns above expansive views of Utah's southern desert and Capitol Reef National Park.

GETTING THERE

From Hanksville, drive 28 miles west on State Route 24 to Notom Road, just before the entrance to Capitol Reef National Park. Go south on Notom Road for 13.5 miles to Sandy Ranch Junction. Turn left (east) onto Bull Creek Pass Backcountry Byway at the well-marked BLM sign that shows the way to McMillan Spring Campground. From this intersection, the campground is 19 miles east on a well-maintained dirt road, but right away you'll have to ford Sandy Creek, so a high-clearance, four-wheel-drive vehicle may be needed. There are many forks in the road, but the main route is obvious, and BLM signs point the way at major intersections. In spring, you may be able to drive past the campground and park at Dry Lake Flat or Nasty Flat at the base of the South Summit.

THE ROUTE

From McMillan Spring Campground, follow the road as it winds east toward the South Summit. After 2.7 miles of generally flat skinning, you'll reach Nasty Flat at 9581 feet. It's recognizable by the stand of ghostly dead trees near the road. This is a good place to make camp if you packed in overnight gear for a multiday trip in the area.

There is a fork in the road at Nasty Flat. The right fork heads southeast and can be used to access the skiable terrain on the south end of the ridge. Taking the left fork will get you to Bull Creek Pass. To quickly gain the South Summit, go left at the fork and skin for about a quarter mile to the base of a steep sub-ridge. In the spring, wind and sun have likely done their job on the south-facing side of this ridge, so it's a good but strenuous hike on exposed dirt and rock. Strap skis or splitboards to packs and climb the ridge for 1300 feet to the South Summit Ridge of Mount Ellen. Once there, it's a short half-mile traverse northeast on the ridge to the summit proper at 11,419 feet.

The ski and snowboard terrain along the South Summit Ridge is mind blowing. West-facing avalanche chutes and open bowls line up in tidy rows just waiting for you to pick them off one by one. No matter your descent choice, you'll have a 1000-plus-foot run down to the road, where you can easily get back to your ascent ridge for another lap.

For an odd distraction, be sure to check out the abandoned Wayne County school bus, located below the South Summit's west face at 9500 feet. It seems to have been converted into someone's motor home but was left there years ago.

Opposite: *Mount Mellenthin dominates the horizon on a tour to Haystack, La Sal Mountains.*

LA SAL MOUNTAINS

MOAB IS UNDOUBTEDLY the outdoor recreation capital of Utah. Mountain biking, rock climbing, river rafting, four-wheeling, and backpacking, along with two national parks, draw visitors from around the world. You can add backcountry skiing to that list, though most people don't even consider skiing in Moab. Yet the La Sal Mountains, which provide a snowcapped backdrop to Utah's most iconic desert landscapes, hold some of the best ski terrain anywhere.

The La Sals are the second-highest mountain range in the state, with summits rising well above 12,000 feet. The range is divided into three sections—the north, central, and south groups, which are divided by the two mountain passes, Geyser Pass and La Sal Pass. This chapter describes routes in all three groups, but peaks in the far north of the range, such as Manns Peak and Mount Waas, are not included as they are remote enough to be less feasible for day tours (unless you have a snowmobile). Geyser Pass is the primary trailhead for ski touring, and the road is plowed all the way to the parking area. Several big peaks such as Mellenthin and Tukuhnikivatz are mountaineering destinations best ascended in the spring when snowpack is stable and you can make use of crampons and ice axes. For winter tours, the evergreens off the Laurel Highway and in the Corkscrew Glades have protected powder runs.

The south group consists of South Mountain and the South Mountain Glades. This area is a mecca of deep powder skiing but requires a long approach on skins when La Sal Pass Road is snow covered. Two backcountry huts operated by Tag-A-Long Expeditions—the Tomasaki Hut in the north and the Beaver Lake Hut in the south—used to be excellent base camps for exploring remote areas of the range but have sadly been out of service for the last few years. Check back for information about possible reopenings in the future.

NOTES

Land Management. Tours in the La Sal Mountains are located in Manti–La Sal National Forest. Contact the Moab Ranger District for more information. Web address and phone number are found in Resources.

Road Conditions. Geyser Pass Road is regularly plowed, but it can take road crews some time to clear it after a big storm. Even when plowed, however, a 4x4 vehicle or chains is strongly recommended. Check the Utah Avalanche Center Moab advisory or the Forest Service's Moab field office for current road conditions.

Weather. The La Sal Mountains have a continental snowpack, which more closely resembles conditions in Colorado than Utah. This means avalanche danger is notoriously bad in the winter months, with persistent weak layers and wind slabs on upper faces being a primary concern. The upper peaks are often wind scoured to bare rock. Spring is peak season here, when corn skiing is second to none. An epic weekend consists of backcountry skiing the La Sals one day and mountain biking or rock climbing in Moab the next. Check the Utah Avalanche Center's Moab advisory and the National Weather Service for current conditions. See Resources for web addresses and phone numbers.

View of the Corkscrew Glades from Geyser Pass Road

89 Corkscrew Glades

Start Point	Trans–La Sal trailhead, 8990 feet
High Point	Point 10974, 10,974 feet
Trail Distance	5 miles
Trail Time	4 hours
Skill Level	Intermediate
Best Season	Winter
Map	USGS La Sal Junction

The Corkscrew Glades are a northwest-facing series of runs that dot a thick pine forest nestled below Tuk No and the massive Mount Tukuhnikivatz. From a distance, the glades look like a cluster of steep, open meadows that thread down like commas, resembling a spiraling corkscrew. The riding tends to be a good bet for soft winter snow that's protected by the trees, and the approach is a moderate skin on flat, view-laden expanses followed by steep switchbacks to Point 10974. The Corkscrew Glades can be easily combined with Noriegas Peak (Tour 90) for a double-mountain day.

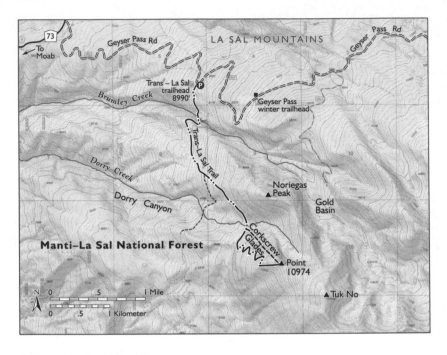

GETTING THERE

From Moab, drive south on US Highway 191 for 7.8 miles to a signed turnoff for Kens Lake–La Sal Loop Road (County Road 73) on the left. In half a mile, turn right and follow the road for 11.5 miles to the intersection with Geyser Pass Road. Turn right onto the plowed dirt road and follow it for another 2 miles to the Trans–La Sal trailhead, located at a large switchback.

THE ROUTE

From the signed trailhead, go straight up on the Trans–La Sal Trail and contour around the hillside, and then descend to Brumley Creek. Cross the creek and skin up the other side. Continue on the trail as it heads southeast. After about 1 mile from the trailhead, get off the summer trail when it goes south into the open meadows. Stay left (east) and along the edge of an aspen grove. Keep going south around the flanks of Noriegas Peak, aiming for the Corkscrew Glades that can be seen at the head of Dorry Canyon.

Around 0.75 mile after leaving the summer trail, you'll cross Dorry Creek, which will likely be under the snow. From here, head straight up into the evergreen trees on a steep skin track with multiple switchbacks as it crosses the glades. Another mile and 1200 vertical feet later, you'll reach the wide, flat top of Point 10974. While it's a short walk to the true summit, there's little reason to go there as the skiing begins at the edge of the flat. Simply ski or ride back down the way you came, or choose one of the many neighboring glades and open hallways for a long descent back to Dorry Creek.

90 Noriegas Peak

Start Point : Trans–La Sal trailhead, 8990 feet
High Point : Noriegas Peak summit, 10,597 feet
Trail Distance : 3 miles
Trail Time : 3 hours
Skill Level : Intermediate
Best Season : Winter
Map : USGS La Sal Junction

Of all the summits in the La Sal Mountains, Noriegas Peak is probably the easiest to get to. A short approach with minimal avalanche exposure makes it an ideal spot for a quick midwinter tour. Low-angle glade skiing is what's on the menu, though you can get crazy on the mountain's extremely avalanche-prone north face. Also, be prepared for some major bushwhacking through pucker brush in the lower elevations. This tour is easy to link with the Corkscrew Glades (Tour 89) for an all-day adventure.

GETTING THERE

From Moab, drive south on US Highway 191 for 7.8 miles to a signed turnoff for Kens Lake–La Sal Loop Road (County Road 73) on the left. In half a mile, turn right and follow the road for 11.5 miles to the intersection with Geyser Pass Road. Turn right onto the plowed dirt road and follow it for another 2 miles to the Trans–La Sal trailhead, located at a large switchback.

Skiing down the low-angle summit of Noriegas Peak

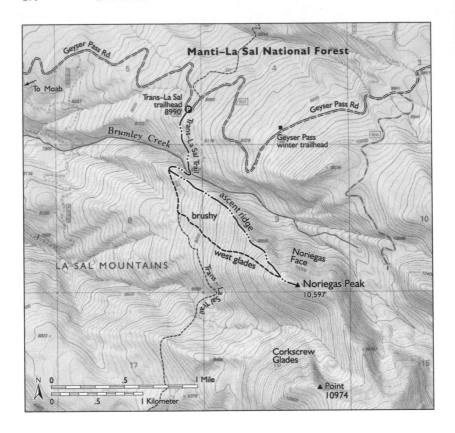

THE ROUTE

From the signed trailhead, go straight up on the Trans–La Sal Trail as it curves around the hillside, and then descend to Brumley Creek. Cross the creek and skin up the other side. At the first switchback out of the creek, about 0.6 mile from the trailhead, turn southeast (left) and head straight up the ridge into the aspens. The trees and brush can become thick and difficult to navigate, and the low angle makes it hard to know if you're still on the ridge, but the foliage eventually thins as the slope angle steepens while you gain elevation.

The best rule of thumb is to keep going southeast, and you'll make it to the 10,597-foot summit after a little over 1.25 miles of skinning from the creek.

The top of Noriegas Peak is a wide, flat area, an ideal perch to soak in the scenery. When you're ready to ski or snowboard down, a safer descent is the west glades, skier's left of your ascent route. Again, the foliage is thick in places, so try to link open meadows together or risk more bushwhacking.

To return, locate the Trans–La Sal Trail and follow it north back to Brumley Creek and the trailhead. You may also continue south on the trail to snag a run on the Corkscrew Glades if time allows.

On the north side of Noriegas Peak is a wide-open bowl that falls back into Brumley Creek. This area is called Noriegas Face, but it's not recommended at all, despite how tasty it may look. This rock-filled avalanche factory is notorious for being the site of massive slides. Like former Panamanian dictator Manuel Noriega, the face is pockmarked and terrifying. Avoid at all costs.

91 Laurel Highway

Start Point : Geyser Pass winter trailhead, 9600 feet
High Point : Mount Laurel summit, 12,271 feet
Trail Distance : 6.5 miles
Trail Time : 4 hours
Skill Level : Intermediate
Best Season : Winter/Spring
Map : USGS Mount Tukuhnikivatz

Laurel Highway is the name locals give to Laurel Ridge, and it's a fitting term as a well-established skin track leads touring parties to some of the best moderate ski terrain in the La Sal Mountains. Laurel Highway is the most popular route that leaves the Geyser Pass winter trailhead, accessing quality tree skiing in the North Woods and Julies Glade, as well as open bowls off Pre-Laurel Peak. You can even use the ridge for mountaineering excursions on Mount Laurel and Mount Mellenthin. Ski and snowboard lines end up in Gold Basin, where flat-tracking on a groomed road gets you back to your car.

Laurel Highway is one of the most popular ascent routes in the La Sal Mountains.

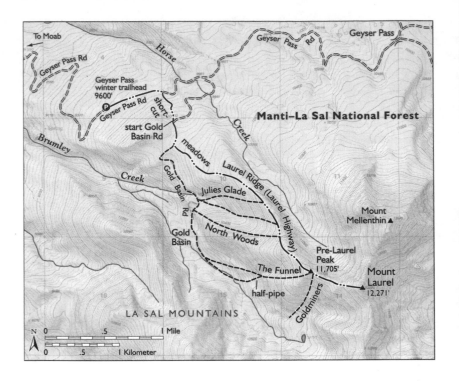

GETTING THERE

From Moab, drive south on US Highway 191 for 7.8 miles to a signed turnoff for Ken's Lake–La Sal Loop Road on the left. In half a mile, turn right and follow the road for 11.5 miles to the intersection with Geyser Pass Road. Turn right onto the plowed dirt road and follow it for another 4.6 miles to the Geyser Pass winter trailhead. Parking is in the large, plowed lot with bathrooms and informational signs. The route starts on the northeast side of the lot.

THE ROUTE

Follow the groomed Geyser Pass Road northeast for about a half mile, and then turn right and head up a narrow swath in the evergreens. This is a good shortcut that saves over a mile of travel and is easy to spot due to the likelihood of a skin track already in place. At the top of the shortcut at 10,060 feet, go right on Gold Basin Road and follow it for less than a quarter mile while keeping an eye out for a skin track on your left that heads into the trees.

Follow the skin track as it contours southeast above the road, where it goes in and out of open meadows and the aspen-evergreen forest that covers Laurel Ridge. It's a splendid ascent as views of Mount Tukuhnikivatz and Tuk No to the south are plentiful and spectacular along the way.

After the last large meadow, 1.75 miles from the trailhead at about 10,700 feet, the trees get thicker and the route now follows the top of the ridge, though it isn't long before you get above tree line on a broad, rounded shoulder at 11,300 feet. This open shoulder is the start of good ski and snowboard runs that fall northwest into the North Woods and Julies Glade. This is a good place to descend if avalanche danger is a concern, as the trees provide a more anchored snowpack and hold powder against the constant La Sal Mountain wind. You can spend the day doing yo-yo laps here or continue up Laurel Ridge.

To reach Pre-Laurel Peak, continue following the undulating terrain another mile to the summit at 11,705 feet, which is marked by a small weather station. This is the end point for most tours, though you can stay on the ridge to climb Mount Laurel. It takes another 0.5 mile and 566 feet to get there, and the route follows obvious switchbacks on the shale-covered southwest face. It's a worthy summit, but wind usually scours snow to the rock, which means good skiing (and easy climbing) is rare.

To ski or snowboard from the top of Pre-Laurel Peak, you have two good options. First, make turns down a run called Goldminers, an open bowl located southeast of the summit that ends in upper Gold Basin. The second, and my favorite, is the Funnel, a wide, west-facing shot that funnels into a natural half-pipe as it loses elevation. It's a super fun line that drops 1600 feet to the bottom of Gold Basin. Getting back to the trailhead requires skinning or skate-skiing back along the flat Gold Basin Road to the Geyser Pass winter trailhead.

92 Mount Tukuhnikivatz

Start Point : Geyser Pass winter trailhead, 9600 feet
High Point : Mount Tukuhnikivatz summit, 12,482 feet
Trail Distance : 8 miles
Trail Time : 6 hours
Skill Level : Advanced/Expert
Best Season : Spring
Map : USGS Mount Tukuhnikivatz

No skier has ever visited Moab for mountain biking or rock climbing and looked to the horizon at the snow-covered La Sal Mountains without thinking that they'd like to ski there someday. And of all the peaks visible from Moab's red rock paradise, Mount Tukuhnikivatz is the pyramid that stands out the most, with a vertical relief that will make any skier or snowboarder salivate. Locals just say "Mount Tuk" for short, but the full, hard-to-pronounce name—*Tu-kuh-ni-ki-vatz*—is a Native American word that roughly means "where the sun sets last." As for the tour, climbing and sliding down Mount Tuk is a springtime tradition when stable corn snow allows safe travel on this prize of a desert peak.

Mount Tukuhnikivatz is the premier ski-mountaineering summit in the La Sals.

GETTING THERE

From Moab, drive south on US Highway 191 for 7.8 miles to a signed turnoff for Kens Lake–La Sal Loop Road on the left. In half a mile, turn right and follow the road for 11.5 miles to the intersection with Geyser Pass Road. Turn right onto the plowed dirt road and follow it for another 4.6 miles to the Geyser Pass winter trailhead. Parking is in the large, plowed lot with bathrooms and informational signs. The route starts on the northeast side of the lot.

THE ROUTE

Follow the groomed Geyser Pass Road northeast for about a half mile, and then turn right and head up a narrow swath in the evergreens. This is a good shortcut that saves over a mile of travel and is easy to spot due to the likelihood of a skin track already in place. At the top of the shortcut at 10,060 feet, go right on Gold Basin Road and follow it into Gold Basin.

From the top of the shortcut, it's another 2 miles of skinning on Gold Basin Road to the base of Mount Tukuhnikivatz. Along the way, you'll pass through sparsely wooded aspen and evergreen forests below the massive ski terrain of Tuk No, the smaller satellite peak that's just north of Mount Tuk. To ski Tuk No, leave the bottom of the canyon at road's end and ascend south up Tuk No's north ridge. The first 700 vertical feet through the trees is very steep, so booting up is the most feasible technique. At around 10,900 feet, the ridge angle mellows considerably. Continue climbing an additional 0.5 mile and 1150 vertical feet to the summit. As with all ridges in the La Sals, much of it will likely be wind scoured down to the rock.

Tuk No has a few descent options, and all are very steep. The north face is a massive avalanche path called Exxons Folly, because the oil giant drilled at the base of the mountain. But the phrase "avalanche path" should set off warning bells—this is only safe in the most bomber of snowpacks. The northeast side is a long couloir that splits

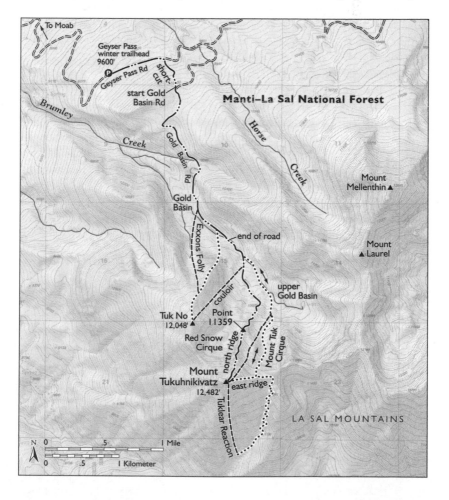

the upper half of the mountain before widening into the lower face. It's a long, uninterrupted run that many consider to be among the most classic descents in the La Sals.

For Mount Tukuhnikivatz, continue skinning beyond the end of Gold Basin Road and follow the creek bed southeast. At 10,600 feet, you'll reach the toe of Mount Tuk's intimidating north ridge, which splits Mount Tuk Cirque to the east and Red Snow Cirque to the west. This is the primary mountaineering route to gain the summit. Skin or boot pack nearly 550 feet up the steep slope from the bottom of the ridge to the top of Point 11359, a broad hump distinguished by a small stand of straggly trees. This is a good spot for a snack break and to do an avalanche stability assessment. The rest of the ridge is pretty straightforward to navigate as it's an obvious boot pack or scramble up loose, snow-covered rocks for 1123 vertical feet to the Tukuhnikivatz summit.

In the spring when avalanches are of less concern, skinning up Mount Tuk's northeast face in Mount Tuk Cirque is a faster and easier option. To get there, bypass the north ridge and continue into the flats of upper Gold Basin at 10,600 feet. Head south directly toward the mountain and switchback up the broad bowl to the base of some vertical rock ribs. Strap skis or boards to packs and hike the remainder to Tukuhnikivatz's east ridge at around 12,000 feet. To bag the summit, traverse the ridge west for 0.25 mile and enjoy dizzying views of the red desert far below as you boot pack up the summit pyramid until there is nothing left to climb.

To descend, you can pretty much ski or snowboard off the summit in any direction, but the easiest way to return to your vehicle on a sweet run is to make turns down the ascent route on Tuk's northeast face, Mount Tuk Cirque, back into upper Gold Basin and retrace your skin track to the car. Red Snow Cirque, between Tuk and Tuk No, is gnarly stuff: 50-degree slopes littered with cliffs. Many people ascend directly up the face from the bottom of Gold Basin to the cliffs and ski down from there.

Another classic spring descent is Tuk's southeast face, an epic run that locals call "Tuklear Reaction." This legendary 2500-foot slope holds perfect, smooth corn after basking in the morning sun. You can ride down as far as you want and then skin back up to the saddle on Tuk's east ridge, where you can descend Mount Tuk Cirque and Gold Basin all the way back to the car.

93 Mount Mellenthin

Start Point : Geyser Pass winter trailhead, 9600 feet
High Point : Mount Mellenthin summit, 12,645 feet
Trail Distance : 8 miles
Trail Time : 6 hours
Skill Level : Advanced/Expert
Best Season : Spring
Maps : USGS Mount Tukuhnikivatz, Mount Peale

Mount Mellenthin is the second-highest peak in the La Sal Mountains and is also among the most popular to ski because of relatively easy access. Still, getting to the

The approach to Mount Mellenthin from the north ridge

summit along the north ridge and then skiing down chutes and bowls on her classic north face is no cake walk. The ascent ridge is steep and covered in loose talus, and the ski down requires careful navigation of summit cliffs and rock outcroppings. But if you arrive when there is plenty of snow, the winds are light, and the blue sky is filled with the brilliant desert sun, then Mellenthin will treat you to the La Sals' fantastic views and al dente spring corn skiing that are always worth the effort to get there.

GETTING THERE

From Moab, drive south on US Highway 191 for 7.8 miles to a signed turnoff for Kens Lake–La Sal Loop Road on the left. In half a mile, turn right and follow the road for 11.5 miles to the intersection with Geyser Pass Road. Turn right onto the plowed dirt road and follow it for another 4.6 miles to the Geyser Pass winter trailhead. Parking is in the large, plowed lot with bathrooms and informational signs. The route starts on the northeast side of the lot.

THE ROUTE

Follow the groomed Geyser Pass Road northeast for 1 mile. At the intersection with Gold Basin Road, stay left and continue on Geyser Pass Road as it undulates into the evergreen trees. In 1.5 miles from the trailhead, you'll begin to see Mount Mellenthin through the trees, looming south of the road. Stay on the road as it slowly descends into a drainage and wraps around to the south.

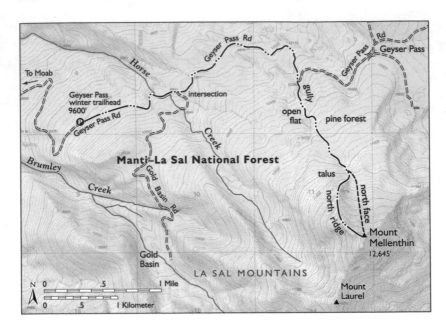

At 2.5 miles from the trailhead, leave the road at the bottom of the drainage where the road makes a very sharp switchback. Skin south up the gully toward Mount Mellenthin. You'll soon cross a flat, open area that is popular with snowmobilers. Follow the tracks to the end of the open field, and stay left (east) before you enter a bowl. Climb a short hill into the evergreen forest at 10,600 feet, and keep going south on relatively flat terrain for 0.5 mile until you exit the trees at the base of Mellenthin's north ridge.

The bottom of the north ridge is very steep, so you'll have to kick steps up the snow and talus. It's often wind scoured and difficult to find purchase. At 11,700 feet, the ridge finally levels and you can put your skis or splitboard back on and skin easily for about a quarter mile until the terrain gets steep once more. Another 200-vertical-foot hike on talus and then a short but stunning walk on the knife-edge summit ridge completes the climb to the top.

The best skiing and snowboarding is down Mellenthin's north face. A series of steep chutes that converge in an open bowl are guarded by cliffs and rocks just below the summit ridge. If snow coverage is good, you can find an alley through rock outcroppings to pick through with your skis on. Otherwise, carefully downclimb to the snow until the coast is clear for a long, classic La Sal descent. But tread lightly because this is serious avalanche terrain. If you have any concern about the snowpack, retrace your ascent route on the north ridge.

To return, follow your ascent track through the evergreens back to Geyser Pass Road. Note that the rolling terrain on the way back may be difficult for snowboarders to get through without skinning.

94 Haystack Mountain

Start Point : Geyser Pass winter trailhead, 9600 feet
High Point : Haystack Mountain summit, 11,641 feet
Trail Distance : 7 miles
Trail Time : 6 hours
Skill Level : Intermediate/Advanced
Best Season : Spring
Maps : USGS Mount Tukuhnikivatz, Mount Peale, Mount Waas

Haystack Mountain is one of the easiest major peaks in the La Sal Mountains to summit and then ski or snowboard. This lower-elevation peak has mellow ascent slopes and straightforward access, which makes it a good tour for intermediate backcountry skiers and splitboarders looking to bag a desert summit without getting all gnarly. Spring is an ideal time for a tour on Haystack, as south- and east-facing aspects bathe in corn-creating sunlight, and the north bowl stays cold, keeping snow well into late spring. The ascent route does cross into major avalanche terrain, so a stable snowpack is key to a successful tour. You may also need an ice ax and crampons on spring mornings when the snow is hard, especially on one particularly steep section below the summit ridge.

Skiing down Haystack's north bowl with Moab's red rock desert sprawling to the horizon is an unforgettable experience.

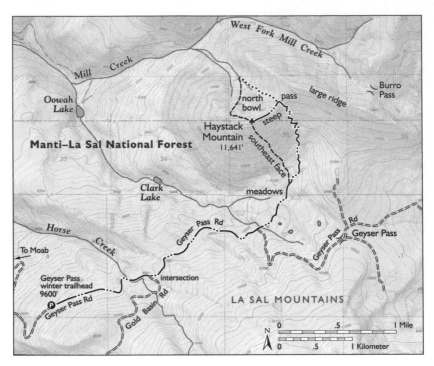

GETTING THERE

From Moab, drive south on US Highway 191 for 7.8 miles to a signed turnoff for Kens Lake–La Sal Loop Road on the left. In half a mile, turn right and follow the road for 11.5 miles to the intersection with Geyser Pass Road. Turn right onto the plowed dirt road and follow it for another 4.6 miles to the Geyser Pass winter trailhead. Parking is in the large, plowed lot with bathrooms and informational signs. The route starts on the northeast side of the lot.

THE ROUTE

Follow the groomed Geyser Pass Road northeast for 1 mile. At the intersection with Gold Basin Road, stay left and continue on Geyser Pass Road as it undulates into the evergreen trees. Just over 2 miles from the trailhead, leave the road where it curves sharply south. To the north, you'll see large meadows at the foot of Haystack Mountain. Descend a short, treed slope down to the meadows, and skin north along the east side of the clearing, keeping well away from the avalanche terrain on Haystack's south face.

The meadows gradually ascend to the foot of the mountain over a half mile and begin to be more aggressively steep at around 10,500 feet. Keep skinning around Haystack's southeast face and go up between the mountain and a large ridge that separates Haystack from Burro Pass. It's another 0.6 mile and 800 vertical feet to a small pass, which tops out at around 11,300 feet.

From this saddle, go directly up Haystack's east flank. The slope is steep, so it's usually easier to boot pack up the 200 vertical feet to the summit ridge. If the snow is hard, you may need crampons and an ice ax or Whippet. Once there, it's an easy, low-angle walk to the flat, indistinct summit at 11,641 feet. Drink in the view, because it's most impressive.

There are two main ski or snowboard descents that you can do, depending on snow and avalanche conditions. The biggest line with an edge-of-the-world view of Moab's red rock desert belongs to the massive north bowl. This steep line falls for more than 1000 vertical feet and is divine during stable powder days, but the snow can be hard Styrofoam on spring mornings. At the bottom, returning to the pass is easy. Simply skin southeast up through the evergreens by making steep switchbacks for just under a half mile and 700 vertical feet to the pass.

In early spring, when there's still a deep enough snowpack, the corn skiing on Haystack's southeast aspect is a must-do. Ascend to the summit from the east pass as described above, and then make wide turns down the open face back to the meadow you traversed on the ascent route. It's over 1200 vertical feet of corny goodness with a spectacular view of Mount Mellenthin over your right shoulder.

To return, retrace your ascent route by skiing down the low-angle meadow and skinning back up to Geyser Pass Road, where you can skate-ski all the way back to the trailhead. Note that the rolling terrain on the way back may be difficult for snowboarders to get through without skinning.

95 South Mountain Glades

Start Point : La Sal Creek winter trailhead, 7800 feet
High Point : Point 11142, 11,142 feet
Trail Distance : 12 miles
Trail Time : 8 hours
Skill Level : Advanced
Best Season : Winter/Spring
Maps : USGS Mount Tukuhnikivatz, Mount Peale

The South Mountain Glades are a bit of a locals secret. Found in the south group of the La Sal Mountains near La Sal Pass, the glades are located on Point 11142, a small, wooded peak just southeast of South Mountain. Several meadows spill down from the top, so many in fact that, when viewed from a distance, the mountain looks almost like a ski resort with cut runs. These open spaces offer long vertical on protected aspects within evergreen forests that shelter powder snow for weeks after a storm. Also, the South Mountain area gets more snow than the rest of the range, making this Moab's own powder paradise. Unfortunately, La Sal Pass Road isn't plowed, so the approach from the trailhead is long. The upside is that practically no one skis here, so you can have the place all to yourself.

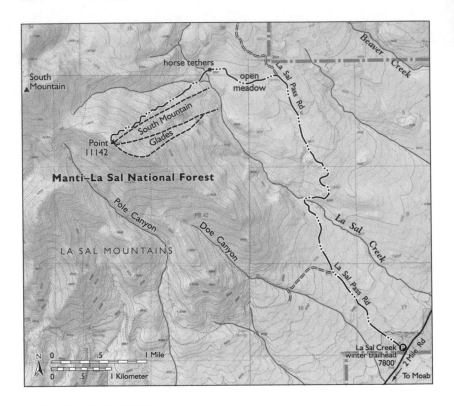

GETTING THERE

From Moab, drive south on US Highway 191 for 22 miles to the intersection with SR 46. Turn left (east) toward the town of La Sal, and in 9 miles, you'll pass through this tiny town. Continue east for another 3.5 miles, and turn left onto 2 Mile Road. In 2 miles, you'll come to La Sal Pass Road on the left. There is a plowed parking area with signs that mark this as the La Sal Creek winter trailhead. Park here unless La Sal Pass Road is drivable. If that's the case, drive up the road as far as you can safely make it. For the purposes of this route description, mileage will start at the winter trailhead.

THE ROUTE

From the La Sal Creek winter trailhead, go northwest on La Sal Pass Road. If it's snow covered, there will probably be tire trenches from jeeps and snowmobile tracks that will make skinning fast and easy. In 1.25 miles, you'll come to a signed fork. Left goes to Doe and Pole canyons. Stay right toward La Sal Pass and the South Mountain trailhead.

Two miles from the car, the road dips down into the La Sal Creek drainage. Keep following the road as it comes up the other side and switchbacks to about 8600 feet. As you continue on the road, Mount Peale will dominate the skyline before you, with Mount Tukuhnikivatz in the distance. After 3.8 miles from the trailhead, when the foliage turns from scrub oak to aspens and evergreens, leave the road at around 8960 feet where you can see a gigantic, open meadow to the west. It will likely be covered in snowmobile tracks. Head west across the meadow toward Point 11142 and South Mountain. This is a good place to scope out your line in the obvious glades.

Flat-track across the meadow to the other side, where you can find wooden horse tethers (assuming they're not completely buried under snow). Keep going west down to La Sal Creek, where there is a good crossing. You are now at the bottom of the South Mountain Glades.

Skin west and ascend through the forest on the northeast face of Point 11142. There may already be an established skin track, but if you're breaking trail, keep heading west through the forest for 0.6 mile until you finally break free of the trees at the bottom of open meadows at about 9600 feet.

Now that you can see the runs you will be skiing, switchback up the side of the glades while checking for snowpack stability all the way to the top of Point 11142. It's nearly 1 mile and 1550 vertical feet of skinning from the bottom of the glade to the summit, and the upper 500 feet is forested with large evergreens, making it difficult to determine if you've made it to the true summit. Most locals tend to simply lap the open meadows without bothering to push for the mountain's view-obscured crown.

Descent options are everywhere as several glades dot the entire northeast aspect. These meadows fall nearly 2000 feet to the creek bottom and hold the deepest, most protected snow in the La Sal Mountains. To get the most bang for your buck, it's best to just ski or snowboard several laps on the glade you ascended. Be careful though,

View of Point 11142 and the South Mountain Glades from the meadow near La Sal Pass Road

as many of these open spaces are boulder fields that can be dangerous during periods of low snow.

To return, ski down to the creek and retrace your skin track back to La Sal Pass Road. You may be tempted to follow La Sal Creek down to where it intersects the road, but the drainage gets narrow and brushy. Even though it adds mileage, it's actually faster to ski the road down to the trailhead.

96 South Mountain

Start Point : La Sal Creek winter trailhead, 7800 feet
High Point : South Mountain summit, 11,817 feet
Trail Distance : 14 miles
Trail Time : 10 hours
Skill Level : Advanced
Best Season : Winter/Spring
Maps : USGS Mount Tukuhnikivatz, Mount Peale

At 11,817 feet South Mountain is among the smallest peaks in the range, but stands out like a lonely mountain, separate from her sisters to the north, Mount Peale and Tuk. While the bigger mountains get all the love from skiers, due to size and accessibility from Gold Basin, South Mountain is harder to appreciate. The approach is

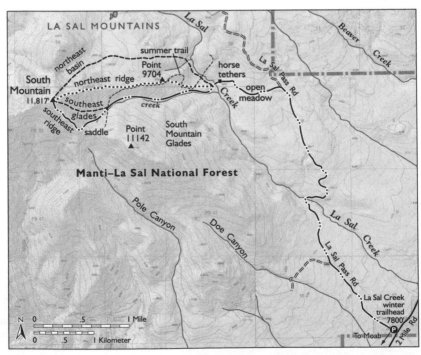

extremely long for day tours, and the summit is a full 1000 feet shorter and barely goes above tree line. But if you're looking for powder, South Mountain is the place to be. For some reason, this area gets more snowfall than the rest of the La Sal Mountains, and therefore has better powder skiing. Descents include enormous glades and meadows that spill down to La Sal Creek and are prime for meadow-skipping, while the steep northeast basin is a marquee line. The skiing doesn't get much better than this.

GETTING THERE

From Moab, drive south on US Highway 191 for 22 miles to the intersection with SR 46. Turn left (east) toward the town of La Sal, and in 9 miles, you'll pass through this tiny town. Continue east for another 3.5 miles, and turn left onto 2 Mile Road. In 2 miles, you'll come to La Sal Pass Road on the left. There is a plowed parking area with signs that mark this as the La Sal Creek winter trailhead. Park here unless La Sal Pass Road is drivable. If that's the case, drive up the road as far as you can safely make it. For the purposes of this route description, mileage will start at the winter trailhead.

THE ROUTE

From the La Sal Creek winter trailhead, go northwest on La Sal Pass Road. If it's snow covered, there will probably be tire trenches from jeeps and snowmobile tracks that will make skinning fast and easy. In 1.25 miles, you'll come to a signed fork. Left goes to Doe and Pole canyons. Stay right toward La Sal Pass and the South Mountain trailhead.

Two miles from the car, the road dips down into the La Sal Creek drainage. Keep following the road as it comes up the other side and switchbacks to about 8600 feet. As you continue on the road, Mount Peale will dominate the skyline before you, with Mount Tukuhnikivatz in the distance. After 3.8 miles from the trailhead, when the foliage turns from scrub oak to aspens and evergreens, leave the road at around 8960 feet where you can see a gigantic, open meadow to the west. It will likely be covered in snowmobile tracks. Head west across the meadow toward Point 11142 and South Mountain.

Flat-track across the meadow to the other side, where you can find wooden horse tethers (assuming they're not completely buried under snow). Keep going west down to La Sal Creek, where there is a good place to cross the water. At this point, you're at the convergence of La Sal Creek and a small creek that comes down from between South Mountain and Point 11142. Follow this smaller drainage west as it winds through a thick evergreen forest. It's best to sidehill above the creek to avoid the terrain trap whenever possible.

By following the creek, it's a relatively easy 2-mile ascent to the 10,800-foot saddle between Point 11142 and South Mountain's summit. Once you gain the saddle, it's a safe and quick half-mile skin up the southeast ridge to the top.

Another way to the summit is via the northeast ridge. This route is more direct but is steeper and exposed to the wind, which deposits crusty snow piles all along the ridge. The toe of the ridge is at the La Sal Creek crossing, where you can skin up through the forest and basically follow the summer trail route. In 0.5 mile, you'll pass below

Elaborate tree graffiti on the approach to South Mountain's summit

Point 9704, where the trail continues on the wide ridge. When the trail curves south at around 10,260 feet, keep right to stay on the ridge and follow it for another 0.75 mile to the summit. The upper part of the ridge can be difficult due to wind-blown snow and undulating terrain, but it provides a good view of the mountain's northeast basin, where you can scope out possible descent lines.

At the top, enjoy unparalleled views of red rock desert all around, broken up by islands of mountains like the Abajo Range to the south, Colorado's San Juan Mountains far to the east, and the imposing south faces of Mount Tuk and Mount Peale to the north.

There are a few descent options from the top. The biggest line that will earn you bragging rights is the northeast basin. This huge amphitheater of rock and snow is steep and long as it spills down toward La Sal Creek. Of course, this line is highly avalanche prone and should only be skied when the snowpack is very stable. At the bottom of the basin, ski east through the woods until you reach La Sal Creek, and follow it back to your ascent track for the return to the trailhead.

The safest skiing and snowboarding options are the glades on South Mountain's southeast aspect. These open meadows can be sun affected, but the well-spaced trees between the glades protect the snow, with deep, soft powder lasting for days after a storm. One of the best powder runs of my life was a nearly 2000-foot shot in those glades from the summit to the creek.

To return, ski down to La Sal Creek and retrace your skin track across the meadow back to La Sal Pass Road. You may be tempted to follow La Sal Creek down to where it intersects the road, but the drainage gets narrow and brushy. Even though it adds mileage, it's actually faster to ski the road down to the trailhead.

Opposite: *The old platter-lift line at Old Blue Mountain Ski Resort is one place snowmobilers won't go, which means the powder remains untracked.*

ABAJO MOUNTAINS

THE SOUTHERNMOST MOUNTAIN RANGE in this book is the Abajo Mountains, located west of Monticello. Also known locally as the Blue Mountains, this series of 11,000-foot peaks rises from the unpopulated high desert of southeastern Utah. The remote location and lack of winter infrastructure means you're more likely to find snowmobiles instead of skis or snowboards. But if conditions are good and you make the effort to get there, you can find untracked winter powder or spring corn on open bowls or gladed evergreen and aspen forests—and have it all to yourself.

The highest point is 11,360-foot Abajo Peak. A summer-only road climbs to the top, where dozens of communication towers have been built. It's a popular drive for sightseeing and is among the best paragliding areas in the state. In the winter, the mountain is empty. Huge bowls spill east from the summit, and north- and west-facing tree runs keep snow cold and deep. The Old Blue Mountain Ski Resort, located at the base of Abajo Peak, is a great place for lapping abandoned ski runs alongside crumbling lifts. Farther into the range, Horsehead Peak has some of the best terrain in southern Utah. Viewed from town, the Horsehead is named after an evergreen forest shaped just like a horse's head. On the mountain, a massive, northeast-facing bowl alongside the head is the ultimate ski objective when avalanche conditions are low.

There are many other skiable mountains in the Abajos, such as South Peak, but access is limited due to dirt roads that are snowbound in the winter. Come spring, however, it's an excellent place to explore on your own with a topo map. There is a lot of untapped potential and new interest in these mountains—even rumors of proposed backcountry huts. So keep an eye on the Abajos as they could become the next "it" place.

NOTES

Land Management. Tours in the Abajo Mountains are located in Manti–La Sal National Forest. Because the range is a watershed for the towns of Blanding and Monticello, the Forest Service has banned backcountry camping around the high peaks. Contact the Monticello Ranger District for more information. Web address and phone number are found in Resources.

Road Conditions. North Creek Road is plowed up to the Harts Draw winter trailhead, near Dalton Springs Campground. All other access roads require snowmobiles or a long day on skins. Some dirt roads in lower elevations can melt off in early spring.

Weather. The Abajo Mountains are lower in both elevation and latitude compared to most ranges in the state. In fact, *abajo* means "down" or "low" in Spanish. As a result, expect to find less snowfall amounts in this desert range. However, big southern storms can drop dozens of feet of snow here when the Wasatch gets nothing, so always check that forecast! Unfortunately, the Abajos share the Utah Avalanche Center's Moab advisory despite being more than 50 miles south. Always supplement with your own snowpack assessment before skinning into the backcountry, and check the National Weather Service for current conditions. See Resources for web addresses and phone numbers.

97 Old Blue Mountain Ski Resort

Start Point : County Road 118 turnoff, 8340 feet
High Point : Point 10837, 10,837 feet
Trail Distance : 5 miles
Trail Time : 4 hours
Skill Level : Intermediate
Best Season : Winter
Map : USGS Abajo Peak

The Old Blue Mountain Ski Resort is exactly that—an abandoned ghost resort with lift shacks, cables, and a faded platter lift still intact. This tiny ski area shut down in the early '80s because of a lack of snow. The few cut runs are now home to snowmobilers, families on sledding trips, and backcountry skiers. The slopes in and around the resort are some of the most accessible in the Abajo Mountains, which makes this a great spot for short half-day tours. Longer tours can also be linked to the upper reaches of Abajo Peak.

Snowboarding untracked powder along the abandoned platter lift at the Old Blue Mountain Ski Resort

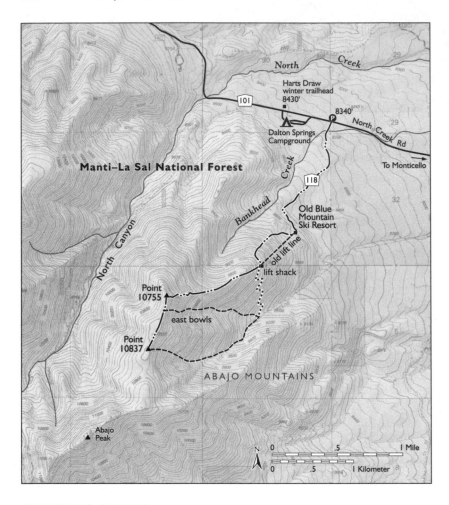

GETTING THERE

In the town of Monticello, as you drive south on US Highway 191, turn right (west) on 200 South. A sign will direct you to Harts Draw Loop Road. Follow the street for three blocks where it will curve around a neighborhood and become Abajo Drive. Continue west. When you leave the town limits, the road becomes North Creek Road (County Road 101). Follow it up into the foothills for 4 miles until you reach the turnoff for CR 118 on the left. It will likely be snow covered and plowed in. Park here along the side of the road. If you come to the Harts Draw winter trailhead by Dalton Springs Campground, you've gone too far.

THE ROUTE

Head south on CR 118, which is the unmaintained road to the Old Blue Mountain Ski Resort. The snow will probably be packed down from snowmobiles, so you can bang out the 1 mile of skinning with little issue. The road ends at what used to be the parking lot for the ski area. Here, you can check out the abandoned lift shack, towers, and surface lift that are frozen in time.

From the bottom of the resort, skin up the cut run as it curves climber's right around the evergreen trees. The run is a quick and efficient way to ascend and will likely be tracked out by snowmobiles. The upper part of the run has become overgrown with small trees, so the machine access stops here. When you reach the evergreens, trend left on an old cat track to the upper lift shack. It's only 0.5 mile and 800 vertical feet from the resort base to this point.

From here, you can ski the cut run you ascended, or, if it's too tracked out, make turns down the narrow lift line. This line is usually untouched because it's too cramped for snowmobiles. Just be wary of the old lift cable sagging to the ground or just under the snow surface as you can easily run into it.

For a longer tour, from the upper lift shack continue west up the ridge in an evergreen forest. It starts out as a low-angle walk but becomes pretty steep when the trees thin out at about 10,200 feet. Keep going up the ridge by making tight switchbacks to the top of Point 10755. From here, go south on the ridge, where large, east-facing bowls await your skis or snowboard. These 800- to 1000-vertical-foot shots between Point 10755 and Point 10837 are fun but are in serious avalanche terrain. Be confident of snowpack stability before dropping in.

To return, skin north about 700 vertical feet back up to the ascent ridge to where you can ski down the Old Blue Mountain Ski Resort, and then skate-ski on the road back to your vehicle.

You can also use this ridge as an alternate route to Abajo Peak. From Point 10755, it's about 1.5 miles of up-and-down skinning southwest to the communication towers on the summit (see Abajo Peak, Tour 98).

98 Abajo Peak

Start Point : Harts Draw winter trailhead, 8430 feet
High Point : Abajo Peak summit, 11,360 feet
Trail Distance : 9 miles
Trail Time : 7 hours
Skill Level : Intermediate/Advanced
Best Season : Winter
Map : USGS Abajo Peak

Abajo Peak is the tallest mountain in the range and has some of the most eye-catching ski and snowboard terrain in southeastern Utah. Huge bowls on her southeast face are perfect for corn tours in the spring when the snowpack calms down, and the evergreen and aspen forests on north aspects hold good powder and glade skiing all winter long. While the approaches from North Creek or the Old Blue Mountain Ski Resort

An array of communication towers crowds the summit of Abajo Peak.

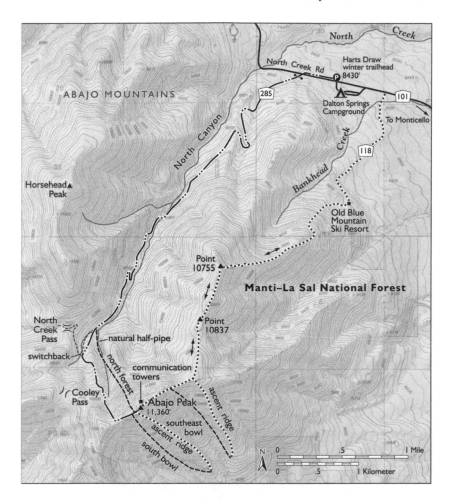

are long, and the gigantic communication towers on the summit ruin the solitary backcountry experience, Abajo Peak's ample ski terrain is totally worth the effort.

GETTING THERE

In the town of Monticello, as you drive south on US Highway 191, turn right (west) on 200 South. A sign will direct you to Harts Draw Loop Road. Follow the street for three blocks where it will curve around a neighborhood and become Abajo Drive. Continue west. When you leave the town limits, the road becomes North Creek Road (County Road 101). Follow it up into the foothills for 4.3 miles to the Harts Draw winter trailhead, right across the road from Dalton Springs Campground. There is a large parking area and Forest Service outhouse.

THE ROUTE

From the parking area, skin up snow-covered CR 101 for 0.25 mile to CR 285. Go left, pass an open metal gate with a ROAD CLOSED sign on it, and enter North Canyon. From the turnoff, continue skinning up the road, which will probably be packed down by snowmobile tracks, for 3.4 miles. You'll gradually gain elevation as you travel past views of Horsehead Peak to the west and the obvious Abajo Peak summit with her communication towers to the south. At the top of the canyon, you'll reach a major switchback near North Creek Pass.

From this switchback, leave the road and skin southeast toward Abajo Peak into a forest filled with pine, fir, spruce, and aspen. The foliage is thin enough for easy routefinding, but the slope gets steeper as you gain elevation. From the switchback, it's about a half mile of steep skinning to the summit ridge, where a super-short traverse northeast gets you to the top.

Alternatively, you can reach the summit of Abajo Peak from the ridge above the Old Blue Mountain Ski Resort. Ascend the route as described in the Old Blue Mountain tour (Tour 97), but when you reach Point 10837 continue following the ridge south for another 1.2 miles to the top. This route is shorter mileage-wise than using North Creek, but it is steeper and the ridge undulates, making cross-country travel more difficult.

There are two primary descent options from the summit of Abajo Peak. First, if snow conditions warrant, a run down the wide-open, south- and southeast-facing bowls is a must-do. These massive bowls fall 2000 feet and are separated by sub-ridges that can be used to skin back up to the summit. But be warned that while these runs are tasty, each bowl ends in a serious avalanche terrain trap and should only be skied during the most stable of snowpacks.

The other descent option is off the north side. That evergreen forest you used to ascend is also prime tree skiing, as this sheltered aspect holds soft, cold snow. The best line is a wide swath in the trees that becomes a small drainage with an exit onto the road in North Canyon. You can find the start of the run between Abajo Peak's summit and Cooley Pass. It begins steep with thicker trees but opens up into a very fun line with playful terrain features that ends in a natural half-pipe above the road. Of course this also is a terrain trap, so make a careful avalanche assessment here.

To return, ski back down CR 285 all the way to the Harts Draw winter trailhead.

 **99** Horsehead Peak

Start Point : Harts Draw winter trailhead, 8430 feet
High Point : Horsehead Peak summit, 11,209 feet
Trail Distance : 7 miles
Trail Time : 5 hours
Skill Level : Advanced
Best Season : Winter
Map : USGS Abajo Peak

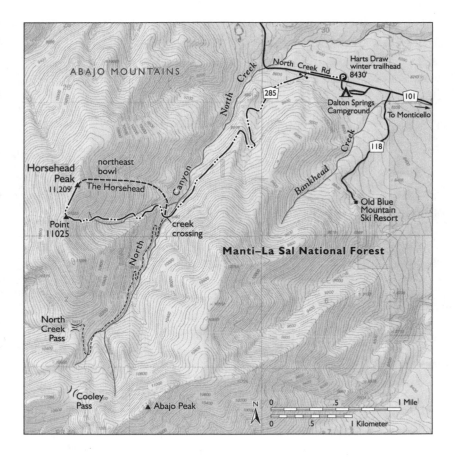

Horsehead Peak is a local landmark around Monticello. The mountain gets its name from a formation of evergreen trees and snow on the northeast aspect that forms the shape of a horse's head. It's quite obvious when viewed from town, and it also makes a good point of reference for ski touring in the range. As far as skiing and snowboarding on the mountain, access is straightforward from North Canyon, and long, 2000-vertical-foot descents can be had on enormous open bowls with perfect fall lines. If you time your trip when snow conditions are prime, you'll have a run of a lifetime by riding the Horsehead.

GETTING THERE

In the town of Monticello, as you drive south on US Highway 191, turn right (west) on 200 South. A sign will direct you to Harts Draw Loop Road. Follow the street for three blocks where it will curve around a neighborhood and become Abajo Drive. Continue west. When you leave the town limits, the road becomes North Creek Road (County Road 101). Follow it up into the foothills for 4.3 miles to the Harts

You can see how the evergreens on the left form a horse's head in this view of Horsehead Peak from North Canyon.

Draw winter trailhead, right across the road from Dalton Springs Campground. There is a large parking area and Forest Service outhouse.

THE ROUTE

From the parking area, skin up the snow-covered CR 101 for 0.25 mile to CR 285. Go left, pass an open metal gate with a ROAD CLOSED sign on it, and enter North Canyon. From the turnoff, continue skinning up the road as if you're heading to Abajo Peak or North Creek Pass. The skin should be easy as the road will probably be packed down by snowmobile tracks.

After about 1.5 miles of fairly level skinning, you'll get a good view of the "horsehead" on Horsehead Peak to the west. Continue up the road until it crosses North Creek at 2 miles from the trailhead and an elevation of 9400 feet. As soon as you cross the creek, ascend west straight up the mountainside into a steep side-drainage. Unless there is already a skin track, you'll have to break trail through a thick evergreen forest that eventually opens up into meadows at about 10,000 feet.

When you reach the meadows south of the peak, keep climbing alongside the trees as much as possible to avoid avalanche terrain on the way to the summit ridge at Point

11025. From the creek crossing to the ridge, it's about a 1-mile, 1600-vertical-foot climb. Once you gain the ridge, traverse north for a final 0.25 mile to the broad, rocky summit.

There are two main descent options from the top of Horsehead Peak. The first is to ski or snowboard down the slopes you skinned up. This descent has wide-open bowls and tree skiing at the bottom, but the southeast aspect means the window of good snow is small.

The best line off the top is the epic northeast bowl that falls alongside the horsehead formation. This run is a huge 2000-foot drop with an almost perfect fall line. Ski it on a powder day and you'll think you've died and gone to heaven. The main issue with this descent, however, is that the bottom becomes a narrow gully (avalanche terrain trap) that is choked with thick brush (bushwhack). To avoid getting tangled up in that mess, stay skier's right in the evergreen trees as you near the bottom and traverse back to the spot where you left the road by the creek on your ascent.

To return to your vehicle, simply follow the road back to the Harts Draw winter trailhead.

RESOURCES

ROAD CONDITIONS
Utah Department of Transportation (UDOT), (866) 511-8824, www.udot.utah.gov
Wyoming Department of Transportation (WYDOT), (888) 996-7623, www.dot
.state.wy.us

AVALANCHE AND WEATHER CONDITIONS
Utah Avalanche Center, www.utahavalanchecenter.org
National Weather Service, www.weather.gov
Salt Lake City National Weather Service Forecast Office, www.wrh.noaa.gov/slc
Cottonwood Canyons Forecast, www.wrh.noaa.gov/slc/snow/mtnwx
    /mtnforecast.php
Wasatch Snow Info, www.wasatchsnowinfo.com
Utah Ski Weather, www.utahskiweather.com

AVALANCHE EDUCATION PROVIDERS
American Avalanche Institute, (307) 733-3315,
    www.americanavalancheinstitute.com
Utah Mountain Adventures, (801) 550-3986,
    www.utahmountainadventures.com
White Pine Touring/AIARE, (435) 649-8710, www.whitepinetouring.com
    /avalanche-training.php

AVALANCHE BEACON PRACTICE PARKS
Canyons Training Center, www.canyonsresort.com/mountain/safety.aspx#
    /BeaconPark
Snowbasin Resort, https://snowbasin.com/mountain/mountainsafety/rescue/
Snowbird Rescue Training Center, www.snowbird.com/winter/activities/atc/
Solitude Mountain Resort, www.skisolitude.com/mountain/ski_patrol.php

The avalanche beacon practice parks are made possible by Wasatch Backcountry
    Rescue, (801) 933-2156, www.wbrescue.org/public-education-awareness
    /rescue-training-center

Opposite: *Abandoned lift towers make touring in Old Blue
Mountain Ski Resort an eerie experience.*

NATIONAL FORESTS

Fishlake National Forest
115 East 900 North
Richfield, UT 84701
Phone: (435) 896-9233
www.fs.usda.gov/fishlake

Manti–La Sal National Forest
599 West Price River Drive
Price, UT 84501
Phone: (435) 637-2817
www.fs.usda.gov/mantilasal

Uinta-Wasatch-Cache National Forest
857 West South Jordan Parkway
South Jordan, UT 84095
Phone: (801) 999-2103
www.fs.usda.gov/uwcnf

RANGER DISTRICTS

Beaver Ranger District
575 South Main Street
Beaver, UT 84713
Phone: (435) 438-2436

Evanston Mountain View Ranger
District
Evanston Office
1565 Highway 150 South, Suite A
Evanston, WY 82930
Phone: (307) 789-3194

Heber-Kamas Ranger District
Heber Office
2460 South Highway 40
Heber City, UT 84032
Phone: (435) 654-0470

Heber-Kamas Ranger District
Kamas Office
50 East Center Street
Kamas, UT 84036
Phone: (435) 783-4338

Logan Ranger District
1500 East Highway 89
Logan, UT 84321
Phone: (435) 755-3620

Moab Ranger District
62 East 100 North
Moab, UT 84532
Phone: (435) 259-7155

Monticello Ranger District
496 East Central
Monticello, UT 84535
Phone: (435) 587-2041

Ogden Ranger District
507 25th Street, Suite 103
Ogden, UT 84401
Phone: (801) 625-5112

Pleasant Grove Ranger District
390 North 100 East
Pleasant Grove, UT 84062
Phone: (801) 785-3563

Salt Lake Ranger District
6944 South 3000 East
Cottonwood Heights, UT 84121
Phone: (801) 733-2660

Spanish Fork Ranger District
44 West 400 North
Spanish Fork, UT 84660
Phone: (801) 798-3571

STATE PARKS

Antelope Island State Park
4528 West 1700 South
Syracuse, UT 84075
Phone: (801) 773-2941
www.stateparks.utah.gov/parks
/antelope-island

BUREAU OF LAND MANAGEMENT AND PRIVATE OWNERS

BLM Utah State Office
440 West 200 South, Suite 500
Salt Lake City, UT 84101
Phone: (801) 539-4001
www.blm.gov/ut/st/en.html

Cardiff Canyon Owners Association
www.cardiffcanyon.org

Henry Mountains Field Station
380 South 100 West
Hanksville, UT 84734
Phone: (435) 542-3461

Salt Lake Field Office
2370 South Decker Lake Boulevard
West Valley City, UT 84119
Phone: (801) 977-4300

GUIDE SERVICES AND YURTS

Bear River Outdoor Recreational Alliance (BRORA), (307) 789-1770,
    www.brorayurts.org
Park City Powder Cats and Heli-Ski, (435) 649-6596, www.pccats.com
Powder Ridge Ski Touring, www.sites.google.com/site/powderridgeskitouring
Salt Lake County Parks and Recreation, Big Water Yurt, (801) 483-5473, www
    .parks.slco.org/
Splitboard Education Collective, (801) 694-7933, www.splitboardeducation.com
Tag-A-Long Expeditions, (435) 259-8946, www.tagalong.com
Tushar Mountain Tours, (435) 438-6191, www.skitushar.com
Utah Mountain Adventures, (801) 550-3986, www.utahmountainadventures.com
Utah State University Yurt, (435) 797-3264, www.usu.edu/camprec:/htm/orp
    /yurt
Wasatch Powderbird Guides, (801) 742-2800, www.powderbird.com
White Pine Touring, (435) 649-8710, www.whitepinetouring.com

SKI RESORTS

Alta Ski Area, (801) 359-1078, www.alta.com
Beaver Mountain Ski Area, (435) 946-3610, www.skithebeav.com
Brighton Ski Resort, (801) 532-4731, www.brightonresort.com
Eagle Point Resort, (435) 438-3700, www.eaglepointresort.com
Park City Mountain Resort, (435) 649-8111, www.parkcitymountain.com
Powder Mountain, (801) 745-3772, www.powdermountain.com
Snowbasin Resort, (888) 437-5488, www.snowbasin.com
Snowbird Ski and Summer Resort, (801) 933-2222, www.snowbird.com
Solitude Mountain Resort, (800) 748-4754, www.skisolitude.com
Sundance Mountain Resort, (866) 259-7468, www.sundanceresort.com

INDEX

ABOUT THE AUTHOR

(Photo courtesy Adam Symonds)

JARED HARGRAVE is a freelance outdoor writer with articles published in *Backcountry Magazine*, *Ascent Backcountry Snow Journal*, *Utah Adventure Journal*, and the *Mountain Gazette*. He is also the founder and editor of UtahOutside.com, an outdoor adventure website featuring trip reports, recreation guides, gear reviews and outdoor news in Utah. In addition, he produces *KSL Outdoors*, a half-hour television show broadcasted on Utah's NBC affiliate, KSL 5.

Hargrave lives, writes, and backcountry skis from his Salt Lake City home, which he shares with his wife, Callista, and son, Ridge.

MOUNTAINEERS BOOKS is a leading publisher of mountaineering literature and guides—including our flagship title, *Mountaineering: The Freedom of the Hills*—as well as adventure narratives, natural history, and general outdoor recreation. Through our two imprints, Skipstone and Braided River, we also publish titles on sustainability and conservation. We are committed to supporting the environmental and educational goals of our organization by providing expert information on human-powered adventure, sustainable practices at home and on the trail, and preservation of wilderness.

The Mountaineers, founded in 1906, is a 501(c)(3) nonprofit outdoor activity and conservation organization whose mission is "to explore, study, preserve, and enjoy the natural beauty of the outdoors." One of the largest such organizations in the United States, it sponsors classes and year-round outdoor activities throughout the Pacific Northwest, including climbing, hiking, backcountry skiing, snowshoeing, bicycling, camping, paddling, and more. The Mountaineers also supports its mission through its publishing division, Mountaineers Books, and promotes environmental education and citizen engagement. For more information, visit The Mountaineers Program Center, 7700 Sand Point Way NE, Seattle, WA 98115-3996; phone 206-521-6001; www.mountaineers.org; or email info@mountaineers.org.

Our publications are made possible through the generosity of donors and through sales of more than 600 titles on outdoor recreation, sustainable lifestyle, and conservation. To donate, purchase books, or learn more, visit us online:

MOUNTAINEERS BOOKS
1001 SW Klickitat Way, Suite 201 • Seattle, WA 98134
800-553-4453 • mbooks@mountaineersbooks.org • www.mountaineersbooks.org

Mountaineers Books is proud to be a corporate sponsor of the Leave No Trace Center for Outdoor Ethics, whose mission is to promote and inspire responsible outdoor recreation through education, research, and partnerships. • The Leave No Trace program is focused specifically on human-powered (nonmotorized) recreation. • Leave No Trace strives to educate visitors about the nature of their recreational impacts and offers techniques to prevent and minimize such impacts. • Leave No Trace is best understood as an educational and ethical program, not as a set of rules and regulations. • For more information, visit www.lnt.org or call 800-332-4100.

OTHER TITLES YOU MIGHT ENJOY FROM MOUNTAINEERS BOOKS

Staying Alive in Avalanche Terrain
2nd edition
Bruce Tremper
"No one who plays in mountain snow should leave home without having studied this book."—*Rocky Mountain News*

Avalanche Essentials: A Step-by-Step System for Safety and Survival
Bruce Tremper
The fundamentals of avalanche awareness

Avalanche Pocket Guide: A Field Reference
Bruce Tremper
A waterproof, fold-out quick reference for evaluating and managing avalanche danger

Backcountry Skiing: Skills for Ski Touring and Ski Mountaineering
Martin Volken, Scott Schell, and Margaret Wheeler
The definitive manual of backcountry skiing

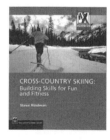

Cross-Country Skiing: Building Skills for Fun and Fitness
Steve Hindman
For the novice to intermediate cross-country skier: instruction by a member of the national Nordic Demonstration Team

Don't Freeze Out There! Deck
Tips and skills for winter outdoor survival in a functional and water-resistant pack of playing cards

www.mountaineersbooks.org